\

Learning and Teaching in the Early Years

Learning and Teaching in the Early Years provides a comprehensive, contemporary and practical introduction to early childhood teaching in Australia. A strong focus on the links between theory, policy and practice firmly aligns this text with the Early Years Learning Framework.

Written for students of early childhood programs, this book covers learning and development, as well as professional practice in teaching children from birth to eight years. In recognition of the evolving role of early childhood teachers, topic areas include learning, teaching, working with families, leading, advocating and researching. Each chapter contains learning objectives, key terms and reflection points. Detailed case studies document the intersection between research, policy and practice, enhancing pre-service and practicing early childhood teachers' appreciation of how a policy-aligned approach reinforces learning and development in the early years.

Learning and Teaching in the Early Years draws on the latest Australian and international research to examine the features of effective practice and to present children's learning as a dynamic and active process requiring specific, intentional teaching behaviours.

Jane Page is Senior Lecturer at the University of Melbourne.

Collette Tayler is Chair of Early Childhood Education and Care at the University of Melbourne.

Learning and Teaching in the Early Years

Edited by

Jane Page

Collette Tayler

CAMBRIDGE
UNIVERSITY PRESS

CAMBRIDGE
UNIVERSITY PRESS

477 Williamstown Road, Port Melbourne, VIC 3207, Australia

Cambridge University Press is part of the University of Cambridge.

It furthers the University's mission by disseminating knowledge in the pursuit of education, learning and research at the highest international levels of excellence.

www.cambridge.org
Information on this title: www.cambridge.org/9781107697188

First published 2016

Cover designed by Leigh Ashforth, watershed art + design
Typeset by Aptara Corp.
Printed in Singapore by Markono Print Media Pte Ltd

A catalogue record for this publication is available from the British Library

A Cataloguing-in-Publication entry is available from the catalogue of the National Library of Australia at www.nla.gov.au

ISBN 978-1-107-69718-8 Paperback

....

For Rod and Pam, Christopher, Laura and Dominic (JP)
For my grandson, Hugo, and all his contemporaries (CT)

....

Foreword

When I was documenting my own thoughts of the 2007 Federal Labor Government and its achievements in early childhood policy, it was Collette Tayler who said to me: 'we're involved in a decade-long effort. If we hold our nerve, we're on track to achieve something fine in this country'. Then, as now, I loved the optimism and ambition of this statement. This publication, guided so ably by Collette, Jane Page and many other academic colleagues, is an important and timely compilation. It explores the raison d'être behind Australia's renewed investment in the early years of a child's life, and details the policy framework and research ideas that govern learning and development in all care settings – be it pre-school, family or long day care.

As described across these chapters, there is now a national focus on policy goals, and a set of standards and regulations against which we can judge the quality of the services provided for Australian children. There has been fine-tuning, to be sure, but there now exists, across the disparate jurisdictions that make up the Commonwealth of Australia, a recognition that the Australian National Quality Framework for Early Childhood Education and Care is a core foundational document.

Within this volume the authors have also considered the many critical issues that are needed to achieve an optimal pedagogical environment. They include the recognition that young children are learners with rights, that *intentional* teaching is the way to help children achieve the skills they need to succeed to life, and importantly an acknowledgement that families are the 'first' partners in the learning process.

Readers of this publication will emerge with a finer appreciation of the complexity, hard work and critical thinking that now informs practice by teachers and families. We know that children are born hard-wired to learn and that the major life phase that represents early childhood is a period of astonishing development. That so many of our talented academic thinkers, policy makers and practitioners are working collaboratively is testament to the open spirit and sense of opportunity that is shared across the early childhood education and care sector.

They are inspired by a singular goal – to help nurture a generation of children who are happy, confident life-long learners.

Maxine McKew
Parliamentary Secretary Early
Childhood – Rudd Labor Government

Contents

Contributors

Editors

Jane Page (PhD) is Senior Lecturer in the Melbourne Graduate School of Education at the University of Melbourne. She has worked in the early childhood profession for over 20 years covering a range of roles both as a practitioner in early childhood services and also as a teacher in the university sector, including Program Coordinator Master of Teaching (Early Childhood) for seven years. Jane has been actively engaged with State and local governments and the Victorian Curriculum Assessment Authority (VCAA) in the development and implementation of a number of projects that focus on early childhood teachers' pedagogical practices. Her research focuses on the application of human rights principles in early childhood settings. Jane is currently managing research projects concerned with quality pedagogy and the impact of evidence-based interventions on children and families experiencing vulnerable circumstances, and is Chief Investigator of an Australian Research Council Linkage Grant *Building a Bridge into Preschool in Remote Northern Territory*, in partnership with the Northern Territory Government's Department of Education and Operations Manager of the Victorian Advancing Early Learning Research Project.

Collette Tayler (PhD) is Chair in Early Childhood Education and Care in the Melbourne Graduate School of Education at the University of Melbourne. She is Chief Investigator in the Australian Research Council National Science of Learning Centre, Project Leader of the E4Kids longitudinal study and its related Victorian Advancing Early Learning studies, and leader of the 3*a* (Abecedarian Approach Australia) group of development projects, at the Melbourne Graduate School of Education. Collette also served as the Deputy Chair of the Australian Children's Education and Care Quality Authority from 2012–2015, and is a board member of the VCAA and the Victorian Children's Council. Collette's teaching, educational research and development work spans 40 years in different parts of Australia, addressing effective early years teaching and learning, with studies conducted in home-, centre- and school-based programs within culturally and linguistically diverse urban, regional and remote communities.

Chapter authors

Amelia Church (PhD) is Lecturer in the Master of Teaching (Early Childhood) in the Melbourne Graduate School of Education at the University of Melbourne, where she leads subjects in qualitative research methodologies, and coordinates the Master of Teaching Research Option and Postgraduate Certificate in Educational Research. Amelia holds a PhD in Linguistics from Monash University and published this research as *Preference organization and peer disputes: How young children resolve conflict* (2009). Most recently, collaborations with other researchers will be published in *Children's Knowledge-in-interaction: Studies in Conversation Analysis* (2016), edited with Amanda Bateman. Her current research interests include communicative competence in early childhood, peer interaction, developmental pragmatics and conversation analysis in institutional settings.

Caroline Cohrssen (PhD) is Senior Lecturer in the Melbourne Graduate School of Education at the University of Melbourne. She edited the writing of the evidence paper for *Practice Principle 1: Family-centred practice* published by the Department of Education and Early Childhood Development (DEECD) in 2010 to support the *Victorian Early Years Learning and Development Framework*. Caroline's subsequent research has investigated quality adult–child interactions to support mathematics learning, the influence of the home learning environment on children's numeracy skills, and children's spatial thinking and academic self-concept in the year prior to school entry. Her work is aimed at equipping families, pre-service early years students and teachers to recognise mathematical thinking, plan playful activities and interact purposefully to support and extend children's emerging skills and understanding. She believes that small-group, play-based mathematics activities provide opportunities for adults to support individual children's skills and understanding as they transition into formal school education, and that equipping children with the skills to achieve success contributes to a child's sense of belonging to a community and a broader society.

Jan Deans (PhD) is Director of the Early Learning Centre, the University of Melbourne's research and demonstration pre-school. She is also Senior Lecturer at the Melbourne Graduate School of Education, taking the role of Professional Partnership Coordinator for the Master of Teaching (Early Childhood) program. She is a long-time advocate for teaching and learning through the arts, and has worked both locally and internationally in early childhood, primary, tertiary and special education settings. She has broad-based expertise in relation to early childhood education and service delivery, and her recent research interests include learning through dance, social emotional competence and learning through music. In 1997, she established Boorai – The Children's Art Gallery to present the voices of young children as expressed through their art and narratives. Boorai collaborates with educational and community organisations locally, nationally and internationally.

Frank Niklas (PhD) is a researcher and Lecturer at the University of Würzburg, Germany and Senior Research Fellow in the Melbourne Graduate School of Education at the University of Melbourne. He is a developmental and educational psychologist with research interests in how children learn in the context of families (Home Learning Environment). In 2010, Frank completed his PhD at the University of Würzburg, where he investigated precursors of reading, writing, and mathematical abilities as well as school readiness in children. He was granted a two-year post-doctoral fellowship by the German Academic Exchange Services (DAAD) in August 2013. In his honorary appointment at the University of Melbourne he works on projects such as 'Effective Early Educational Experiences for Kids' (E4Kids study) and 'Enriching the home learning environment'. In August 2015 he returned to the University of Würzburg.

Tim Gilley (PhD) lectures in the Master of Teaching (Early Childhood) and the Master of Teaching (Early Years) courses in the Melbourne Graduate School of Education at the University of Melbourne. He is also Partner Investigator for the Victorian Department of Education and Training on a major Australian longitudinal study on the impact on children's outcomes of their participation in early childhood education and care (ECEC) programs in the years before school – the E4Kids study. He has a PhD in early childhood education and a Master of Social Work. Tim has worked in a wide range of government organisations (local, State and Commonwealth) and non-government agencies, and has broad experience and expertise in the areas of public administration, social work, social research and social policy. A key element across all roles has been as an advocate for social justice, particularly for families and children from disadvantaged backgrounds.

Karen Weston is Director of Early Learning and Development Reform Branch at the Department of Education in Victoria. Karen has over 25 years experience in early childhood policy and sector development. Her recent work has included leading, in collaboration with many others, the development of the Early Years Learning Framework (EYLF), the *Victorian Early Years Learning and Development Framework*, the *Education and Care Services National Law Act 2010* and its Regulations, and the 2014 Review of the National Quality Framework (NQF), which has established new benchmarks for quality in the provision of education and care in Australia.

Susan Wright (PhD) is Chair of Arts Education and Director of the UNESCO Observatory of Arts Education in the Melbourne Graduate School of Education at the University of Melbourne. Prior to this, she was Professor and Head of Early Childhood and Special Needs Education at the National Institute of Education in Singapore, and the Director of the Centre of Applied Studies in Early Childhood at the Queensland University of Technology. Susan's research interests include semiotics within artistic domains, including narrative genres, and non-verbal modalities, such as gesture, dance, graphic representation and music. A common thread running through much of this work is temporal–spatial–embodied knowing, meaning making and communication. Her books include *Children, Meaning-Making and the*

Arts (2012), *Understanding Creativity in Early Childhood* (2010) and *The Arts, Young Children and Learning* (2003). She has published numerous chapters in research handbooks and books, and journal articles on various topics related to arts education.

Case study authors

Jeff Borland (PhD) is Truby Williams Professor of Economics at the University of Melbourne. One of his major topics of research is on evaluating policies and programs that are intended to assist skill development. His roles in Early Years Education Research Project (EYERP) are to assist with the design of the trial and data analysis.

Isabel Brookes is Research Fellow in the Melbourne Graduate School of Education at the University of Melbourne. Her recent work includes the implementation of a targeted intervention to support Indigenous children's English language learning, leading an early years improvement strategy at a remote early childhood site and the development of online resources to support pre-service teacher education. Isabel is a PhD candidate with the Science of Learning Research Centre, investigating the effect of adult prompts and feedback on children's learning.

Tamera Clancy is Senior Clinical Psychologist with postgraduate training in perinatal psychiatry and infant mental health. Tamera joined the EYERP in 2012, bringing specialised training in developmental assessment and significant experience with families experiencing stress and adversity. Tamera's clinical and research interests include infant–parent relationships, child development and early intervention.

Louise Cooke is the Family Educator for the Families as First Teachers (FaFT) Program at Gunbalanya School and has worked in a number of leadership roles in the FaFT program since 2009. Louise has worked in remote Indigenous early childhood setting since 2004. Prior to her current role, she was Abecedarian Manager (Indigenous Early Learning Programs) in the Department of Education, Northern Territory Government for two years.

Nichola Coombs (PhD) has a clinical background in infant, child and family mental health. She is the Senior Clinical Research Associate for the EYERP, managing the data collection process – including recruitment, engagement and sustained participation of trial participants – and collection of clinical observational data.

Kate Cotter is Chair of the Working Group and a former Children's Protection Society (CPS) board member. Kate has worked as a strategy consultant on major reform programs for public sector organisations and brings extensive experience in project management, service delivery reform in social welfare and public policy development to the research team.

Rachel Flottman has been a lecturer in the Melbourne Graduate School of Education at the University of Melbourne. She is currently completing a PhD on the implementation of the EYLF. Prior to this, she was Policy Adviser in the Victorian Education Department for six years, taking a lead role in the development of the *Victorian Early Years Learning and Development Framework*.

John Haisken-DeNew (PhD) is Professorial Research Fellow at the Melbourne Institute of Applied Economic and Social Research at the University of Melbourne. His research interests include empirical economic analyses of education, economic expectations, health, labour and welfare/subjective well-being.

Alice Hill (PhD) founded the Early Years Education Program (EYEP) and the EYERP (on which she continues to serve) during her time as Chair of the Board of the Children's Protection Society. A Director of the Antipodean Family Foundation, she is a former World Bank economist and McKinsey and Frontier Economics consultant.

Natalie Jones is Senior Kindergarten Teacher and Team Leader at the University of Melbourne's Early Learning Centre. Natalie's experience in the early childhood field spans 20 years and has seen her work in long day care, tutoring in Indigenous Australian Studies at the University of Melbourne and guest lecturing on a range of topics including the Reggio Emilia approach to education, Indigenous perspectives in early childhood and anti-bias curriculum.

Brigid Jordan (PhD) is a social worker and infant mental health clinician/researcher. She is Associate Professor of Paediatric Social Work at the Royal Children's Hospital and University of Melbourne and heads the Social and Mental Health Group at the Murdoch Children's Research Institute. She has been involved in the design and implementation of both EYEP and EYERP.

Anne Kennedy (PhD) has extensive experience in early childhood education as an academic, advocate, writer, teacher, trainer and consultant and is an honorary fellow of the Melbourne Graduate School of Education at the University of Melbourne. She is the Chairperson of Community Child Care Association, Victoria, a member of the EYEP research group and is the Curriculum Consultant for the CPS EYEP. Anne was a member of the Charles Sturt University writing team that developed the EYLF.

Gerry Mulhearn (PhD) is a member of the Research Institute for Professional Practice Learning and Education at Charles Sturt University, and an independent consultant. Previously, as Director in the South Australian Department of Education and Child Development, she played a lead role in the development of the EYLF, the National Early Childhood Development Strategy and the NQF assessment and rating process.

Carmel Phillips is Manager of the Early Years Unit, VCAA. In this role she supports the implementation of the *Victorian Early Years Learning and Development Framework*. This includes reviewing and developing curriculum and assessment resources, and program evaluations. From 2012, a key focus of her role has been the development and delivery of inquiry based professional learning with practitioners, policy makers and researchers in multidisciplinary early years networks to improve outcomes for children.

Nicole Pilsworth holds a Master of Educational Leadership and Bachelor of Education (Early Childhood). She has experience in a variety of ECEC settings over the last 25 years in New South Wales and Victoria including supporting the implementation of the EYLF and the National Reform Agenda. Nicole is the Albert Felton Early Childhood Education Fellow in the Melbourne Graduate School of Education at the University of Melbourne in research focusing on the impact of professional learning on teachers' interactions and young children's learning outcomes.

Rachel Pollitt is a graduate of the Master of Teaching (Early Childhood) program at the University of Melbourne. She was the recipient of the School of Early Childhood Study Funds Award 2014 in her final year of study. She is a PhD Candidate (AAP) in the Melbourne Graduate School of Education at the University of Melbourne, undertaking research on spatial reasoning and assessment in early childhood teaching practice.

Gracie Pupillo holds a Bachelor in Early Childhood Studies, which has enabled her to work in a variety of early childhood settings including both long day care and kindergarten over the past 20 years. Her recent experience has been in leading the implementation of the 3a strategies (Abecedarian Approach Australia) and Victorian Advancing Early Learning (VAEL) Study with Melbourne University. Gracie is currently working as the educational leader across three services for the Moonee Valley City Council while teaching at a sessional kindergarten.

Carol Rasborsek was a graduate of the Master of Teaching (Early Childhood) program at the University of Melbourne. She was the recipient of the Ada Mary a'Beckett Award in her final year of study. She has fifteen years experience working with children in kindergarten and long day care settings. She is Clinical Specialist in the Master of Teaching (Early Childhood) program at the University of Melbourne and a consultant for the Early Years Unit at the Victorian Curriculum and Assessment Authority.

Joseph Sparling (PhD) is Honorary Professorial Fellow in the Melbourne Graduate School of Education at the University of Melbourne and Senior Scientist Emeritus at the Frank Porter Graham Child Development Institute at the University of North Carolina. With Professor Craig Ramey, he developed the Abecedarian Approach. Forty years of research shows that implementation of this program early in life has a positive long-lasting impact for children and parents experiencing vulnerability and disadvantage.

Sophia Stirling is a graduate of the Master of Teaching (Early Childhood) program at the University of Melbourne. She currently works as a graduate teacher at the

University of Melbourne Early Learning Centre. Sophia's experience with children spans 15 years and has seen her work as a dance teacher's assistant and a teacher in child care, primary school and long day care settings.

Jennifer Sumsion (PhD) is Foundation Professor of Early Childhood Education and Director of the Research Institute for Professional Practice, Learning and Education at Charles Sturt University. In previous leadership roles, she has been Co-Director of the Excellence in Early Years Education Collaborative Research Network and co-leader of the national consortium that was contracted to develop and trial the EYLF.

Yi-Ping Tseng (PhD) is Senior Research Fellow at the Melbourne Institute of Applied Economic and Social research at the University of Melbourne. She is a labour economist with specific interest on program evaluation and social policies. Yi-Ping is a member of the CPS research group.

Wan Yi Lee is a graduate of the Master of Teaching (Early Childhood) program at the University of Melbourne. This case study was conducted in partial fulfillment of the Master's program in which she was awarded the School of Early Childhood Fund Prize 2014 for best overall course results. She is a PhD scholarship recipient of an Australian Research Council Linkage Project, currently situated in the Melbourne Graduate School of Education at the University of Melbourne.

Diana Warren (PhD) is an economist at the Australian Institute of Family Studies in Melbourne. Her research focuses on the application of longitudinal data analysis for complex survey data, particularly using the LSAC and HILDA. Her main research interests are economics of education and labour economics.

Sarah Young is a lecturer in early childhood education at the Melbourne Graduate School of Education at the University of Melbourne. She also works with children and adults in a variety of community and educational settings focusing on teaching and learning in the early years, with a particular emphasis on the arts. Sarah is currently completing her PhD, which examines the kindergarten teacher's role in play.

INTRODUCTION

Learning and teaching are two of the most honourable pursuits in life. In the first eight years, a child's learning is nothing short of remarkable, and it is conditioned on the context in which each child lives. This text explores the many opportunities that exist for early childhood teachers to promote, support and maximise young children's learning and development. The authors draw upon contemporary Australian and international research into child development and education, social and educational policy, and professional practice in order to highlight the active ingredients of learning and teaching young children. Forming and sustaining positive and strong learning and teaching relationships is at the heart of human engagement. The quest of any early childhood teacher is to enable every child to progress along optimal and equitable learning pathways as children engage with others, including their families and members of the broader communities in which they live and grow.

Each chapter of this text highlights both conceptual and practical information to support early childhood teachers in their role, especially to promote young children's learning. Collectively the authors of all chapters are drawn together through a broader unity of purpose – the coalescence of evidence-based principles and priorities for working with young children (infants, toddlers, pre-schoolers and children in school). In different ways, the authors profile opportunities for promoting learning in a range of educational contexts that serve children in the first eight years of life. Research, policy and practice case studies are integrated throughout the text to illustrate specific developments and projects, and to highlight the potential intersections of learning, research, policy and practice.

Learning and teaching in the early years is shaped by how we, as teachers, understand the child as a learner. This book is constructed around an image of young children as strong, competent learners with the capacities to be knowledgeable about their worlds and subjects of interest. This image underscores the importance of viewing young children as capable contributors and thinkers who thrive in the context of warm, secure and interesting environments with respectful, knowledgeable and engaged teachers. It speaks to the importance of early childhood teachers promoting children's active participation in the learning process, listening and responding to children's perspectives and lived experiences, and adopting pedagogical practices that support the realisation of the general principles outlined in the *United Nations Convention on the Rights of the Child* (1989).

The context in which young children learn and develop holds the key to every child's success as a life-long learner. Bronfenbrenner's systems theory gives voice to an ecological model (see Figure 0.1) revealing the layered personal, social, political and economic contexts surrounding the child, and the opportunities to refine, improve, replenish or refocus the conditions that support young children's learning, development and well-being. Children are a key part of social systems that aspire to ensure quality of life for all. A Bronfenbrenner-based framework offers teachers a useful conceptual device to consider the unique context of the child and the actions that may be possible or necessary to afford each child the optimal opportunities and conditions for learning. Considering the contexts in which young children learn and develop supports teachers to learn about and engage with the kinship, community networks and cultural environments that shape young children in the first eight years of life. There is integrity in considering the contextual enablers and barriers in young children's lives and reaching deeper understandings of the ways

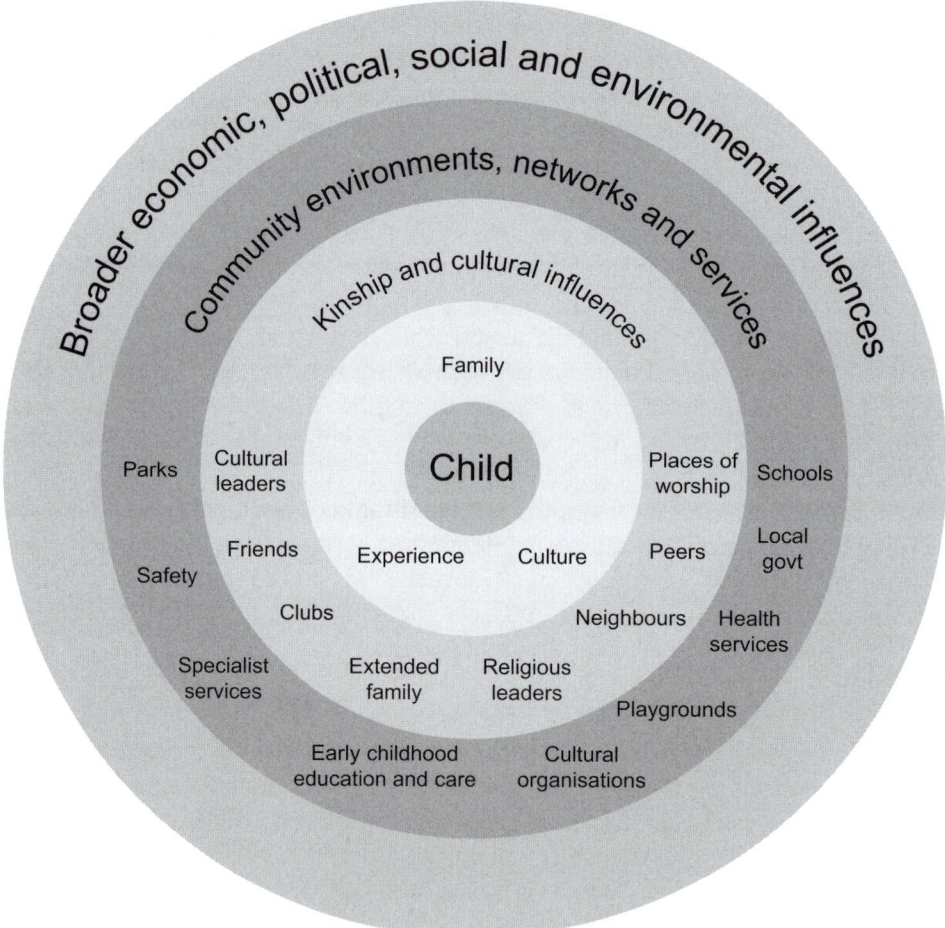

Figure 0.1: Ecological model of child development (adapted from Bronfenbrenner, 1979; reproduced from the *Victorian Early Years Learning and Development Framework*, 2016, with permission from the Department of Education and Training (Victoria) and the Victorian Curriculum and Assessment Authority.

in which young children's learning and development are shaped by personal, family and cultural histories. Teachers can and do create learning environments every day. Those that are inclusive and strong in providing all young children with equal opportunities to learn make a positive difference. Engaging with children, children's families, professional colleagues, organisations and agencies to advocate for optimal life conditions and experiences of young children is an honourable pursuit. Collective effort can deepen effectiveness when there is a clear common vision about supporting young children's learning and development.

Addressing teaching and learning from birth to eight years of age – the major life phase that represents early childhood – is critical. These years are when strong foundations for learning are laid, and where inequalities in learning opportunities can occur and play out throughout young children's lives into adulthood. Ensuring continuity as the child grows emotionally, physically, intellectually and socially across the many educational contexts in which young children and families engage is paramount. Using the findings of research into very early learning and development to guide practice affords the best opportunities for young children to thrive, build a strong sense of identity, contribute in their social worlds, and feel secure and able to progress their learning and communication capacities. Building strong skills, dispositions and outlooks in the early years of life supports young children as they navigate a range of educational settings and contexts throughout their lives.

The process and practice of educating young children in the early years is a specialist area, derived from empirical research into early learning, development, health and well-being. There is a range of theoretical perspectives to inform and guide planning and practice, and a feast of well-defined strategies and approaches that have been found to make a difference. No single method or approach alone will match the individual circumstances of a child's learning. Rather, a variety of teaching and learning strategies that speak to individual children's interests, learning approaches and understandings can be utilised by teachers in their daily interactions with young children. Education is a life-long process for learners and teachers. Teachers who keep abreast of contemporary research and policy are well placed to reflect on their vision of high-quality care and education, and turn vision into effective practice. Reflecting on the joys and challenges of learning and teaching can shape individuals' work practices, and strengthen the capacity of professional learning communities to sustain young children's learning.

Readers will find within this volume information about children and their learning from infancy, about teaching and the strategies that may be adopted, about collaborative relationships with families and colleagues, about the processes and background characteristics that mediate and moderate learning, about leadership, about continuing to learn through questioning, reading, testing, researching or exploring theories, and about advocating for the optimal and sustainable conditions for all children to learn. The first three chapters offer the learning, policy and child frames that are central to rich discussion and debate about the active agents of young children's learning. Research, policy and practice intersections are embedded throughout this book to illustrate some pathways for teachers working with young children across a range of early childhood settings.

Engaging with contemporary research and theory on learning and teaching in the early years may open new opportunities and possibilities for understanding human learning and development in and beyond the first eight years of life. Exploration, critique, trialling, revising and starting over are what it means to be an effective teacher of young children. The impact of this work cannot be underestimated.

Jane Page
Collette Tayler

CHAPTER 1

Learning and teaching in the early years

Collette Tayler and Jane Page

LEARNING OBJECTIVES

In this chapter you will:

1. apply an education lens and articulate features of human learning that contribute to children's well-being and their social and academic achievements, acknowledging that values underpin what is learnt in any society
2. consider the make-up of high-quality early childhood programs and the quality of teaching necessary to enhance children's personal, social and educational achievements
3. plan to collect evidence about children's learning that will point to the next steps in providing experiences to extend or expand children's capabilities.

Introduction

Learning is vital to each child's sense of well-being and development, and yet, talking about learning in any context – at home, among professional colleagues or peers, with children, in early years centres, or through formal studies – reveals a wide range of understandings of the term and its meaning, and the relevance and significance of learning in the first phase of life. Learning is the bedrock of education and, in the early childhood years from birth to age eight, is both a personal and social enterprise that occurs within all of the formal and informal contexts inhabited by the child. In this chapter, we argue that learning about learning is essential prerequisite knowledge for any adult intending to engage productively with infants, toddlers and young children, whether they are at home or in early years centres and classrooms.

Learning: a personal and interactive process that takes place in the child's mind, facilitating action and developmental change, and the achievement of personal, social and intellectual achievements.

There is also debate about the relationship between learning and development. **Development** is the hallmark of growth and change and may be construed as change or growth in one's capacities or abilities. Development may be demonstrated through changed behaviour, language or action; hence a child's development is subject to observation and monitoring. Theorists profess subtly different ways in which learning and development interact, and while it is apparent that learning and development are closely interrelated, development may be construed as being conditional on necessary maturation of the brain and as an outcome of learning. Learning, particularly the learning of skills, is linked primarily to a child's immediate environment and the interactions that take place within that environment. Suffice to say that prevailing theories of the relationship between learning and development continue to refine and change in light of further research and debate. The chapters of this book each address young children's learning in the early years from birth, and the optimal ways in which adults around the child can promote children's learning and development.

Development: the change that occurs in children as they grow and build their physical, intellectual, emotional and social capabilities.

Prevailing **learning theories** and perspectives on educating the very young are typically built from evidence and research findings that have come from a range of disciplines: educational science; neuroscience; cognitive, behavioural, social and cultural psychology; and the medical sciences. At this time, theories about young children's learning reflect the agency of babies, toddlers and young children to reach out, relate to others, observe and absorb information, since recent decades of research have changed thinking about early human capacity. In reviewing writings on child psychology at the millennium, Cole (2000) notes the wealth of scholarship on early cognition and the movement towards a 'relational interpretation of persons and environments' (p. 371). The scale of research driven by theories emphasising the active, relational role of humans

Learning theories: formulations about how information is absorbed, processed and retained.

in the environment provokes the challenge of thinking 'in terms of "and/but" in place of "either/or" (Cole, 2000, p. 372) if we are to realise the interrelationship of person and context in any learning situation. Contemporary learning theory that is applied to the study of infants, toddlers and young children is no longer principally based upon waiting for the child to mature. Hence, the evidence presented in this chapter is selected to help shed light on what makes a positive difference to young children's learning in formal and informal education settings. We reaffirm the value of play as a core context for learning in early childhood, consider play in light of *promoting* learning and development, and take heed of application – applying knowledge about learning to the teaching of children from birth to about the age of eight years.

Preferred approaches to promoting young children's learning also reflect the history and culture of the society in which they are applied. Evidence is selected in regard to the development of citizens in a democracy, and hence, democratic values are embedded. The values within democratic cultures promote certain ways of being and thinking – to use Bruner's words 'mind could not exist save for culture' (1996, p. 3). Drawing upon contemporary learning theories, research and early childhood policy, this chapter promotes the role of **teachers** as catalysts who afford the very young every opportunity to realise their full potential and develop a love of learning.

> **Teachers:** for the purposes of this chapter and text, early childhood educators and teachers are referred to as teachers. This is deliberate: to define the act of teaching as intentional, inclusive of intentional assessment and planning.

Features of learning in the early years

How do we best support young children in their learning and development processes? When might adults step in or intervene in children's activity, and when might they stand back and observe? While there are not simple answers to such questions, teachers who improve their knowledge about young children's learning and development are better able to make decisions as they engage in promoting children's learning and ensuring their well-being. For the very young, learning is relational and rapid. Infants, toddlers and pre-schoolers engage with everyday objects, and people around them influence what children learn and understand about the world. From the outset, infants attune to people and objects, and through this process each child's attention, memory, reasoning, communication skills, and physical and aesthetic capacities are shaped and developed. There is an excellent opportunity to make a difference to children's developmental outcomes in the earliest phase of life – from infancy. Working to understand human **learning mechanisms** and processes helps to give infants, toddlers and young children optimal support. Learning processes and mechanisms are by no means a clear and resolved science, yet there is evidence from numerous studies to guide teachers' choices about early years' curriculum and pedagogy.

> **Learning mechanisms:** the neurological processes within the brain that underlie learning and the development of memory.

Understanding children's learning and cognition: contributions from neuroscience, educational and psychological sciences

A range of studies stemming from various disciplines verify that both genetic and environmental endowments play a part in learning and development. Rutter (2002) was a leader in highlighting that the workings of the human mind are based on the functioning processes within the brain. He noted the substantial role of genetics in 'the origins of individual differences with respect to all psychological traits, both normal and abnormal' (2002, p. 2). Both genes and experience in the environment account for individual learning and achievement, and play a part in the variation of achievement and ability within any group (Asbury & Plomin, 2013). Research into **epigenetics** indicates that a person's genetic make-up and early experiences interact to shape the structure and functioning of the brain. Further, neuroplasticity is at a peak in the very early years of life. What infants, toddlers and young children experience, and the relationships they have with people around them, help to shape brain functioning – who they are – and the way their thinking develops (Tayler & Sabastian-Galles, 2007).

Epigenetics: the study of the transmission of a person's heritable information that can influence the function of genes over and above traditional genetic mechanisms, thereby establishing how environmental and genetic factors intersect and contribute to a person's make-up. See, for example, Schuurmans and Kurrasch (2013).

In early childhood classrooms, this underscores the value of responsive teachers who establish warm and loving environments, and secure attachments, to help to build children's sense of belonging and well-being (Laevers, 2005). During the early life phase, there is an excellent opportunity to positively influence a child's overall development (Blakemore & Frith, 2005; National Scientific Council on the Developing Child, 2007).

Forming the mind: learning as mental activity

The experience of having repeated positive thoughts and emotions is found to strengthen the areas in the brain that stimulate optimism, and ultimately enhance a child's long-term resilience (Shonkoff & Phillips, 2000). However, exposure to repeated negative thoughts and experiences strengthens negative neural pathways. Chronic negativity that is manifest through stress, anger, fear, sadness and helplessness eventually hardwires automatic negative thought processes inside the brain (National Scientific Council on the Developing Child, 2007). These findings mark the importance of warm caring relationships early in life. Children thought to be at risk of poor outcomes because of particular genetic endowments or environmental circumstances *can* be supported by giving special attention to the range and frequency of particular kinds of early experiences.

Randomised controlled studies that have intervened in the early learning and development of disadvantaged children, by providing experiences to strengthen foundational learning, have been found to raise children's social and intellectual achievements (Pungello et al., 2010). Those who engage with the child have an excellent opportunity to make a positive difference, especially when genetic endowment or local environments are less than ideal. However, not all children are exposed to research-validated programs proven to optimise early learning and development. Effective programs may not be well understood, they may be unavailable or unaffordable in some regions, or they may be seen as unnecessary. Notwithstanding the advances in knowledge about early human learning, adults largely determine the kinds of exposure infants, toddlers and young children have to different experiences – adults play a strong part in forming the mind of the child.

Memory and learning capability

Teachers working with the very young are challenged to review research across a wide range of disciplines – since early childhood is a phase of life rather than a discipline in itself – in order to keep pace with current knowledge about early learning and development, and discern the optimal processes for supporting children as they learn and grow. Rovee-Collier and Cuevas (2009) note this problem by illustrating old and new knowledge regarding memory:

> The belief that the memories of infants and adults are fundamentally different is treated as a fact in general psychology and child development texts, in the popular press, and even by well-known scientists. Our common inability to recollect what happened when we were infants ('infantile amnesia') lends credence to this belief – but it is wrong. (p. 11)

From infancy a child's developing memory aligns closely with learning. Recent research demonstrates astonishing memory development over the first few years of life, verifying that infant memories are activated both directly and indirectly. Over a short period they readily form new and relatively permanent associations between objects or events that are present and events or objects that are absent (Rovee-Collier & Cuevas, 2009). Such work illustrates change in understandings about the formation of children's minds. Accumulating information over successive learning episodes relies on the skill to recall experience within earlier episodes, retrieve similar representations and integrate information from different sources that may be available in the present and the past. Verbal and non-verbal measures of infant and toddler memory attest to competence and confirm that memory is expressed 'in a manner appropriate to the age at encoding' (Rovee-Collier & Cuevas, 2009, p. 34).

As infants and toddlers build memory, their capacities rapidly increase. Research within cognitive neuroscience explains that 'the processes involved in building a memory trace, and the time-course of development of the neural structures involved has contributed to the generation of specific predictions regarding the sources of age-related change' (Bauer, 2009, p. 138). Significant age-related variance in long-term memory stems from the encoding and consolidation processes that occur early in life – a profound illustration of the importance of exploring how best to support children as they develop memory through processes of encoding, consolidating, storing and retrieving. Teachers can make a difference, for example, through reminders about prior objects, actions or events. Ornstein and

Haden (2009) highlight the value of imitation sequences as prompts for a child to demonstrate actions that have been demonstrated before. Such sequences can be built into back-and-forth exchanges with children, where adults provoke 'you show me' responses from the child. However, the authors point out that a child's recall by about one year of age, while already having undergone major change, is still limited. They note: 'In contrast to the 2-step events that are remembered by 9- and 10-month olds, children at 24 months of age can produce sequences of five steps in length' (Ornstein & Haden, 2009, p. 371). Further, 20-month-old children can recall sequences after one month elapses, and some remember them after delays of a year (Bauer et al., 2000).

A child's passage through infancy, toddlerhood and early childhood phases is momentous for building event knowledge. Both experience with objects and social interaction play a part in the development of memory and use of event knowledge that helps children to operate in a complex world: 'Goal directed, temporally organised actions form the core of event representations from infancy on … [and] with age, event knowledge develops from simple sequence representations to nested hierarchical structures that organise many types of knowledge and can be accessed through multiple paths' (Hudson & Mayhew, 2009, p. 85). Adults around the child can assist when they highlight and repeat basic routines and events while attuning their words and actions to those of the child's – repeated experiences play a key part in the child's development of memory.

Maturation, memory and learning

Children develop strategic approaches to the conduct of everyday tasks as they mature, yet maturation alone, and child exploration or free play without the engagement of others (including adults), neglects the influential relational role of people in children's learning. Simply waiting for a young child to mature – 'ready in her own good time' – before expecting the use of memory strategies, for example, is a practice based on theories that have since been proven wanting. It is inaccurate to assume that toddlers and pre-schoolers cannot use memory strategies, such as rehearsal, organisation and retrieval (Bjorklund, Dukes & Douglas Brown, 2009), to manage and complete activities.

Some traditions in the practice of early childhood teaching and the expectations of teachers are changing in light of these (and similar) research findings. For example, it is now clear that young children are able to demonstrate a wider range of mathematical abilities than previously tested under Piagetian theory (Ginsburg et al., 2006). Butterworth (2005) reviewed and assessed the innate numerosity of infants and their general cognitive abilities (Piagetian), noting that infants and the very young can discriminate visual arrays of items, and detect change in numerosity through their visual world, by using object tracking and continuous quantity systems. This affords opportunities for play involving two, three or four items, and the manipulation of sets or items in view. Progression to the development of counting occurs from about age two, this representing '… the first bridge from the child's innate capacity for numerosity to the more advanced mathematical achievements of the culture into which she is born' (p. 7).

Teachers who prompt very young children to use rehearsal strategies help their memory performance, since children become inclined to implement strategies even if their ability to use them is limited (Bjorklund et al., 2009). Games that stress the importance of grouping items into categories (organisation) and present the child with cues to help memory (retrieval) produce high levels of performance by children across kindergarten and early school. Such memory cues include sequentially using category cards, telling a child the number of items that matched, and asking the child to recall as many of the items as possible before going on to the next category. The experiments reported affirm the value of using objects and items that children can manipulate (hands-on).

As teachers directly engage with children, they can help build new levels of understanding or strategy use. This behaviour aligns with working in the 'zone of proximal development' (Vygotsky, 1978) and may involve cueing and prompting to help a child remember or overtly talk about remembering strategies or procedures for achieving a task. Yet, there is no clearly established pathway or timing process to help children reach new levels of insight or understanding in situations that require them to remember events, sequences or processes. Biological, cognitive and social processes all play a part in the child's learning, developing memory and perspective taking.

Language and learning as a social relational process

Attraction to and engagement with others is a human characteristic evident from birth. Human babies seek and look intently towards faces from their first weeks of life, and relationship is fundamental in the rapid learning progressions that occur through infancy, toddlerhood and early childhood. Children's relationship experiences are building blocks in a wall of personal, intellectual and social development. Further, language acquisition and development is a unique hallmark of humans, delivering a way to represent the past and future as well as the present.

The onset of language fundamentally alters cognition. MacWhinney (2014) summarised the impact of social structures on children's language learning, including their relations with caretakers. His review highlights that child language learning is supported when the relations are marked by 'trust and identification', 'common ground' and 'cooperativeness'. Further, engagement by caretakers with children that involves 'simple input', 'scaffolding' and 'fine tuning' was found to assure the child's language learning whereas 'extensive rich input' or 'little input at all' has marked effects on the vocabulary levels and subsequent academic achievement of children. Finally, he found that multi-lingual children show 'early sensitivity to the many social conditions determining code selection' (p. 127).

Australian children grow up in a multilingual, multicultural society and, although English is the standard language, learning English as an additional language is the experience of many teachers working with very young children as their language learning explodes between one and three years, and many children are bilingual, developing vocabularies in both (or several) languages during their early years. Recognition and celebration of each child's first language is a vital principle in support of identity, learning and literacy. Direct support in learning English as an additional language is also necessary to ensure a child's education, and future working life, both of which demand fluency in English. Multilingual staff are great human resources in early childhood settings, as are the material resources that guide teachers working with young children (see, for example, Clarke, 2011). Although some effort is made to introduce the learning of languages other than English within the primary years curriculum, this is minor in comparison to Europe where significant support for language learning and the maintenance of linguistic diversity is provided, not only as an impetus for later learning, but also as a means of positively influencing attitudes towards other cultures and languages. In Europe, early language learning includes 'systematic awareness raising or exposure to more than one language taking place in an early childhood education and care setting, and an early start ... considered essential to gaining native speaker intonation and competence' (European Commission, 2011, p. 6). This policy recognises the intellectual merit of language learning and learning through language, values an early start, capitalises on diversity, enhances multilingual and intercultural awareness, and builds the base of effective cross-cultural communication.

Learning and the growth of self-regulation

Relating well to others involves the regulation of one's own behaviour and emotions wherever engagements with others occur. Learning to moderate and manage one's behaviour in different social settings helps a young child to build a sense of identity and contribute in a community. Tayler (2015) discusses pathways to learning in groups and the importance of self-regulation for a child to effectively engage with others:

> There is a strong case for helping to build the foundations for citizenship by thoughtfully promoting children's engagement and participation during pre-school activities. Such promotion helps to build each child's executive functions, including inhibitory control, mental flexibility and working memory. Blair and Diamond (2008, p. 908) conclude that 'in acquiring the capacity for self-regulated learning, social–emotional skills that foster the [child's] relationship [with caring trusted others who model the process] and executive function skills that promote self-regulation are quite literally foundational for learning'. In preschool, the fundamentals of self-regulation and internal executive control are encouraged through informal activities of interest to the child. Importantly, the interactions that encourage perseverance when tasks become difficult, maintain attention to goals, and hold information in mind in order to complete preferred steps and sequences are catalysts for promoting a child's self-regulation capacity. Such behaviours have been linked to mindfulness (Kabat-Zinn, 2003), and referred to as 'contemplative practices' (Willis & Dinehart, 2014). Neurobiological conceptions of children's functioning suggest the value of preventing children from falling into patterns of response that are highly reactive, but rather encourage effortful regulation (Blair, 2002), and referred to as 'contemplative practices' (Willis & Dinehart, 2014). In a longitudinal study of 217 four-year-old urban and rural children, McLelland and colleagues (2007) assessed

the behavioural regulation of the children and their vocabulary, emergent literacy and mathematical skills: they found that growth in behavioural regulation predicted increases in vocabulary, mathematics and emergent literacy skills prior to school. (Tayler, 2015, pp. 166–7)

Aggressive and reactionary behaviour can also inhibit the development of friendships and prevent children from learning together. Tremblay's research recognises this kind of behaviour as foundational to exhibiting violent behaviour later in life (Tremblay, 2004). Furthermore, Heberle et al. (2014) tested the effects of a range of contextual variables (including personal, family and neighbourhood factors) on the behaviours demonstrated by toddlers, finding that parenting behaviour and exposure to violence, as well as parent depressive symptoms, were more strongly linked to toddler disruptive behaviour than neighbourhood factors. Relationships matter! 'Prevention programs require the surrounding adults to demonstrate control over their physical aggression and teach young children how not to resort to [physical aggression]' (Tayler, 2015, p. 165).

Values within learning contexts: the teacher role

The role of the teacher is to understand a child's development and to lead and support the child's learning within a warm and stimulating environment. Children's activity and culture influence the particular learning that takes place each day. Both the child's current level of development (the abilities already mastered) and the child's potential are of interest to teachers: knowing what a child can do, and what a child can do with assistance and support, is important in relation to the way in which teachers interact with children. Further, achieving a balance between practising known skills and processes, and building novelty and challenge into children's everyday activity, is part of the decision-making role of teachers.

Values commonly agreed about what is important for children to know and be able to do, learn and experience in the Australian context are translated through learning frameworks as preferred practices and outcomes for all children up to age five. These are addressed in later chapters. All countries have policies that shape the early learning context and teachers need to critically reflect on values embedded within their programs.

RESEARCH CASE STUDY

Joseph Sparling

THE ABECEDARIAN STUDIES: WHAT DO THEY TELL US ABOUT PROMOTING LEARNING IN THE EARLY YEARS?

The Abecedarian Approach is an example of research-validated teaching and learning strategies based on one-to-one or small group interactions. This approach was developed and tested by over 30 years of randomised trials demonstrating its effec-tiveness in promoting positive and long-lasting changes in children's life outcomes (Ramey, Sparling & Landesman, 2012). In Australia, since 2010, Abecedarian materials have been customised to suit local culture and settings under the Abecedarian Ap-proach Australia (3a) initiative. 3a is not a curriculum; rather it is a set of teaching and learning strategies that can be used within many existing curricula. The approach consists of four elements:

1. *language priority*: a commitment to make every experience an opportunity for talking, listening and learning language
2. *LearningGames®*: 200 experiences or games played between an adult and one or two children. A specific, culturally appropriate set of these materials for use with Aboriginal children and families was also developed
3. *conversational reading*: individual and pair reading that emphasises back and forth communication
4. *enriched caregiving*: intentionally adding educational content to the daily, re-peated routines of care.

The synchronicity of adult and child behaviours within shared learning events, and the type and quality of feedback provided by the teacher to the child during the interactions, is at the heart of the 3a Approach, and this is the subject of research engaging very young Aboriginal children (Brookes & Tayler, 2015). Early findings verify that the rate of young children's learning and developmental progress can be mark-edly changed through the use of specific teaching strategies enacted through social interaction between the child and the teacher or a more knowledgeable other; and that the timeliness of adult inputs into children's experiences affects the impact of the learning experiences. 3a includes two strategies based on joint attention between the adult and child: adult-initiated contingent prompts and feedback; and contingent child responses to the adult behaviours. These strategies are called 3S (see, show, say) and 3N (notice, nudge, narrate), and are used to extend children's receptive and expressive language, and their learning.

REFLECTION POINTS

1. How can early education policy makers and teachers ensure policy and practice that reflects a holistic view of nature and nurture, promotes learn-ing for *all* children and guarantees a learning culture within any setting?
2. How will you organise your own early childhood program to ensure support for each child's learning? What aspects must you address?
3. Select a feature of early learning reported in this chapter that you would like to probe in greater depth. Summarise your understanding and draft further questions to explore through a library search or interview with experienced practitioners.

4. Develop a list of practices to support early learning that you might implement with infants, toddlers and/or young children. Compare your list with the practices set out in the Early Years Learning Framework (EYLF) (DEEWR, 2009) or the *Victorian Early Years Learning and Development Framework* (Department of Education and Training (Victoria), 2016).

The active ingredients of high-quality early childhood programs

Early childhood programs address both the personal and the collective dimensions of children's experiences as teachers work to ensure each child's personal well-being, social participation and education. Enhancing children's well-being, learning and development pathways depend on timing, targeting and consistent support across the child's early years. Early childhood education and care settings have the potential to at least partially compensate for disadvantaged and stressful early environments, and can amplify positive early development – yet the quality of programs is paramount.

Research and program evaluations across numerous countries verify that participation in high-quality programs outside the home during early childhood is beneficial both for early socialisation and intellectual development. Particular gains are evidenced in the cognitive and language development of young children living in disadvantaged circumstances. However, 'quality' is a value-laden construct; the level of quality within programs is influenced by the history, culture and values of the local society, and its aspirations for children.

Examining two commonly accepted components of program quality – structure and process – can assist teachers in considering their program and teaching within an early childhood setting. Many tools exist to assess program quality and these take account of either structural or process aspects, or both. Australian programs are assessed against a National Quality Standard (NQS) (ACECQA, 2011) that integrates structural and process aspects through regulation and quality improvement. Structural quality refers to the facilities, resources, adult-to-child ratios and staff qualifications that set the background for children's learning within a setting. Typically these are easily measurable and normally controlled by forces outside the setting such as government regulation, financing and curriculum-setting. Process quality refers to the nature of interactions within the setting, including the nature of pedagogical leadership. For a review of observational measures of quality, see Ishimine and Tayler (2013).

The structural characteristics of early childhood programs

Evidence of the effects of structural characteristics, such as group size, ratios of adults to children and qualifications of staff on children's learning outcomes, is inconsistent. In the US, group size has been modestly associated with higher levels of cognitive development (NICHD Early Child Care Research Network & Duncan,

2003), with larger group sizes found to moderate the relationship between long periods of time in care and children's externalising behaviour (McCartney et al., 2010). Inconsistent findings may be explained by the complexity of the pathway between each child's exposure to an environment and a child's subsequent development. Ratios have also been found to be significant predictors of children's learning outcomes, as well as the level of qualification of staff (see, for example, Howes, 1997); however, direct pathways to positive child outcomes most likely depend on the way in which adults engage with them.

Because the relationship between program quality and the outcomes for children is complex, singling out individual aspects of quality and definitively attributing one aspect alone to child outcomes is problematic. Better measurement at the room and child level is needed, yet a wide range of studies confirm that the quality of program does indeed make a difference.

The process characteristics of effective programs

The emotional, organisational and instructional domains of adult–child interactions in early childhood classrooms are process characteristics that make a difference to children's outcomes. For example, Mashburn et al. (2008) analysed evidence from classrooms in different parts of the US, findings strong relationships between the type and intensity of adult–child interactions in classrooms and the level of children's academic and language performance. When studying the progress of children who were determined to be at risk of doing poorly through their display of problem attentional, academic or social behaviours, Hamre and Pianta (2005) found similar results. Positive experiences in classrooms have been found to promote behaviours that support children's learning and well-being. Over time, researchers focused on the organisational, emotional and instructional aspects of classroom interactions characterise effective teaching in the early years as 'responsive teaching', and in turn, responsive teaching has been found to clearly promote both the social and cognitive development of young children (Hamre et al., 2014).

Planning for learning

There are empirically validated educational strategies and interventions that work to change child outcome trajectories and, hence, there is merit in teachers selecting and implementing evidence-based strategies. Adopting an early learning framework that ensures a mix of freedom, guidance and direction is the backdrop of Australian early childhood education – the main goal being attending to children's learning.

Teachers need to articulate the theoretical bases of their programs in order to be clear about purpose when working with children. Tayler (2015) notes that:

> early childhood educators experience difficulty in articulating the theoretical bases for their pedagogical practices, and they frequently revert to broad developmental theories to guide their practice (Hedges & Cullen, 2012; Stephen, 2010). Levers of development such as age and maturation have long influenced the way in which educators set up the environments for infant, toddler and kindergarten-age children's play – natural materials, equipment and objects are selected having regard to stages of development and

the indoor and outdoor play spaces within any early childhood setting ... Ideally, play spaces afford rich engagements with objects and people, and spontaneous learning is facilitated according to the interests of the very young child. (Tayler, 2015, pp. 163–4)

The approach selected by each teacher is a reflection of the philosophy that teachers adopt and what they see as their purpose. In Australian settings, planning for learning is a common endeavour albeit manifest in different ways according to the preference of teachers within a local community.

RESEARCH CASE STUDY

E4KIDS: ASSESSING THE EFFECTIVENESS OF AUSTRALIAN EARLY CHILDHOOD EDUCATION AND CARE EXPERIENCES

Effective Early Educational Experiences for Kids (E4Kids[1]) was a five-year longitudinal study that assessed the contribution of participation in early childhood programs on the cognitive and social development of some 2500 three and four year olds. Early childhood programs in Australia are not compulsory – parents decide on the relevance, timing and amount of their children's attendance (which is also dependent on the ability of families to pay).

Consider the findings below and the questions they raise for the provision of high-quality, effective early learning programs.

Regarding children's access and usage of programs

Higher parental education predicted the earlier entry of children into early childhood education and care (ECEC) programs three and four years before school. Low-quality home learning environment, alongside having both parents in the paid workforce, also predicted earlier ECEC program usage. 'These data suggest that even among those children attending ECEC programs at age 3–4 years there remains a significant group of children who either do not attend ECEC programs in the formative first three years of life or who attend at a level (under 10 h per week) which is unlikely to lead to significant developmental benefit' (Gilley et al., 2015, p. 9).

Regarding program quality

The average quality within programs varied systematically across the type of service. The average long day care classroom is lower in quality than pre-school classrooms by about three quarters of a standard deviation, and 'we found evidence that Australian pre-school settings are slightly stronger in the areas of classroom organisation

---

1   E4Kids is a project of the Melbourne Graduate School of Education at the University of Melbourne and is conducted in partnership with Queensland University of Technology. The study was funded by the Australian Research Council Linkage Projects Scheme (Grant LP0990200), the Victorian Government Department of Education and Training, and the Queensland Government Department of Education and Training.

and instructional support, yet even in these areas our standardised, internationally validated rating tools returned overall scores that averaged in the low-to-medium range' (Tayler et al., 2013, p. 20).

Regarding program availability and quality

> On average programs in lower SES [socio-economic status] areas exhibit lower adult–child interaction quality as measured by the three CLASS domains … Long day care services are the key source of the lower availability of ECEC in low-SES areas, an important finding, as long day care services represent more than two thirds of all available ECEC spaces. These findings are consistent with previous findings in the US related to the undersupply of ECEC services in low-SES areas. They do not, however, support the findings of Small and Stark (2005) that identified for-profit services as the source of undersupply. Instead, there is an equiproportional distribution of management types across SES neighborhoods in Australian ECEC services. (Cloney et al., 2015, p. 13)

Regarding the type of children's experience and their skills development

While age and intelligence proved to be important predictors of both children's initial performance and the further development of competencies, typical SES measures did not predict the child outcomes well when all variables were included in the analyses. Rather, what adults do with children is the key (Hildenbrand et al., 2015).

Regarding children at risk of poor progress

In everyday ECEC programs, young children who may be at risk of making poor progress because of predictive variables within family or local community, and because of their absolute level of ability, are:

> at persistent risk of doing poorly over time. In this non-experimental data drawn from the progression of children through typical everyday ECEC programs, children who do not receive specific interventions early continue to perform below the level expected by normative data and relative to their more advantaged peers, albeit having an ECEC program dosage that may be below what is needed to ensure solid progress. These findings offer compelling background and justification for giving more attention to assessing skills and abilities early. In the least this would support the learning of children who are at risk of poor performance and aid the design of individualised programs that are known to accelerate development. (Tayler, Cloney & Niklas, 2015, p. 59)

REFLECTION POINTS

1. How can teachers play an active role as advocates for quality ECEC in the case of young children who may not be enrolled into ECEC programs by their parents until about four years of age? What 'learning promotion' options may be pursued in local communities to engage families in children's learning from birth?

2. What kinds of program and child assessment and tracking processes will you use as a teacher? How can you ensure early attention for children whose learning would be enhanced by timely and focused support?

3. Summarise what you know about the provision of effective instructional supports to very young children, and find three further research papers that include findings about how teachers can improve their pedagogical practices in support of rich and meaningful early learning.

Collecting evidence of learning to build teaching effectiveness

To take on a role that has **learning promotion** at its heart, effective teachers rely on sound evidence of what each child knows and can do in order to be clear about what might be added to a child's experience to consolidate skills, deepen understandings and extend knowledge. Evidence about each child's development, combined with critical reflection on the role the teacher can play in promoting learning, is fundamental to the preparation of appropriate, stimulating learning experiences to engage the child. Concurrently building children's agency and control of their learning, and children's motivation to keep learning, is likely to help them to persist and take on new challenges. With learning promotion as a teacher's mission, a world of opportunities to engage and help to expand knowledge and skills unfolds. Yet, no matter the activities that arise, teachers' professional work demands sensitivity to each child's behaviours, interests and capabilities.

> **Learning promotion:** the active support of a person's learning by those who engage with the person.

The ideas presented below about assessment, and the collection of evidence about children's knowledge, skills and understandings, were drawn from review papers by Tayler, Ishimine and Raban (2011) and Marbina et al. (2015). Readers are encouraged to use these ideas to further their own research into assessment and design an assessment strategy that may be deployed when working with infants, toddlers or young children.

Effective assessment needs a clearly defined purpose

In order to provide an informed understanding of children's abilities, teachers need to know what they are assessing, and for what purpose. Having a clear understanding of indicators of learning and well-being progression (and each child's developmental trajectory) supports teachers to be specific and explicit in assessments. There are a range of typical developmental trajectories that may serve as a guide for working with young children, and expanding knowledge of what children know and can do. Be aware that, sometimes, children surprise adults who assume that developmental milestone charts best represent what an individual child knows and can do: these are merely a gauge to begin observation, for example, with the purpose of learning about individual children's capabilities through games and joint explorations.

Effective assessment of cognition and well-being is based on multiple sources of information

Assessment practices that involve adopting a mixed methods approach, across multiple contexts, administered at different times and by different people, give the most balanced account of a child's capacity. Where existing measures only provide a checklist of observed behaviours, additional descriptive information proves valuable in planning for further learning and learning promotion activities.

Assessment must be sensitive to the individual setting

A holistic approach to assessment takes account of the learning environment and the wider philosophy adopted and promoted. Children who feel comfortable and secure are more likely to participate with others and demonstrate their interests and capabilities.

Sound assessment practice includes children's own reports

Children are reliable experts on their own experiences. Assessment strategies that are currently used include discussions with children about their experiences, incorporating what they have learned and what else they would like to know. Such discussions provide ample evidence of further learning promotion opportunities. Drawing, photography, role play, use of puppets, topic-focused discussions or brainstorms during group or circle time can each inform teachers about children's capabilities and interests.

Assessment of children's progress includes evidence from parents or primary caregivers

Families are children's first teachers. Parental involvement in any assessment strategy ensures that the dispositions and skills of each child are best revealed, and that children's competencies and the challenges they face are apparent. Families observe children in a wide range of settings beyond the ECEC program.

Assessment is an opportunity for multidisciplinary collaboration

In the early years, children and families utilise a range of services, including maternal and child health clinics, community play groups, cultural groups, family day care schemes, long day care centres, general and paediatric health services, pre-school/kindergartens, out-of-school-hours care, and early intervention support. Developing a shared understanding of what children's learning and development looks like in the early years, and a common language for how it is described and supported, not only enhances professional conversations, but also supports consistency of practice for families, providing reassurance that everyone is working together in the interest of the child.

Different tools offer different kinds of knowledge on children's learning and development

Some tools focus on the children's program at an *environment* or *whole room level* to gain a picture of the overall climate of a given environment; other tools focus on the *individual child level* whereby individual children are observed and assessed against particular indicators with an aim to promote the individual child's learning and development. Selecting tools that are validated for the purpose intended and pitched towards the unit of analysis that is of greatest interest is an important aspect of any assessment strategy. There is value in using a range of lenses to deepen understanding of learning and point towards next steps in promoting each child's learning, as well as the learning of a group of children.

REFLECTION POINTS

1. What principles would characterise your own approach to the assessment of children? Develop a personal list of fundamentals about assessment that you wish to further explore in order to build your own knowledge about young children from birth to the age of eight years.
2. Review the practice principles that are contained in any early years curriculum or framework for learning (see, for example, EYLF, 2009). What is said or not said about assessment? How is very early learning construed? Is there any reference to the promotion of learning? What is the scope? How are families involved?
3. Obtain a copy of the NQS from www.acecqa.gov.au. Critique the content of the standards and write a short summary of the quality areas that you determine to be of particular importance.

Conclusion

Children develop at an extraordinary rate in the early years. There are many types of early childhood programs for infants, toddlers and pre-school-age children, most of which pay attention to children's overall development. Teachers have a rich array of research literature on how children learn and develop, and implementation literature on how to play a positive part in promoting children's learning. Importantly, keeping abreast of the research on children's learning is fundamental to enacting optimal curriculum and pedagogy. Common myths regarding the minds of very young children are being dispelled in an era of multidisciplinary inquiry into learning, growth and development, and yet fundamentals, such as having a sense of security, well-being, and engagement with others, remain at the heart of children's progress.

Further reading

Blair, C. & Diamond, A. (2008). Biological processes in prevention and intervention: the promotion of self-regulation as a means of preventing school failure. *Development and Psychopathology, 20*(3), 899–911. DOI: http://doi.org/10.1017/S0954579408000436

Center on the Developing Child, Harvard University. (2011). Building the brain's 'Air Traffic Control' system: how early experiences shape the development of executive function. Working Paper No. 11. Retrieved from www.developingchild.harvard.edu

Currie, J. (2009). Healthy, wealthy and wise: socio-economic status, poor health in childhood and human capital development. *Journal of Economic Literature, 47*(1), 87–122.

Nelson, K. (2005). Evolution and development of human memory systems. In B. J. Ellis & D. F. Bjorklund (Eds.). *Origins of the Social Mind. Evolutionary Psychology and Child Development* (pp. 354–82). New York: The Guildford Press.

Piaget, J. (1952) *The Child's Conception of Number*, translated by C. Gattegno and F. M. Hodgson. London: Routledge & Kegan Paul.

References

Asbury, K., & Plomin, R. (2013). *G is for Genes*. Chichester, West Sussex: John Wiley and Sons.

Australian Children's Education and Care Quality Authority (ACECQA). (2011). *Guide to the National Quality Standard*. Retrieved from http://files.acecqa.gov.au/files/National-Quality-Framework-Resources-Kit/NQF03-Guide-to-NQS-130902.pdf

Bauer, P. J. (2009). The cognitive neuroscience of the development of memory. In M.L. Courage & N. Cowan (Eds.). *The Development of Memory in Infancy and Childhood* (pp. 115–44). New York: Psychology Press.

Bauer, P. J., Wenner, J. A., Dropil, P. L., & Wewerka, S. S. (2000). Parameters of remembering and forgetting in the transition from infancy to early childhood. *Monographs of the Society for Research in Child Development, 65*(4), Serial No. 263, i–iv and 1–23.

Bjorklund, D. F., Dukes, C., & Douglas Brown, R. (2009). The development of memory strategies. In M. L. Courage & N. Cowan (Eds.). *The Development of Memory in Infancy and Childhood* (pp. 145–75). New York: Psychology Press.

Blakemore, S. J., & Frith, U. (2005). The learning brain. Lessons for education: a précis, *Developmental Science, 8*(6), 459–71.

Brookes, I., & Tayler, C. (2015). 'The effect of adult prompts and feedback on children's language learning and development'. Poster for Science of Learning Research Centre Symposium, Melbourne.

Bruner, J. (1996). *The Culture of Education*. Cambridge, MA: Harvard University Press.

Butterworth, B. (2005). The development of arithmetical abilities. *Journal of Child Psychology and Psychiatry, 46*(1), 3–18.

Clarke, P. (2011). *Learning English as an Additional Language in the Early Years (Birth to Six)*. Melbourne: VCAA.

Cloney, D., Cleveland, G., Hattie, J., & Tayler, C. (2015). Variations in the availability and quality of early childhood education and care by socioeconomic status. *Early Education and Development*. DOI: http://doi.org/10.1080/10409289.2015.1076674

Cole, M. (2000). Struggling with complexity: the handbook of child psychology at the millennium. *Human Development, 43*(6), 369–75.

Department of Education and Training (Victoria) and the Victorian Curriculum and Assessment Authority. (2016). *Victorian Early Years Learning and Development Framework*. Melbourne: Department of Education and Training (Victoria).

Department of Education, Employment and Workplace Relations (DEEWR). (2009). *Belonging, Being & Becoming: The Early Years Learning Framework for Australia*. Canberra: DEEWR for COAG.

European Commission. (2011). *Language Learning at Pre-primary Level: Making it Efficient and Sustainable*. Brussels: European Commission.

Gilley, T., Tayler, C., Niklas, F., & Cloney, D. S. (2015). Too late and not enough for some children: early childhood education and care (ECEC) program usage patterns in the years before school in Australia. *International Journal of Child Care and Education Policy, 9*(9), 1–15. DOI: http://doi.org/10.1186/s40723-015-0012-0

Ginsburg, H., Kaplan, G., Cannon, J., et al. (2006). Helping early childhood educators to teach mathematics. In M. J. Zaslow & I. Martinez-Beck (Eds.). *Current Issues in Early Childhood Professional Development* (pp. 171–202). Baltimore, MD: Brookes Publishing.

Hamre, B. K., & Pianta, R. C. (2005). Can instructional and emotional support in the first-grade classroom make a difference for children at risk of school failure? *Child Development, 76*(5), 949–67.

Hamre, B., Hatfield, B., Pianta, R., & Jamil, F. (2014). Evidence for general and domain-specific elements of teacher–child interactions: associations with preschool children's development, *Child Development, 85*(3), 1257–74.

Heberle, A. E., Thomas, Y. M., Wagmiller, R. L., Briggs-Gowan, M. J., & Carter A. S. (2014). The impact of neighbourhood, family and individual risk factors on toddlers' disruptive behaviour. *Child Development, 85*(5), 2046–61.

Hedges, H., & Cullen, J. (2012). Participatory learning theories: a framework for early childhood pedagogy. *Early Child Development and Care, 182*(7), 921–40. DOI: http://doi.org/10.1080/03004430.2011.597504

Hildenbrand, C., Cohrssen, C., Niklas, F., & Tayler, C. (2015). Children's mathematical and verbal competence in different early education and care programs in Australia. *Journal of Early Childhood Research*. DOI: http://doi.org/10.1177/1476718X15582096

Howes, C. (1997). Children's experience in center-based care as a function of teacher background and adult: child ratio. *Merrill-Palmer Quarterly, 43*(3), 404–25.

Hudson, J. A., & Mayhew, E. M. Y. (2009). The development of memory for recurring events. In M. L. Courage & N. Cowan (Eds.). *The Development of Memory in Infancy and Childhood* (69–91). New York: Psychology Press.

Ishimine, K., & Tayler, C. (2013). Assessing quality in early childhood education and care. *European Journal of Education, 49*(2), 272–90.

Kabat-Zinn, J. (2003). Mindfulness-based interventions in context: past, present and future. *Clinical Psychology: Science and Practice, 10*(1), 144–56.

Laevers, F. (2005). *SICs; Well-Being and Involvement in Care. A Process-Oriented Self-Evaluation Instrument for Care Settings*. Retrieved from www.kindengezin.be/img/sics-ziko-manual.pdf

MacWhinney, B. (2014). What we have learned. *Journal of Child Language, July, 14 Supplement, 41*, 124–31.

Mashburn, A. J., Pianta, R. C., Hamre, B. K., et al. (2008). Measures of classroom quality in prekindergarten and children's development of academic language and social skills. *Child Development, 79*(3), 732–49.

Marbina, L., Mashford Scott, A., Church, A., & Tayler, C. (2015). Assessment of Wellbeing in Early Childhood Education and Care: *Literature Review*. Victorian Early Years Learning and Development Framework. Melbourne: VCAA.

McCartney, K., Burchinal, M. R., Clarke-Stewart, A., et al. (2010). Testing a series of causal propositions relating time in child care to children's externalizing behavior. *Developmental Psychology, 46*(1), 1–17.

McLelland, M. M., Cameron, C. E., McDonald Connor, C., et al. (2007). Links between behavioural regulation and pre-schoolers literacy vocabulary and math skills. *Developmental Psychology, 43*(4), 947–59.

National Scientific Council on the Developing Child. (2007). *The Science of Early Childhood Development: Closing the Gap Between What We Know and What We Do*. Cambridge, MA: National Scientific Council on the Developing Child. Retrieved from www.developingchild.net

NICHD Early Child Care Research Network, & Duncan, G. (2003). Does quality of child care affect child outcomes at age 4½? *Developmental Psychology, 39*(3), 451–69.

Ornstein, P. A., & Haden, C. A. (2009). Developments in the study of the development of memory. In M. L. Courage & N. Cowan (Eds.). *The development of memory in infancy and childhood* (pp. 367–85), New York: Psychology Press.

Pungello, E. P., Kainz, K., Burchinal, M., et al. (2010). Early educational intervention, early cumulative risk and the early home learning environment as predictors of young adult outcomes within a high-risk sample. *Child Development, 81*(1), 410–26.

Ramey, C. T., Sparling, J., & Landesman, S. L. (2012). *Abecedarian: The Ideas, the Approach and the Finding.* Los Altos, CA: Sociometrics Corporation.

Rovee-Collier, C., & Cuevas, K. (2009). The development of infant memory. In M. L. Courage & N. Cowan (Eds.). *The Development of Memory in Infancy and Childhood* (pp. 11–41). New York: Psychology Press.

Rutter, M. (2002). Nature, nurture and development: from evangelism through science toward policy and practice. *Child Development, 73*(1), 1–21.

Schuurmans, C., & Kurrasch, D. M. (2013). Neurodevelopmental consequences of maternal distress: what do we really know? *Clinical Genetics, 83*(2), 108–17.

Shonkoff, J. P., & Phillips, D. A. (2000). *From Neurons to Neighbourhoods: The Science of Early Childhood Development.* Washington DC: Office of Educational Research and Improvement.

Stephen, C. (2010). Pedagogy: the silent partner in early years learning. *Early Years: An International Research Journal, 30*(1), 15–28. DOI: http://doi.org/10.1080/09575140903402881

Tayler, C. (2015). Learning in early childhood: experiences, relationships and 'learning to be'. *European Journal of Education, 50*(2), 160–74. DOI: http://doi.org/10.1111/ejed.12117

Tayler, C., & Sabastian-Galles, N. (2007). The brain, development and learning in early childhood. In OECD (Ed.), *Understanding the Brain: birth of a learning science* (pp. 161–184). Paris: OECD Publications.

Tayler, C., Ishimine, K., & Raban, B. (2011). Assessment for learning and development in the early years. A discussion paper to inform the development of a Framework for the assessing and reporting of children's learning 0–5 years. Melbourne: VCAA.

Tayler, C., Ishimine, K., Cloney, D., Cleveland, G., & Thorpe, K. (2013). The quality of early childhood education and care services in Australia. *Australasian Journal of Early Childhood, 38*(2), 13–21.

Tayler C., Cloney, D., & Niklas, F. (2015). A bird in the hand: understanding the trajectories of development of young children and the need for action to improve outcomes. *Australasian Journal of Early Childhood, 40*(3), 51–60.

Tremblay, R. (2004). Development of physical aggression during infancy. *Infant Mental Health Journal, 25*(5), 399–407.

Vygotsky, L. S. (1978). Interaction between learning and development. In M. Cole, V. John-Steiner, S. Scribner & E. Souberman (Eds.). *Mind and Society: The Development of Higher Psychological Processes* (pp. 79–91). Cambridge, MA: Harvard University Press.

CHAPTER 2

A policy frame on early learning and teaching

Karen Weston and Collette Tayler

LEARNING OBJECTIVES

In this chapter you will:

1. understand how Australian policy regarding the provision of education and care in the early years is shaped and informed by research evidence
2. explain how the Early Years Learning Framework and National Quality Framework affect learning and teaching
3. describe how Australian policy reform has influenced the role of teachers.

Introduction

Government policy sets out a vision and a program of ideas about what governments want to do, and the governance for implementation. In this way, government policy is positioned both to frame the social discourse that takes place across communities around a topic, and change the context and practice within the area of interest or concern. Government policy formation varies in its nature according to political leadership – in brief, democracies differ from autocracies in the way that policy is designed, decreed, legislated and implemented. Furthermore, government policy may set direction across a wide range of areas (e.g. regarding efficiency or accountability), address a population issue (e.g. social well-being) or direct action in a specific area (e.g. child protection).

Decisions to develop or change policy may be motivated by a range of factors including: community pressure; changing societal values; political idealism; information on the status or well-being of the whole or sectors of the population; economic imperatives; a need for better governance, transparency or accountability; and findings from recent research or global trends and developments in the area. Typically, no single factor alone accounts for a decision by government to develop or revise policy in an area of concern or interest.

Policy may be designed to: change the behaviour of businesses, organisations and individuals; solve a particular problem; or improve on policy and systems that are already in place (Victorian Public Sector Commission, 2015; Australian Public Service Commission, 2009). Policy setting is by no means free of controversy! In Australia, the combined and sometimes competing policy interests of investing early to support the long-term human development of its youngest citizens, intervening to protect and ensure the well-being of children living in disadvantaged circumstances, and supporting parental (especially women's) participation in the paid workforce shape the policy design and ongoing adjustment of the National Quality Framework. Within the constraints of a chapter, priority is given to the aspects of early childhood and family policy that pertain to children's learning.

Policy: a set of principles and statements that guide decisions and actions towards certain preferred outcomes.

The mechanisms of government policy typically include legislation, regulation and programs. Policy makers within western democracies use a wide range of policy mechanisms, beyond the traditional model of government solely devising and implementing policy. Mechanisms include involving third parties such as entrepreneurs, industry associations, financial institutes and non-government organisations. Policy may be implemented through instruments such as government action, regulation, education and information campaigns, funding and partnership arrangements, and sometimes, combinations of these instruments (Mamouney, 2014; Althaus, Bridgman & Davis, 2013).

Early childhood education and care (ECEC) provision is in itself a mechanism used by governments to achieve policy goals that may relate to education, equity, health, social welfare and inclusion, and the economy. In a democratic and federated country such as Australia, policy making and policy change is also confounded by multiple layers of government having uniquely defined powers to act. Therefore, some policy initiatives take extraordinary cooperation across federal, state, territorial and local levels of government. Achieving whole-of-country policy change involves wide-range planning, collaboration, and negotiation and mutual action through the machinery of many governments.

On an international stage, the Australian National Quality Framework for Early Childhood Education and Care (NQF) policy that is outlined in this chapter is a remarkable achievement. In the period from 2009–12, Australia put into place wide-ranging reform of early childhood provision, and the levers of this reform (legislation, regulation, funding and adjustment) continue. No other federated country has attempted and achieved such coordination and change in the provision of ECEC services, although this has not always been recognised or acclaimed (McKew, 2012).

Teachers may find out about policy through media announcements or by reading the large array of documents published by governments, such as funding information and guidelines, guidance materials that support implementation of legislation or even the legislation itself, curriculum documents, and through guidelines and letters by professional colleagues. Good government policy is developed through active engagement and consultation with the community and particularly the stakeholders involved in the proposed change. Australian teachers and families have participated in consultation about the national reform of the early childhood sector.

A detailed explanation and analysis of Australian policy in ECEC follows, including some international evidence that supports the design of the reforms that relate to promoting young children's learning and the changing role of the teacher.

Direction from research: some influences and dilemmas of Australian early childhood policy

Research findings from across the educational, social and behavioural sciences propelled Australian policy makers to affirm the importance of early life experiences, understand the interplay of genetic and environmental factors in brain development and human behaviour, and realise the opportunity to advance every child's potential. The landmark report, *From Neurons to Neighbourhoods: The Science of Early Childhood Development* (Shonkoff & Phillips, 2000) confirmed that 'children are born wired for feelings and ready to learn' (p. 4) and that basic brain architecture and function is established in early childhood (McCain, Mustard & Shanker, 2007), increasing the likelihood of favourable developmental outcomes through well-planned interventions. Cross-disciplinary knowledge about child development (see also Chapter 1) revealed elements that are expected to produce positive impacts, including highly skilled teachers; relatively small group sizes and high adult-to-child ratios for close relationships; age-appropriate curricula and stimulating materials in a safe phys-ical setting; a language-rich environment; warm, responsive interactions between staff and children; and high and consistent levels of child participation (Center on the Developing Child, 2007; National Research Council, 2001).

Evidence from the Effective Pre-School and Primary Education Project (EPPE) in the UK demonstrated that pre-school education has a lasting effect on children's development and can help alleviate social disadvantage (Sylva et al., 2010). The EPPE study found that children made greater developmental progress in settings with more highly qualified staff (especially qualified teachers) and where cognitive and social-behavioural development were viewed as of equal importance. Settings chosen for their provision of high-quality programs demonstrated an effective ped-agogy for learning, described as 'shared sustained thinking' where two-thirds of the activities were child-initiated with about half of these activities extended by teachers (Siraj-Blatchford, 2010). These findings, among others from model pro-grams (Rinaldi, 2001; Pianta et al., 2009), have influenced early childhood policy in Australia.

Australian policy makers engage with local and international researchers and early childhood professionals, accessing international evidence from research and policy in multiple jurisdictions. Contemporary early childhood policy has been in-fluenced by comparative research into early childhood systems and international benchmarking reports of government spending (Economist Intelligence Unit, 2012; OECD, 2013), as well as rich ideas drawn from national and regional thinktanks, reviews and consultations, and local studies. At no other time in history has there been so much information available to guide policy.

Government policy and investment in early childhood provision is also in-fluenced by economics-focused reports that promote investment in early child-hood learning as more cost effective than investment at older ages (Heckman, 2003; Cunha et al., 2005). Heckman (2003) argues that learning starts in infancy and that once children fall behind in their learning, they are likely to remain behind: 'early learning begets later learning' (p. 1). It is argued that school en-vironments play only a small role in reducing achievement differences, while parenting practices have strong effects on children's emotional development and motivation (Heckman, 2003). Furthermore, a focus on early childhood provision is advocated also to help reduce child poverty and exclusion. *Starting Strong II* (OECD, 2006) concluded that early childhood policies should provide access and participation for all young children to learning in partnership with education sys-tems. Recommendations included increasing public investment with appropriate accountability, system reform integrating education and care, coordinated vision and quality standards set through participatory approaches which emphasise educational program and practice, including development of curriculum, and on-going research into the effects of provision on children's learning and well-being.

Globalisation and neo-liberal influences (particularly in western English-speaking nations) have led to convergence in early childhood and education policy. For example, education and life-long learning are now positioned as tools for creating and maintaining a 'competitive edge' in world markets, yet Ball (1998) and others challenge the convergence of globalisation, and the 'marketisation' of education as a cost effective and flexible policy solution. The use of market mechanisms, such as choice and accountability, is questioned, particularly if implementation is undertaken by entrepreneurs rather than by the state (Henry et al., 1999; Ball, 2006). Entrepreneurial services shape access and equity outcomes unless there are tight regulatory controls, and the steering capacity of governments is considerably weaker if funding is through subsidies to parents rather than provided directly to services (OECD, 2006). The Australian early childhood system represents a 'mixed-market' model established after the 1970s, comprising private, community and government-supplied programs and delivering both strengths and shortcomings. Policy effort operates within this context.

Promoting children's learning and supporting women's participation are of mutual and overlapping interest to policy makers (Pianta et al., 2009; OECD, 2006, 2013; Penn, 2011).Women's participation in the paid labour market is a key driver of the Australian Government's interest in expanding early childhood services, with women contributing to national productivity. The intersection of workplace participation policies and early childhood policies poses numerous opportunities and challenges for innovation, and there is a wealth of research and policy evidence to better integrate child, family and labour market policy initiatives.

Australia's federated system of government

Australia has a federated system of government, where all levels of government are involved in policy, funding, providing and regulating ECEC services. The Australian Constitution aimed to limit Commonwealth powers to make laws that united the federation and Australia's relations with the outside world (Fenna, Robbins & Summers, 2014). Each state retains its own sovereignty and the power to make laws (over matters not controlled by Commonwealth), and thus, nine different governments are involved in policy making in Australia. Federalism has evolved and there is debate as to whether our system of government is ineffective and indecisive, or whether it provides great opportunity for constitutional innovation and experimentation among its various governments (Fenna et al., 2014).

A key challenge is the imbalance in revenue-raising capacities, with the Commonwealth having more ability to pay for reform (McClintock, 2013), and reason for increased Commonwealth involvement in the nation's affairs (National Commission of Audit, 2015). The focus of the federated system shifts between conflict and cooperation (Fenna, 2014) with debates about clarifying roles and responsibilities (McClintock, 2013), or collaborating through intergovernmental forums and agreements that seek to re-distribute Commonwealth funding with appropriate accountability measures for the achievement of outcomes.

Under the federated system, State and territory governments are responsible for education and have the power to legislate for standards in education and early childhood. Each jurisdiction, however, may implement policy differently, illustrated by the historically different approaches to the delivery of pre-school, with some states providing pre-school within their schooling system while others provide funding to non-government organisations for pre-school to operate in a range of settings. Coordination of early childhood policy in Australia is challenging, all the more reason for heralding the NQF as an example of extraordinary achievement and cooperation by nine governments.

Policy on early learning

The Commonwealth Government provides subsidies to parents to assist in making early learning and care affordable (Elliott, 2006; Brennan, Blaxland & Tannous, 2009; Tayler, 2011; Productivity Commission, 2014). After the 2007 Federal Government election, improving ECEC became a national priority, with a focus on integrating early learning and care under the education portfolio. The government proposed a universal right to access pre-school in the year before school, under new Commonwealth legislation, and states and territories instead agreed to a national partnership to implement this reform (COAG, 2008).

In the period between 2007 and 2012, both levels of government developed and agreed on *Investing in the Early Years – A National Early Childhood Development Strategy* (COAG, 2009) – a national vision for all children by 2020. This overarching framework outlined actions to improve child outcomes, and contribute to social inclusion, human capital and productivity for the nation. Through intergovernmental agreements, children gained improved access to early education, and outcomes for children (birth to five years) were defined through the first ever national learning framework. Further, the quality of services was also assessed, with the ratings published, and other partnership agreements gave further specific attention to supporting Indigenous children, and the status of the early childhood workforce.

Through the **Council of Australian Governments (COAG)**, strategic policy for early childhood programs rests with the **Education Council** where Education Ministers acknowledged, for the first time, their responsibility for 'the development and strengthening of early childhood education, to provide every child with the opportunity for the best start in life' in the *Melbourne Declaration on Education Goals for Young Australians* (Ministerial Council on Education, Employment, Training and Youth Affairs, 2008, p. 11). This follows the international trend of designating education as the lead ministry for children from birth (United Nations Educational Scientific and Cultural Organization, 2007; Penn, 2011; OECD, 2013). This approach increases attention on children's learning and the streamlining of systems through to the early years of school. However, since early childhood education is non-compulsory, it can struggle for attention and adequate funding within an education bureaucracy (UNESCO, 2007).

Council of Australia Governments (COAG): the peak forum for collaboration across Commonwealth, State and local Government. COAG promotes and oversees significant national policy reforms with support from ministerial councils.

Education Council: a forum for ministers with portfolio responsibility for school education and early childhood development to coordinate strategic policy at a national level.

The *National Partnership Agreement on Early Childhood Education* (COAG, 2008) is a leading example of effective collaboration in a federated system where

Commonwealth funding added to state and territory funding for pre-schools and increased the number of places and hours of access for more children.

For younger children not accessing a pre-school program, undoubtedly the market-based policy framework has helped to expand places (Newberry & Brennan, 2013) and 22 per cent of children under the age of two years and 54 per cent of two- and three-year-olds attended early childhood programs (ABS, 2014).

RESEARCH CASE STUDY

Diana Warren and John Haisken-DeNew

EARLY BIRD CATCHES THE WORM: THE CAUSAL IMPACT OF PRE-SCHOOL PARTICIPATION AND TEACHER QUALIFICATIONS ON YEAR 3 NAPLAN COGNITIVE TESTS

This research case study demonstrates an effective research and evaluation partnership between government (Department of Education) and the Melbourne Institute of Applied Economic and Social Research (University of Melbourne), to produce the first analysis of the impact of pre-school programs for Australia.

This research used data drawn from Waves 1 and 3 of the Longitudinal Survey of Australian Children (LSAC), and matched Year 3 nationwide NAPLAN tests (2008) in the domains of numeracy, reading, spelling, writing and grammar, to look at the causal impact of attendance at pre-school in the year prior to starting formal schooling. It also examined the impact effect of pre-school teachers with diploma and degree level qualifications on Year 3 NAPLAN scores.

The key findings are outlined below.

- After controlling for a rich set of socio-demographic characteristics, including 'Who am I?' ability scores, attendance at pre-school has a significant positive impact on later NAPLAN outcomes, particularly in the domains of numeracy, reading and spelling.
- The direct causal effects of pre-school attendance are equivalent to 10 to 20 NAPLAN points, or 15 to 20 weeks of schooling at the Year 3 level, three years after attending pre-school.
- Children whose NAPLAN test scores for numeracy are at the higher end of the distribution benefit the most from attending pre-school. However, for reading and spelling, children whose test scores are just above the national minimum standard benefit most from having attended pre-school.
- Children whose pre-school teacher had a diploma or degree in early childhood education or child care gained the most from attending pre-school – the level and specialisation of pre-school teacher qualifications are important.
- Children whose pre-school teacher had only a certificate-level qualification in child care or early childhood teaching or had no relevant childcare qualification showed no significant benefit from attendance at pre-school.

REFLECTION POINTS

1. What factors receive prime consideration in formulating government policy on early childhood learning at any point in time: investment, affordability, access, workforce capability, regulation, values? How might these factors compete or confound early childhood learning policy outcomes?
2. Consider the influences on early childhood policy internationally: economics, globalisation, research, practice, leadership, sustainability, rights.
3. What evidence can policy makers use to justify public expenditure?
4. How can governments ensure equitable outcomes for all children, including those from disadvantaged and culturally diverse backgrounds?

The Early Years Learning Framework

Australia's first national curriculum framework – *Belonging, Being & Becoming: The Early Years Learning Framework for Australia* – was a collaborative policy initiative led by COAG, with input from the profession, early childhood academics and all levels of government. The Early Years Learning Framework (EYLF) defines curriculum as 'all the interactions, experiences, activities, routines and events, planned and unplanned, that occur in an environment designed to foster children's learning and development' (DEEWR, 2009a, p. 9). The aim of the document is to 'extend and enrich children's learning from birth to 5 years' (DEEWR, 2009b, p. 5.).

The EYLF integrates play, learning and teaching (Greishaber, 2010) and some argue privileges learning over play (Ortlipp, Arthur & Woodrow, 2011). It departs from a tradition of child developmental theories that value play, discovery and exploration, to 'learning through play' and intentional teaching for defined outcomes for children's learning, straddling social pedagogy and school readiness traditions (Greishaber, 2010; OECD, 2006; Bennett, 2005; Monash University, 2011).

The diverse cultural contexts of young children in Australia supported moving away from developmental theories and domains of development, to a focus on the social nature of young children's learning and the importance of building strong relationships (VCAA, 2008). The EYLF mandates five broad and observable outcomes for children in settings providing home-based and centre-based early learning and care.

1. Children have a strong sense of identity.
2. Children are connected with and contribute to their world.
3. Children have a strong sense of well-being.
4. Children are confident and involved learners.
5. Children are effective communicators.

There has been some resistance to an outcomes-based learning framework (Ortlipp et al., 2011) and opposition to content knowledge being emphasised (Grieshaber,

2010), as well as the child. The outcomes are organised as general capabilities, with content knowledge woven through, permitting a revisiting of the debates around subject area knowledge, concepts and processes in early childhood pedagogy (Kreig, 2011; Raban & Scull, 2013). The outcomes were included based on evidence about closing the cognitive and social learning gaps for disadvantaged children (Burchinal & Cryer, 2003) and to support 'intentional teaching' of literacy, science and mathematics concepts.

The EYLF also promotes assessment practices that gather and analyse information about what 'children know, can do and understand' (DEEWR, 2009b, p. 17) as part of an ongoing cycle of planning, documenting and evaluating children's learning. Program documentation in Australia has been influenced by narrative stories that interpret learning (Carr, 2011) and the pedagogical approaches of Reggio Emilia in Italy, renowned for documenting children's learning (Rinaldi, 2001). Pedagogical documentation has the potential to improve children's learning, contribute to teacher's awareness of learning processes and help parents to gain a greater understanding of young children's learning (Buldu, 2010).

The framework challenges the role of the teacher in promoting young children's learning through play. Debates describe tensions between play and learning and whether the concepts of 'play-based' and 'teacher-directed' are actually opposites or a pedagogical binary (Munn, 2010; Thomas, Warren & de Vries, 2011), while some see 'play as a valuable context for learning and teaching' (Van Oers & Duijkers, 2013, p. 512.). There is, however, an expectation that teachers will engage in 'sustained shared thinking' and provide 'a balance between child led, child initiated and teacher supported learning' (DEEWR, 2009b, p. 15).

POLICY CASE STUDY
. . . .

Gerry Mulhearn and Jennifer Sumsion

DEVELOPING THE EARLY YEARS LEARNING FRAMEWORK

We conceptualise policy development as a set of practices (Ball, 1993), and concur with Taylor et al. (1997), in seeing policy as having three key elements – context, text and consequences – rather than being confined to a technical exercise of producing a policy text in isolation. Along with many of our colleagues, we welcomed the development of Australia's first national early years curriculum framework, made available publicly in 2009, as the initial component of the NQF as it signalled children's learning and development as being at the heart of the national reforms. We felt it was important to learn from international experience, but that it would be naïve to directly apply what had been produced in other places, particularly as the project brief required a distinctively Australian framework. We anticipated complicated policy processes, given the federated nature of policy making in Australia, in which nine state, territory and Commonwealth jurisdictions committed to collaborate in the initiative.

The EYLF was developed within a complex context. In 2009, there were diverse qualifications and role requirements across the ECEC field, with between 60 and 70 per cent of staff holding formal approved qualifications (DEEWR, 2009a). It had fallen largely to the staff with teaching degrees or diploma qualifications to plan the children's program, with all staff working with the children to operationalise it. Since then, the National Quality Standard (NQS) has progressively introduced requirements for all teachers to be qualified and involved in planning and enacting the curriculum. Teachers work in diverse settings, including long day care, family day care and sessional pre-school, with many services offering a mix of programs in a variety of configurations and geographic locations, with a range of theoretical paradigms and approaches about supporting young children's learning.

The authors, respectively a senior administrator representing one state jurisdiction as a member of the EYLF Government Working Group and the leader of the national consortium that was contracted to develop and trial the EYLF, were faced with a variety of policy starting points from different jurisdictions. Some states had a long history of curriculum development in early childhood while others had not pursued this as a policy issue, even though practitioners were operating programs focusing on children's learning. Learning for children under two years of age was not a strong focus across the country. Acknowledging the different starting points contributed new learning for all of us and highlighted sensitivities in meeting both state and national interests concurrently.

A challenging time frame was set, with the process of development and consultation taking approximately 12 months. Tenders were called in August 2008 for development and trialling of the draft framework, which was submitted to the EYLF Working Party in May 2009. The working party appointed the consortium, whose task was to build upon the two previous literature reviews (Wilks et al., 2008; Edwards, Fleer & Nuttall, 2008) and the group was able to draw from feedback from national consultations based on a discussion paper (Productivity Agenda Working Group, 2008), as well as written submissions. Targeted consultations with a diversity of teachers and critical friends and a six-week trial in 28 practice settings were then undertaken.

'Our most valuable lesson came from opportunities to discuss the vastly different expectations, imperatives, conventions, structure and constraints under which academics and bureaucrats work, and to experience a common sense of purpose and trust that can nevertheless develop across often deep divides' (Sumsion et al., 2009, p. 11).

Our common sense of purpose came to the fore during the drafting phases with some of the broad issues being around assumptions about foundational theories for early learning, definitions of curriculum, and concepts about outcomes and standards. We were challenged by tensions, such as how to define families in an inclusive way without unwittingly excluding some, through using a limited range of examples. We pondered on how to ensure that working with children under two could be acknowledged in a broad framework.

As Ball (1993) points out, texts are the result of compromises, negotiations and serendipity. We were mindful that the EYLF was to be just that – a framework – and that a policy text, once implemented, is beyond the control of the author or authority because there is a multiplicity of interpretations.

The text that has resulted is a relatively short document. In line with OECD recommendations, the EYLF is intended to be an open framework that does not rely on one theory alone, but acknowledges the richness of approaches that teachers bring to their practice. It provides contemporary guidance about quality practice and is designed to promote the professional judgement of teachers and ongoing reflection about practice. Importantly, while it outlines five broad learning outcomes for children, it describes a set of principles and practices that will assist teachers to support the achievement of those outcomes.

The EYLF has now been in use for almost six years. A baseline evaluation (DEEWR, 2011; Fleer, Shah & Peers, 2011) reveals a positive reception overall. While professional development about its implementation has been widely available, specific aspects have been raised as requiring a greater focus for support. The most recent Australian Children's Education and Care Quality Authority (ACECQA) snapshot of assessments and rating of services shows that 'Quality Area 1' relating to program and practice has a significant percentage of assessed services at the 'working towards NQS' level (ACECQA, 2015, p.12). For us, this raises questions about what needs to be done next and reminds us that policy is not a static exercise.

Reflecting on our experience in developing the EYLF, we remember our work in revisiting drafts with a view to getting a framework as good as we could agree, one that would be relevant, educative and stimulating for teachers, as well as being politically acceptable at that point in time. We recall the 'substantial and cumulative toning down' of each version (Sumsion et al., 2009, p. 7) as we strived to deliver a framework that took account of much of the feedback, incorporated learnings from contemporary research and fitted within the policy parameters.

We are also reminded of the dynamic nature of policy and that a temporary settlement at a point in time is always part of that dynamic cycle.

The National Quality Framework and Standard

Dahlberg, Moss and Pence (1999) have argued that quality is a subjective, value-based, relative and dynamic concept, and the OECD (2006) recommends effective government steering on one hand and participatory and voluntary approaches to quality on the other. The design of Australia's national quality system builds upon the former, world-recognised childcare accreditation system that was established in 1993 (National Childcare Accreditation Council, 2009; Press & Hayes, 2000).

The genesis for change grew from several nationwide reviews which established that the multi-layered approach of national accreditation and disparate standards across pre-school and childcare settings were too fragmented and complex for a marketised system. All promoted a more qualified and professional workforce to achieve a vision of high-quality early education for children (Press & Hayes, 2000; Elliott, 2006; Tayler et al., 2006; Brennan et al., 2009). Stakeholder feedback advocated for an integrated system of regulation and accreditation that raised standards, considered the experience for the child, and included curriculum and learning (Tayler et al., 2006). Pressure mounted for reform of the quality system and, in 2006, the Commonwealth announced an overhaul of the accreditation system, introducing spot checks, an amalgamation of the three separate accreditation systems (long day care, family day care and outside school hours care), and replacement of peer validators with employed professionals (Brough, 2006). A Victorian Government report advocated for a unified and more consistent approach to quality in centre-based services, and for more information for parents about the aspects of quality to support parent choice (Allen Consulting Group, 2007). The Rudd Labor Government election commitment was to introduce a tough set of national child care standards to accredit and rate service quality (ALP, 2007).

In a landmark decision that transformed the governance of ECEC provision, COAG agreed to establish a 'jointly governed unified national quality framework' to replace the 'existing separate licensing and quality assurance processes' (Morand, 2010, p. 3593) and released a discussion paper for consultation (DoE, 2008). The development of the NQF and its legislative framework required the cooperation of ministers in every jurisdiction. COAG decisions on the NQF were guided by the report of an expert advisory panel (DEEWR, 2009a), which considered the Australian context and the international evidence on the aspects of quality (OECD, 2006). The panel recommended levels of staff qualifications, ratios of staff to children and group size as important structural aspects of quality, noting these elements are proxy indicators for process quality (positive and sensitive staff–child interactions), which is associated with positive child outcomes. The NQF introduced significant changes to the structural elements of quality, with staged improvements to ratios and qualifications (so more qualified teachers work with children with a qualified teacher in every centre-based service).

The Framework emphasises educational program and practice concepts, and embeds the approved learning frameworks (*Belonging, Being & Becoming: The Early Years Learning Framework for Australia*, *My Time, Our Place* – for school-age children – and others like the *Victorian Early Years Learning and Development Framework* (VEYLDF) (Department of Education and Training (Victoria), 2016)), thus prescribing consistent curriculum entitlements and learning across pre-school and childcare settings.

A NQS was also developed and introduced to apply to centre-based services, settings caring for school-age children, and the home environments that deliver family day care services. The NQS is defined for the Australian context to address:

- educational program and practice
- children's health and safety
- physical environment
- staffing arrangements
- relationships with children
- collaborative partnerships with families and communities
- leadership and service management.

The NQS is used to assess and rate services, including assessment of process quality through observation. The rating system summarises a service's achievements in a meaningful way (including program quality and implementation of the EYLF), provides robust information to families about quality, and drives quality improvement and innovation (DEEWR, 2009a). The ratings are published at one of five levels to give families better information to compare services and make program choices for their child. There is some debate that relying on parents as informed consumers may collectively diminish the capacity of parents to agitate for an equitable system of high-quality early education, especially if this raises fees (Fenech, 2013).

The NQF legislation was passed in the Victorian parliament and applies as state law in other states and territories, except Western Australia where corresponding law is enacted. The objectives are: to integrate education and care; promote children's health, safety and well-being; and promote best practice and continuous improvement in services. It is founded on principles of the rights and best interests of children, respect for families, equity, inclusion, and valuing of Aboriginal and Torres Strait Islander cultures (Parliament of Victoria, *Education and Care Services National Law Act 2010*).

The ACECQA was established to oversee and guide implementation of the Framework; to publish national registers of approved services online with their rating; and to approve early childhood qualifications at the national level (ACECQA, 2015).

A recent review identified widespread views that the NQF is supporting ongoing practice improvement, more consistency in the regulation of quality standards and professionalising of the workforce. Focus groups indicated that parents noted improvement in the quality of their child's services (Deloitte Access Economics, 2014). The review highlights further work to reduce administrative burden, improve consistency in assessing and rating outcomes, and in educating the community about the importance of early childhood education.

The NQF is a coordinated, world-leading quality system, designed through consultation and research for the Australian context of mixed provision, and based on streamlining previous regulation and accreditation systems. The approach aims to achieve 'the right balance' between affordability, improving quality and providing access to information about ECEC services (Morand, 2010).

The impact of reform on teachers and teaching

The Australian early childhood reforms continue to impact and raise demand for a qualified and professional workforce. An Early Years Workforce Strategy for Australia (Standing Council on School Education and Early Childhood, 2012) called on peak bodies, unions and training providers to collaborate with government to enhance professionalism and leadership, and to grow a diverse, qualified and responsive workforce.

The introduction of the EYLF challenged teachers to actively promote children's learning and move from pedagogy that privileged 'free play', where teachers set up the environment according to children's interests (Grieshaber, 2010). The EYLF has, through its language, the potential to shape the identity of early childhood professionals, positioning them as 'teachers' and 'intentional teachers', rather than carers (Ortlipp et al., 2011). An evaluation of the implementation of the aligned VEYLDF (Garvis et al., 2013) introduced the concept of the Educational Change Model (Pendergast et al., 2005) to encourage policy makers and professionals alike to acknowledge that educational reform takes time, and implementation can be inhibited or enabled by leadership, support for the profession and resistance to change from teachers and the community.

Given the differing starting points in each jurisdiction at the outset of the NQF reforms in 2012, there remains considerable variation across jurisdictions, particularly in attracting qualified teachers to regional and remote areas; supporting Indigenous staff to gain qualifications; and for all professionals to build cultural competence. Further, advice to government is conflicted about whether it should invest support in the pedagogical and regulatory reforms and inclusion of children with diverse backgrounds (Productivity Commission, 2011) or whether employers should accept primary responsibility for funding and supporting ongoing professional development (Productivity Commission, 2014).

The early childhood workforce has grown and is more qualified. In 2006, only 45 per cent of teachers held a diploma or above qualifications (DEECD, 2007), while current data indicate that around 82 per cent of teachers hold an early childhood qualification, with 16 per cent of these holding early childhood teacher degrees (PricewaterhouseCoopers Australia, 2014; The Social Research Centre, 2014). There are more early childhood professionals per child, and a large majority of professionals are implementing the learning frameworks, responding to assessment and rating processes, and attending professional development. The effort to 'deliver a sustainable, highly qualified and professional workforce' (SCSEEC, 2012, p. 1) is policy work in progress.

REFLECTION POINTS

1. How can families' and children's voices be heard in designing policy?
2. How does contemporary Australian early childhood policy affect early years professional roles?
3. How can a teacher use professional judgement and knowledge in a time of policy reform?
4. Does policy reform improve children's learning?
5. How can policy makers improve implementation of reforms, communication, professional development, data and research?
6. What steps will you take when designing and implementing a local ECEC policy? How can understanding the development of Australian early childhood systems policy help you to develop and implement policies within a centre or school?

Conclusion

Early childhood learning has been a focus of significant reforms in the ECEC sector in Australia since 2009.

Key outcomes include the following:

- children access 15 hours of pre-school in the year before school
- a unified NQF that regulates centre-based and home-based services across Australia
- consistent national standards on the structural components of quality (ratios, qualifications, curriculum) are in place in every jurisdiction
- teachers delivering programs to children are more qualified and more is known about this workforce
- services are focused on quality improvement
- services are assessed and rated against a NQS, with ratings published
- outcomes for children are planned for in all settings through the national curriculum framework (EYLF)
- data systems can describe children's access to early learning and child care and how they are faring developmentally.

While design of the system to support children's learning occurred at a national level, across both tiers of government, informed by multidisciplinary research evidence and program evaluations, it is the early childhood sector with all its diversity in programs, teachers and providers, that has implemented the reforms at the local level. It is the teachers who interact with children and families every day, and local leaders who have made this policy reform successful and remarkable. Debate will continue about the integration of education and care, Australia's investment in early learning and the orientation towards early childhood education as an entitlement.

Further reading

Allen, L. & Kelly, B. (Eds). (2015).*Transforming the Workforce for Children Birth Through Age 8: A Unifying Foundation, for Committee on the Science of Children Birth to Age 8: National Academy of Sciences*. Washington DC: National Academic Press.

Council of Australian Governments (COAG). (2009). *National Partnership Agreement on the National Quality Agenda for Early Childhood Education and Care*. Agreed 7 December 2009. Canberra: COAG.

Department of Education and Early Childhood Development (DEECD). (2008). A research paper to inform the development of An Early Years Learning Framework for Australia. Melbourne: DEECD.

Productivity Commission. (2013). Childcare and early childhood learning. Productivity Commissioner Issues Paper, December 2013. Canberra: Australian Government.

Productivity Commission. (2015). *Report on Government Services. Volume B: Child Care, Education and Training*. Chapter 3: Early childhood education and care, Table 3.1: Preschool programs in Australia. Canberra: Australian Government. Retrieved from http://pc.gov.au

Salamon, L. M. (Ed.). (2002). *The Tools of Government. A Guide to the New Governance*. New York: Oxford University Press.

References

Allen Consulting Group. (2007). *Quality Time: Regulating for Quality in Early Childhood Education and Care in Victoria*. Melbourne: Victorian Department of Premier and Cabinet and the Department of Human Services.

Althaus, C., Bridgman, P. & Davis, G. (2013). *The Australian Policy Handbook* (5th ed.). Sydney: Allen & Unwin.

Australian Bureau of Statistics (ABS). (2014). '4240.0 Preschool Education, Australia, 2014; 4402.0 Childhood Education and Care, Australia, June 2014'. Retrieved from www.abs.gov.au

Australian Children's Education and Care Quality Authority (ACECQA). (2015). *NQF Snapshot Q3 2015: A Quarterly Report from the Australian Children's Education and Care Quality Authority*. Sydney: ACECQA.

Australian Labor Party (ALP). (2007). *New Directions for Early Childhood Education: Universal Access to Early Learning for 4 Year Olds*. Retrieved from www. walabor.org.au

Australian Public Service Commission (APSC). (2009). *Smarter Policy – Choosing Policy Instruments and Working with Others to Influence Behaviour*. Commissioners Foreword. Retrieved from www.apsc.gov.au

Ball, S. (1993). What is policy? Texts, trajectories and toolboxes. *Discourse: the Australian Journal of Educational Studies*, *13*(2), 10–17.

Ball, S. (1998). Big policies/small world: an introduction to international perspectives in education policy. *Comparative Education*, *34*(2), 119–30.

Ball, S. (2006). *Educational Policy and Social Class*. London: Routledge.

Bennett, J. (2005). Curriculum issues in national policy-making. *European Early Childhood Education Research Journal*, *13*(2), 5–23.

Brennan, D., Blaxland, M., & Tannous, K. (2009). A strategic assessment of the children's services industry. A paper prepared for the Children's Services Subcommittee of the Community and Disability Services Minister's Advisory Council. Adelaide: South Australian Government.

Brough, M. (2006). 'Child care overhaul to boost quality' [Media release]. Retrieved from www.formerministers.dss.gov.au/3455/family_day_care

Buldu, M. (2010). Making learning visible in kindergarten classrooms: Pedagogical documentation as a formative assessment technique. *Teaching and Teacher Education*, *26*(7), 1439–49.

Burchinal, M., & Cryer, D. (2003). Diversity, child care quality and developmental outcomes. *Early Childhood Research Quarterly*, *18*(4), 401–26.

Carr, M. (2011). Young children reflecting on their learning: teachers' conversation strategies. *Early Years: An International Research Journal*, *31*(3), 257–70.

Center on the Developing Child. (2007). *A Science-Based Framework for Early Childhood Policy: Using Evidence to Improve Outcomes in Learning, Behavior, and Health for Vulnerable Children*. Retrieved from http://developingchild.harvard.edu/resources/a-science-based-framework-for-early-childhood-policy/

Council of Australian Governments (COAG). (2008). *National Partnership Agreement on Early Childhood Education*. Agreed 29 November 2008. Canberra: COAG.

Council of Australian Governments (COAG). (2009). *Investing in the Early Years – A National Early Childhood Development Strategy*. An initiative of the Council of Australian Governments. Canberra: Commonwealth of Australia.

Cunha, F., Heckman, J., Locher, L., & Masterov, D. (2005). Interpreting the evidence of life cycle skill formation. Discussion Paper No.1675. Bonn, Germany: Institute for the Study of Labor IZA.

Dahlberg, G., Moss, P., & Pence, A. (1999). *Beyond Quality in Early Childhood Education and Care: Postmodern Perspectives*. Philadelphia, PA: Routledge Falmer.

Deloitte Access Economics. (2014). *Education Council, Regulation Impact Statement for proposed options for changes to the National Quality Framework, COAG Consultation Regulation Impact Statement, November 2014*. Retrieved from www.deloitteaccesseconomics.com.au

Department of Education (DoE). (2008). *Productivity Agenda Working Group, Education. A National Quality Framework for Early Childhood Education and*

Care. A Discussion Paper, August 2008. Canberra: Department of Education and Training.

Department of Education and Early Childhood Development (DEECD). (2007). *National Children's Services Workforce Study (2006)*. Melbourne: DEECD.

Department of Education and Training (Victoria) & Victorian Curriculum and Assessment Authority. (2016). *Victorian Early Years Learning and Development Framework*. Melbourne: Department of Education and Training (Victoria).

Department of Education, Employment and Workplace Relations (DEEWR). (2009a). *Towards a National Quality Framework for Early Childhood Education and Care: Report of the Expert Advisory Panel on Quality Early Childhood Education and Care*. Canberra: Department of Education and Training.

Department of Education, Employment and Workplace Relations (DEEWR). (2009b). *Belonging, Being & Becoming: The Early Years Learning Framework for Australia*. Canberra: DEEWR for COAG.

Department of Education, Employment and Workplace Relations (DEEWR). (2011). *Final Report: Baseline Evaluation of the Early Years Learning Framework (EYLF)*. Melbourne: Monash University Education.

Economist Intelligence Unit. (2012). Starting well: Benchmarking early childhood education across the world. Retrieved from www.lienfoundation.org.publications

Edwards, S., Fleer, M., & Nuttall, J. (2008). A research paper to inform the development of an early years learning framework for Australia. Melbourne: DEECD.

Elliott, A. (2006). *Early Childhood Education: Pathways to Quality and Equity for All Children*. Melbourne: Australian Council for Educational Research.

Fenech, M. (2013). Quality early childhood education for my child or for all children? *Australian Journal of Early Childhood, 38*(4), 92–8.

Fenech, M., Giugni, M., & Bown, K. (2012). A critical analysis of the National Quality Framework: mobilising for a vision for children beyond minimum. *Australian Journal of Early Childhood, 37*(4), 5–13.

Fenna, A. (2014). The Australian system of government. In A. Fenna, J. Robbins & J. Summers (Eds.). *Government and Politics in Australia* (pp. 12–32). Sydney: Pearson Australia.

Fleer, M., Shah, C., & Peers, C. (2011). *Quantitative Report: Baseline Evaluation of the Early Years Learning Framework (EYLF) for the Department of Education, Employment and Workplace Relations*. Melbourne: Monash University Education.

Garvis, S., Pendergast, D., Twigg, D., et al. (2013). The Victorian Early Years Learning and Development Framework: Managing change in a complex environment. *Australasian Journal of Early Childhood, 38*(2), 86–94.

Grieshaber, S. (2010). Departures from tradition: The Early Years Learning Framework for Australia. *International Journal of Child Care and Education Policy, 4*(2), 33–44.

Heckman, J. (2003). Invest in the very young. Conference paper. Public conference, Université de Montréal, Faculty of Arts and Sciences, Centre of Excellence for Early Childhood Development.

Henry, M., Lingard, B., Rizvi, F., & Taylor, S. (1999). Working with/against globalization in education. *Journal of Education Policy, 14*(1), 85–97.

Krieg, S. (2011). The Australian Early Years Learning Framework: learning what? *Contemporary Issues in Early Childhood, 12*(1), 46–55.

Mamouney, L. (2014). Shifting use of policy instruments for environmental problems: New South Wales, Australia, 1979–2010. *Journal of Environmental Assessment Policy and Management, 16*(1), 1–20.

McCain, M., Mustard, J., & Shanker, S. (2007). *Early Years Study 2: Putting Science into Action*. Toronto, ON: Council for Early Childhood Development.

McClintock, P. (2013). COAG's reform agenda, the seamless national economy and accountability for outcomes. *Australian Journal of Public Administration, 72*(1), 66–72.

McKew, M. (2012). *Tales from the Political Trenches*. Melbourne: Melbourne University Press.

Ministerial Council on Education, Employment, Training and Youth Affairs (MCEETYA). (2008). *Melbourne Declaration on Education Goals for Young Australians*. Melbourne: MCEETYA.

Monash University. (2011). *Final Report: Baseline Evaluation of the Early Years Learning Framework (EYLF)*. Canberra: DEEWR for the Council of Australian Governments.

Morand, M. (2010). *Education and Care Services National Law Bill*, Hansard, 2 September 2010, 2nd Reading Speech Victorian Parliament. Retrieved from www.vic.gov.au (p. 3593)

Munn, P, (2010). Play or learning in Early Years curricula? And what about the cultures in which Early Years Education systems are embedded? *International Journal of Early Years Education, 18*(3), 183–4.

National Childcare Accreditation Council. (2009). *Making a Difference for Children: the Australian Journey in Assuring Quality Child Care*. Canberra: Australian Government.

National Commission of Audit. (2015). *3.2 The Operation of the Federation*. Australian Government. Retrieved from www.ncoa.gov.au

National Research Council. (2001). *Early Childhood Development and Learning. New Knowledge for Policy*. Washington DC: National Academy Press.

Newberry, S., & Brennan, D. (2013). The marketisation of early childhood education and care (ECEC) in Australia: a structured response. *Financial Accountability & Management, 29*(3), 227–45.

Organisation for Economic Co-operation and Development (OECD). (2006). *Starting Strong II: Early Childhood Education and Care*. Paris: OECD.

Organisation for Economic Co-operation and Development (OECD). (2013). 'Education indicators in focus: how do early childhood education and care (ECEC) policies, systems and quality vary across OECD countries?' Paris: OECD.

Ortlipp, M., Arthur, L., & Woodrow, C. (2011). Discourses of the Early Years Learning Framework: constructing the early childhood professional. *Contemporary Issues in Early Childhood, 12*(1), 56–69.

Parliament of Victoria. (2010).*Education and Care Services National Law Act 2010.* Retrieved from www.legislation.vic.gov.au

Pendergast, D., Flanagan, R., Land, R., et al. (2005). *Developing Lifelong Learners in the Middle Years of Schooling.* Brisbane: The University of Queensland.

Penn, H. (2011). Policy rationales for early childhood services. *International Journal of Child Care and Education Policy, 5*(1), 1–16.

Pianta, R., Barnett, S., Burchinal, M., & Thorburg, K. (2009). The effects of preschool education: what we know, how public policy is or is not aligned with the evidence base, and what we need to know. *Psychological Science in the Public Interest, 10*(2) 49–88.

Press, F., & Hayes, A. (2000). *ECD Thematic Review of ECEC Policy: Australian Background Report.* Canberra: Australian Government.

PricewaterhouseCoopers Australia (2014). *2013 Early Childhood Education and Care Workforce Review: Workforce Review Report.* Canberra: Department of Education, Australian Government.

Productivity Agenda Working Group – Education, Skills, Training and Early Childhood Development. (2008). A national quality framework for early childhood education and care: a discussion paper. Melbourne: COAG.

Productivity Commission. (2011). *Early Childhood Development Workforce. Productivity Commission Research Report.* Canberra: Australian Government.

Productivity Commission. (2014). *Childcare and Early Childhood Learning. Productivity Commission Inquiry Report.* Overview and Recommendations No.73. Canberra: Australian Government.

Raban, B, & Scull, J. (2013). Literacy in the early years. In D. Pendergast & S. Garvis (Eds.). *Teaching in the Early Years: Rethinking Curriculum, Pedagogy and Assessment* (pp. 69–85). Sydney: Allen & Unwin.

Rinaldi, C. (2001). Documentation and assessment: what is the relationship? In C. Giudici & C. Rinaldi (Eds.). *Making Learning Visible: Children as Individual and Group Learners* (pp. 78–90). Reggio Emilia, Italy: Reggio Children.

Shonkoff, J., & Phillips, D. (2000). *From Neurons to Neighbourhoods: The Science of Early Childhood Development.* Washington DC: National Research Council.

Siraj-Blatchford, I. (2010). A focus on pedagogy: case studies of effective practice. In K. Sylva, E. Melhuish, P. Sammons, I. Siraj Blatchford, & B. Taggart (Eds.). *Early Childhood Matters, Evidence from the Effective Pre-school and Primary Education project* (pp.149–65). Abingdon, Oxon: Routledge

Standing Council on School Education and Early Childhood (SCSEEC). (2012). *Early Years Workforce Strategy: The Early Childhood Education and Care*

Workforce Strategy for Australia 2012–2016. Melbourne: SCSEEC. Retrieved from dss.gov.au

Sumsion, J., Barnes, S., Cheeseman, S., et al. (2009). Insider perspectives on developing The Early Years Learning Framework for Australia. *Australian Journal of Early Childhood, 34*(4), 4–13.

Sylva, K., Melhuish, E., Sammons, P., Siraj-Blatchford, I., & Taggart, B. (2010). *Early Childhood Matters, Evidence from the Effective Preschool and Primary Education project*, Abingdon, Oxon: Routledge.

Tayler, C. (2011). Changing Policy, Changing Culture: Steps Toward Early Learning Quality Improvement in Australia, *International Journal of Early Childhood, 43*(3), 211–25.

Tayler, C., Wills, M., Hayden, J., & Wilson, C. (2006). *A Review of the Approach to Setting National Standards and Assuring the Quality of Care in Australian Childcare Services*. Canberra: Community and Disability Ministers' Committee.

Taylor, S., Rizvi, F., Lingard, B., & Henry, M. (1997). *Educational policy and the politics of change*. London: Routledge.

The Social Research Centre. (2014). *2013 National Early Childhood Education and Care Workforce Census, May 2014*. Melbourne: The Social Research Centre.

Thomas, L., Warren, E., & de Vries, E. (2011). Play-based learning and intentional teaching in early childhood contexts. *Australian Journal of Early Childhood, 36*(4), 69–75.

United Nations Educational Scientific and Cultural Organization (UNESCO). (2007). *Strong Foundations: Early Childhood Care and Education. Education for All (EFA) Global Monitoring Report*. Paris: UNESCO.

Van Oers, B., & Duijkers, D. (2013). Teaching in a play-based curriculum: Theory, practice and evidence of developmental education for young children, *Journal of Curriculum Studies, 45*(4), 511–34.

Victorian Curriculum and Assessment Authority (VCAA). (2008). *Analysis of Curriculum/Learning Frameworks for the Early Years (Birth to Age 8)*. Melbourne: DEECD.

Victorian Public Sector Commission (VPSC). (2015). *Development Guide 13: Contributing to Public Policy*. Retrieved from http://vpsc.vic.gov.au

Warren, D., & Haisken-DeNew, J. (2013). *Early Bird Catches the Worm: The Causal Impact of Pre-School Participation and Teacher Qualifications on Year 3 National NAPLAN Cognitive Tests*, Melbourne Institute Working Paper No. 34/13, Melbourne Institute of Economic and Social Research, The University of Melbourne. Retrieved from http://melbourneinstitute.com/downloads/working_paper_series/wp2013n34.pdf

Wilks, A., Nyland, B., Chancellor, B., & Elliott, S. (2008). *Analysis of Curriculum/Learning Frameworks for the Early Years (Birth to Age 8)*. Melbourne: Victorian Curriculum and Assessment Authority.

CHAPTER 3

Young children as learners with rights

Jane Page and Collette Tayler

....

LEARNING OBJECTIVES

In this chapter you will:

1. explore the key principles underlying the *United Nations Convention on the Rights of the Child* and their implications for young children's learning
2. consider why rights-based principles have been integrated into the documents that comprise the National Quality Framework for Early Childhood Education and Care
3. reflect on the image of the child as a rights holder and the implications this has for teaching values, approaches and practices.

....

Introduction

This chapter will draw on the key principles underlying the *United Nations Convention on the Rights of the Child* (UNCRC) (1989) and research to position young children as dynamic and capable participants in the learning process. It will highlight the key rights-based general principles, policy directives and research studies that underscore the central importance of relationships and interactions between adults and children and the impact that they have for learning and teaching. Against this background, it will examine and profile policy directives, key rights-based principles and research studies that assist teachers to explore their role in promoting children's active **participation** in the learning process.

Participation: stems from the right to be heard, referring to activities and processes in which children play an active role in decision making that can bring about change. For a fuller exploration of this concept, refer to Thomas (2007) and Fleming (2013).

Repositioning young children as active social agents: Australian policy context

Teaching and learning in the early years is predicated on how we, as teachers, understand and construct the child as a learner. In this chapter, and indeed throughout this text, we put forward an image of the child as a holder of rights, and a competent learner from birth with the capacities to learn in and through her relationships with others. In this chapter, we will explore the principles embedded in the UNCRC that assist us to reflect on how we, as teachers, understand and construct children as competent learners and the implications this has for our teaching values, approaches and practices.

The UNCRC is a major international document that has shaped theoretical debates, policy and practice around young children (Cordero Arce, 2015; Woodhead, 2006). In Australia, the key principles underlying the UNCRC have been integrated into the documents that comprise the National Quality Framework for Early Childhood Education and Care (NQF), including national law and national regulations, the National Early Years Learning Framework (EYLF) for children from birth to five years of age and the National Quality Standard (NQS). This, in turn, has given rise to new expectations that teachers enact rights-based principles into their daily practices with young children. It is thus important that teachers understand the purpose and intent of the UNCRC and how it has shaped our roles and responsibilities towards young children in order to respond to this imperative in an active way.

Background to the UNCRC

The UNCRC builds on over 75 years of UN's children's rights and human rights initiatives. Drafting of the Convention began in 1978, in anticipation of the 1979 International Year of the Child, and took 10 years to reach fruition. At the start of the new century, it stands as the most widely ratified human rights treaty in the history of the UN. Unanimously endorsed by the United Nations General Assembly on 20 November 1989, and signed by a record 61 countries on the day it was opened for signature on 26 January 1990, it provides powerful testimony to a global recognition for its pressing need (Page, 2007). Importantly, the UNCRC adds significantly to the scope and power of its precedents. The UNCRC differs, for example, from former declarations and conventions in the ideological and philosophical understanding of children's rights which it encapsulates (Freeman, 2000; Joyniene & Samuelsson, 1999). The 1924 *Geneva Declaration on the Rights of the Child*, for example, presented children's rights predominantly in terms of basic welfare issues. Growing out of the post first world war concerns around rebuilding social and economic stability, the 1924 Declaration focused its attention towards providing the fundamentals of children's well-being and development, such as food, medical care, shelter and spiritual sustenance. It was also directed towards an earlier understanding of children's rights, which viewed children primarily from the perspective of adults in their care-taking roles (Coady, 2000; Limber & Flekkøy, 1995). The 1959 *Geneva Declaration on the Rights of the Child*, likewise, focused on the adult as the main protagonist in protecting young children's rights and well-being.

The UNCRC, by contrast, is an attempt to rebalance this paternalistic conception of rights with an understanding of children as the subjects of rights and full members of society – human beings capable of participating in their social worlds through their relationships with others. This Convention formally recognises and places children's rights on a par with adult rights, and through its adoption children have, for the first time, been granted the same comprehensive range of civil, political, economic, social, cultural and humanitarian rights enjoyed by adults (Archard, 2004). The central image of young children in the UNCRC is as 'social actors from the beginning of life, with particular interests, capacities and vulnerabilities, and ... requirements for protection, guidance and support in the exercise of their rights' (United Nations Committee on the Rights of the Child, 2005, p. 2). It is important to note that this image of young children does not preclude them from protection, but rather recasts this right alongside the view that children are capable of participating actively in the realisation and retention of their rights in the social and cultural contexts in which they engage, including education. Importantly, these rights align with the broader aspirations and principles of the *Charter of the United Nations*: 'recognition of the inherent dignity and of the equal and inalienable rights of all members of the human family is the foundation of freedom, justice and peace in the world' (United Nations, 1989, Preamble, p. 1).

A case for advancing the rights of young children

In Australia, the general principles underlying the UNCRC have been integrated into the key national policies that govern early childhood education and care policies, systems and practices. This, in part, is linked to the fact that ratification of the UNCRC places state parties under a quasi-legal and moral obligation to offer the administrative, legislative, judicial and other means to advance the cause of implementing the 54 Articles outlined in the Convention across a diverse range of settings (United Nations, 1989, Articles 42 & 43). In addition, a monitoring process administered by a United Nations Committee on the Rights of the Child, a group of independent specialists, ensures that the efforts undertaken by each state party to implement the provisions are reported two years after ratification and every five years thereafter (United Nations, 1989, Articles 43, 44 & 45). The UNCRC reviews the reports against independent non-government organisation (NGO) reports concerning the life experiences of children in different nations and has the power to seek additional information, submit written questions, make recommendations and conduct hearings after responses to reports from nations are received (United Nations, 1989, Articles 44 & 45). This legislative power was lacking from all the previous declarations, which were aspirational in their intention and did not obligate state parties to act on the recommendations contained within them (Limber & Flekkøy, 1995). This expectation is significant as it formally pressured state parties to recognise children as bearers of rights. The parties are charged to look beyond their immediate social and economic concerns, and consider how the values underlying rights can be enacted in practice across systems and settings (Archard, 2004), and embedded in the policies and practices of adults working with young children (Woodhead, 2005). Despite this aspirational intent, Byrne and Lundy (2015) caution that there are challenges and complexities in securing children's rights through the processes underlying the formation and enactment of policy.

Reports submitted to the United Nations Committee on the Rights of the Child by signatories highlight the need for a dedicated effort towards enacting *young* children's rights: 'information on the implementation of the Convention with respect to children before the age of regular schooling is often very limited' (Doek quoted in United Nations Committee on the Rights of the Child, United Nations Children's Fund and Bernard van Leer Foundation, 2006, p. vii). This concern led to the development and release of the General Comment No. 7: 'Implementing Rights in Early Childhood' (2005) that sought to 'encourage recognition that young children are holders of all rights enshrined in the Convention and that early childhood is a critical period for the realization of these rights' (p. 1).

The UNCRC and the National Quality Framework for Early Childhood Education and Care

The key discourses embedded in policy impact on the way in which young children live and experience their worlds (Kjørholt, 2013). In Australia, in the past decade, we have witnessed an integration of child rights principles into the suite of legal, policy and practice-oriented documents that comprise the NQF. The documents are aimed at improving the quality of support to young children and their families, and advancing the learning and well-being of the children (Cloney et al., 2013; Flottman & Page, 2012). This process was a deliberate and uniform attempt to 'help ensure that children's rights and needs are at the centre of policy development and service delivery' (Commonwealth of Australia, 2009, p. 7). The NQF comprises a legal and governance system composed of national law and regulations that monitor the quality of early childhood education and care (ECEC) services; a National Early Years Learning Framework (EYLF) for children from birth to five years of age that outlines practice principles and learning outcomes for children; a National Quality Standard (NQS) that contains benchmarks for quality improvement in ECEC and school-aged care services; and a clearly defined ratings system that offers teachers, parents and children information on quality and child outcomes (Cloney et al., 2013). The integration of child rights principles across this suite of documents foregrounds children's rights in the early education and care services system, policies and practices, and raises the accountability of teachers to provide evidence of how they are meeting these standards through their educational programs, and in relationships with young children. In the following section, we will outline how child rights principles are embedded into these documents and what this means for teachers.

The Early Years Learning Framework (EYLF) – *Belonging, Being & Becoming: The Early Years Learning Framework for Australia* (DEEWR, 2009) – is the first curriculum framework for ECEC in Australia. It outlines key principles and practices that promote young children's learning outcomes in the first five years of life. Child rights principles are positioned in the EYLF as central to its aspiration to ensure that all children access and participate in quality teaching and learning experiences. The EYLF outlines expectations of teachers, for example, to 'reinforce in their daily practice the principles laid out in the United Nations Convention on the Rights of the Child' (DEEWR, 2009, p. 26). Child rights principles are also specifically noted as desirable outcomes for young children. Learning outcome 2: 'Children are connected with and contribute to their world', for example, states that 'Children develop a sense of belonging to groups and communities and an understanding of the reciprocal rights and responsibilities necessary for active community' (DEEWR, 2009, p. 26). Participation is noted throughout the EYLF as a means of promoting young children's learning and development, ensuring young children's active role in their learning communities, developing a sense of **agency**, providing access to learning, and enabling children's participation in decision-making processes in their daily education programs. Teachers thus need to be conversant with what these expectations mean, and require of them, in their relationships and daily practices with young children.

> **Agency:** a complex construct that refers to the opportunity afforded to children to 'choose, act and influence' (Mentha, Church & Page, 2015, p. 626). For a fuller exploration of how this concept is referred to in ECEC literature see Mentha et al. (2015).

The NQF has also noted the central importance of children's rights in its aim 'to raise quality and drive continuous improvement in education and care services' (ACECQA, 2011a, p. 7). The *Education and Care Services National Law* and *Education and Care Services National Regulations* note that 'the rights and interests of children are paramount' (p. 8) in the guiding principles to assess and support early childhood education and care services to achieve the NQS. The NQS sets out the quality areas, standards and elements against which ECEC services are assessed. Children's right to participate is directly noted in three standards. Element 1.1.5, for example, states that 'Every child is supported to participate in the program' (ACECQA, 2011a, p. 10). Element 1.1.6 states that 'Each child's agency is promoted, enabling them to make choices and decisions and influence events and their world' (ACECQA, 2011a, p. 10). As part of this process, teachers are expected to develop a Quality Improvement Plan for their service, detailing their plans and actions for ongoing improvement. Centres are required to actively seek out and incorporate children's perspectives in this process: 'It is recommended that services adopt a collaborative approach to self-assessment and the development of their plan, involving wherever possible children, families, teachers, staff members, management and other interested parties' (ACECQA, 2011b, p. 8). Element 3.1.3 requires that 'Facilities are designed or adapted to ensure access and participation by every child in the service' (ACECQA, 2011a, p. 10). Element 6.3.3 'Access to inclusion and support assistance is facilitated' is also linked to ensuring the full participation of every child in educational programs (ACECQA, 2011a, p.11). Collectively, these expectations require teachers to address how they will actively plan for every child's participation in the program and how they can create with children the space, time, materials, equipment and tools that are necessary to support each child's learning outcomes.

Australian documents supporting young children's rights, ethics and advocacy

Prior to the development of the NQF, child rights principles were central to the image of the child outlined in the *Code of Ethics* (the Code) (ECA, 2016). This document is independent of government and non-mandatory, but importantly, it was developed in consultation with teachers and has a high profile in the early childhood profession. The Code is viewed as a guiding framework that supports teachers' reflections on their ethical responsibilities. The image of the child as a rights holder is stated in the core principles: 'Children are citizens from birth with civil, cultural, linguistic, social and economic rights' (ECA, 2016, p. 1). The Code outlines actions for ethically engaging with young children that are founded on this image of the child, and articulates principles to guide relationships and daily practices. Furthermore, the importance of respecting and advocating for young children's rights has recently been reinforced in the ECA and Australian Human Rights Commission (AHRC) publication *Supporting Young Children's Rights: Statement of Intent (2015–2018)* (2015). This document outlines a set of actions and accountabilities to guide teachers and any professional working with young children so that they can systematically enact and advocate for young children's rights in their daily practice.

The naming and integration of rights-based principles in this suite of documents is both recognition by non-government organisations of the importance and value of child rights principles in building and shaping learning relationships and practices, and acknowledgement that the early childhood education and care profession has a key role to play regarding young children's human rights in the teaching and learning process. A central challenge, however, still remains as to how to translate and enact policy statements and principles into daily practice with young children. In the following section of this chapter, we explore how the key principles embedded in the UNCRC build an understanding of how to recognise young children as holders of rights, and ensure there is a culture of participation within the learning process. This discussion is underpinned by the theoretical understanding that children are 'agents in, as well as products, of social processes' (James & Prout, 2015, p. xii) and that equitable relationships in learning between teachers and children are central to enacting young children's rights in early childhood educational settings.

POLICY CASE STUDY

Starting Strong II: Early Childhood Education and Care

In 2006, the Organisation for Economic Co-operation and Development (OECD) published *Starting Strong II: Early Childhood Education and Care*. (Starting Strong (2001) was a formative report of reviews in 12 countries.) The 2006 report synthesised the findings from the thematic review of early childhood education and care systems in 20 OECD countries[1]. The thematic review reports used comparative data to identify the key elements of an effective and sustainable ECEC policy and provision system that could shape access to high-quality early childhood education and care programs, and thereby provide a fair start in life for all children, and contribute to educational equity and social integration (OECD, 2006, p. 3).

As highlighted in Chapter 2, *Starting Strong II* findings influenced the direction and content of the Australian NQF policy. Of key interest to this case study is the way *Starting Strong II* framed children's rights as central to any discussion concerning learning and development. In so doing, the report embodies the broader imperative of the UNCRC, and in particular, Articles 42 and 43 requiring state parties to offer administrative, legislative, judicial and other means to advance the cause of implementing the 54 Articles outlined in the Convention, across a diverse range of settings. Embedding children's rights in ECEC policies, legislation and learning frameworks is a comprehensive method of supporting children's participation in learning.

---

1   Australia is an OECD country.

At a policy level, *Starting Strong II* promotes the development and resourcing of ECEC services that allow *all* children to participate in quality programs. 'Early childhood services are particularly important for children with diverse learning rights, whether these stem from physical, mental or sensory disabilities or from socio-economic disadvantage' (OECD, 2006, p. 17). Policies that aim to increase the participation of children from diverse backgrounds can empower teachers to address inequality in a more targeted way.

At a systems level, *Starting Strong II* encourages national administrations 'to aspire to ECEC systems that support broad learning, participation and democracy… including respect for children's rights, diversity and enhanced access for children with special and additional learning needs' (OECD, 2006, p. 18). This approach is then translated at a central level into key principles where the 'touchstones of a democratic approach will be to extend the agency of the child' (OECD, 2006, p. 18). Within this framework the 'early childhood centre becomes a space where the intrinsic value of each person is recognised, where democratic participation is promoted, as well as respect for our shared environment. *Learning to be, learning to do, learning to learn and learning to live together* should be considered as critical elements in the journey of each child toward human and social development' (OECD, 2006, p. 18).

At a pedagogical level, *Starting Strong II* reinforces that learning is a social and relational process; that it 'springs from social interaction' (OECD, 2006, p. 166). This highlights the value of ECEC teachers adopting a socially oriented and inclusive pedagogy that has child rights at the centre. The report argues for children, through their relationships with teachers and parents, to be afforded the opportunities to participate in learning and for them to experience values and practices that uphold their and other children's rights.

At the child level, *Starting Strong II* speaks of the importance of policy focusing on quality from the child's perspective and 'a need to refocus policy debates on the rights and interests of young children' (OECD, 2006, p. 331). In so doing, the report places value on balancing adult priorities with children's perspectives and lived experiences, and ensuring that children can influence and shape the policies and practices that are directed towards them. *Starting Strong II* further places emphasis on the importance of improving current pedagogical approaches in ECEC settings by focusing on children's learning and holistic development (OECD, 2006, p. 331). In this way, it seeks to promote teaching and learning approaches that are responsive to children's interests and capabilities, and encourage children's participation.

Starting Strong II provided an important impetus for the Australian Government to address young children's rights in an effective and sustainable way through policies, legislation and learning frameworks. As teachers it assists us to understand why rights-based principles have been integrated into the documents that comprise the NQF, and why they are important.

REFLECTION POINTS

1. How familiar are you with the ways in which rights principles are framed in the National Early Years Learning Framework, the NQS and the *Education and Care Services National Law* and *Education and Care Services National Regulations*? What does this mean for your relationships with children? What does this mean for your educational program and practice?
2. How do the Articles and principles outlined in the UNCRC General Comment No. 7: 'Implementing Child Rights in Early Childhood' (2005), and General Comment No. 12: 'The Right of the Child to be Heard' (2009) support you as teachers to enact rights principles in and through your relationships with children?
3. The Code (ECA, 2016) outlines teachers' ethical responsibilities towards young children. How does this document support you to reflect on your values, approaches and practices with young children and their families?
4. *Supporting Young Children's Rights. Statement of Intent* (*2015–2018*) details what enacting young children's rights means for adults and young children. Study this document and reflect on how it builds your understanding of your roles and responsibilities in supporting young children's rights in educational programs and practices.

Young children as holders of rights: implications for teaching and learning

Understanding rights-based conceptions of the child and the core intent underlying the UNCRC is key to teachers exploring how they construct children as learners, and the implications for their teaching values, approaches and practices. In the following section, we explore how children's rights are defined in the UNCRC and the requirements they place on teachers to ensure that young children have multiple opportunities to exercise their rights in educational settings.

The right to life and development

The 54 Articles contained in the UNCRC promote children's rights through four general principles: the right to life and development; the right to be heard; the right to non-discrimination; and the primary consideration of the child's best interests. These general principles are viewed as indivisible, and thus, 'interrelated and mutually reinforcing' (Kaufman & Flekkøy, 1998, p. 16). The right to be life and development as outlined in Article 6 requires state parties to ensure 'to the maximum extent possible the survival and development of the child' (United Nations, 1989, p. 3). In Article 29 education is directed towards 'the development of the child's personality, talents and mental and physical abilities to their fullest potential'

(United Nations, 1989, p. 9) and Article 17 outlines that children are to be provided with 'access to information and material…aimed at the promotion of his or her social, spiritual and moral well-being and physical and mental health' (United Nations, 1989, p. 5). Realising these rights is of special significance in the early years as the research on young children's learning outlined in Chapter 1 reminds us that the first three to five years of life is the time when 'young children experience the most rapid period of growth and change during the human lifespan' (United Nations Committee on the Rights of the Child, 2005, p. 2) and in which important foundations for life-long learning are laid: 'Young children's earliest years are the foundation for their physical and mental health, emotional security, cultural and personal identity, and developing competencies' (United Nations Committee on the Rights of the Child, 2005, p. 2). The extent to which these ideals are realised in early education settings, however, is dependent on adults' beliefs regarding children's development, learning and competence, and the role of the adult and the child in the learning process.

General Comment No. 7: 'Implementing Child Rights in Early Childhood' (2005) notes: 'Respecting the distinctive interests, experiences and challenges facing every young child is the starting point for realizing their rights during this crucial phase of their lives' (United Nations Committee on the Rights of the Child, 2005, p. 3). The General Comment further outlines some key strategies that support adults' implementation of rights principles into daily practice in early years educational settings. These include: forming respectful relationships with children that recognise their capacity to be active members in the learning community; appreciating the diverse social and cultural forces that shape individual children's development and learning identities, and the extent to which all children are provided with opportunities to exercise their rights; providing every child with the emotional support and guidance in ways that respect their individuality and **evolving capacities**; and providing the time and space for children to learn from and with each other through play and exploration. These strategies provoke teachers to provide the foundations for children to participate and engage in their learning. In addition, Schulz (2015) underscores the importance of teachers systematically documenting, assessing and planning for young children's learning. Documentation, he argues, can support teachers to make visible young children's engagement in the processes of learning and how their capacities evolve over time: The ideal of the competent learner requires adequate and systematic documentation, diagnostics and interventions' (p. 209). Documentation, planning and assessment of children's learning thus become a key platform through which teachers can respond meaningfully to individual children's right to development.

Evolving capacities: directly linked to the right to be heard, requiring adults to be mindful of their responsibilities to protect young children from harm, and at the same time, provide opportunities for children to exercise their rights (Lansdown, 2005, p. 30).

The right to non-discrimination

The right to non-discrimination is outlined in a number of Articles in the UNCRC and is an important reminder to teachers to extend all children every opportunity to exercise their rights. Article 1 of the UNCRC, for example, states 'everyone is entitled to all the rights and freedoms set forth therein, without distinction of any kind, such as race, colour, sex, language, religion, political or other opinion, national or social origin, property, birth or other status' (United Nations, 1989, p. 2). The right to non-discrimination is reinforced in Article 2 which states children's right to equal opportunities 'irrespective of the child's or his or her parent's or legal guardian's race, color, sex, language, religion, and political or other opinion; national, ethnic or social origin, property, disability, and birth or other status' (United Nations, 1989, p. 2). Article 30 reinforces that a child also has every right 'to enjoy his or her own culture, to profess and practice his or her own religion, or to use his or her own language' without fear of persecution or discrimination (United Nations, 1989, p. 9). This requirement extends to children of 'ethnic, religious or linguistic minorities or persons of indigenous origin' (United Nations, 1989, p. 9). In addition, Article 29 asserts the importance of developing educational cultures in which 'respect for the child's parents, his or her own cultural identity, language and values, for the national values of the country in which the child is living, the country from which her she may originate, and for civilizations different from his or her own' can flourish (United Nations, 1989, p. 9). These requirements collectively give expression to the broader ideal embedded in the preamble of the UNCRC that asserts the importance of 'Taking due account … of the traditions and cultural values of each people for the protection and harmonious development of the child' (p. 2). In this way, the Articles act as an important reminder that there are ethical and moral dimensions to our roles as teachers in designing learning environments in which all young children can exercise their rights. To do this teachers need to be cognisant of their obligations to every child, active in their intent to ensure that early years learning environments are inclusive, and strong in providing all young children with equal opportunities to learn. Teachers should reflect on their personal values regarding, for example, race, religion, politics, Indigenous and Torres Strait Islander peoples, national, ethnic or social origin, gender, sex and disability. Teachers are encouraged to consider how issues of diversity are profiled and addressed in education programs, and acted out in their daily interactions with young children and their families. They should reflect on how young children's learning and development are shaped by personal family and cultural histories. Further, teachers should carefully monitor how they respectfully welcome, work alongside, listen to and reflect on the learning priorities that all families hold for their children and how they can respond to these in early education programs. It further behoves teachers to reflect on the ways in which children's learning and development are shaped by their personal family and cultural histories.

The right to be heard

The right to be heard is a central platform of the UNCRC. The Article that gives expression to this right is Article 12, stipulating:

> State Parties shall assure to the child who is capable of forming his or her own views the right to express those views freely in all matters affecting the child, the views of the child being given due weight in accordance with the age and maturity of the child. (United Nations, 1989, p. 4)

Article 12 was heralded as one of the most important and radical rights in the UNCRC because it acknowledges the growing capacity of children to independently express their interests and play an active role in exercising their rights in the social and cultural contexts in which they engage, including education. This dimension was missing from earlier declarations and conventions for children. General Comment No. 7: 'Implementing Child Rights in Early Childhood' (2005) reasserts that young children should be afforded the opportunity to be heard:

> The Committee encourages States Parties to take all appropriate measures to ensure that the concept of the child as rights holder with freedom to express views and the right to be consulted in matters that affect him or her is implemented from the earliest stage in ways appropriate to the child's capacities, best interests, and rights to protection from harmful experiencesx. (United Nations Committee on the Rights of the Child, 2005. p. 7)

Freeman (2007) noted that the way in which we as adults interpret young children's competence (or capacity) impacts on the extent to which they are afforded the right to participate in the key contexts in which they engage. As such, it is important that teachers reflect on how their 'image of the child' impacts on the opportunities afforded to children in their educational programs.

Lundy (2007) proposes a model that outlines four factors for teachers to consider when implementing the intent of Article 12 in educational contexts. She speaks of the importance of teachers providing:

1. space – the opportunity for children to express their views in a safe and inclusive environment
2. voice – the information required for children to form and express a view
3. audience – the process to ensure that children's views are communicated to the people with the responsibility and power to make decisions
4. influence – the process to ensure that children's views are heard, taken seriously, and where appropriate, acted upon.

A systematic approach towards implementing and monitoring the rights of young children to be heard in this way can provide an important barometer for assessing the extent to which this is being meaningfully achieved in educational settings.

Several documents outline strategies to support adults in providing young children with the opportunity to be heard. The General Comment No. 7 (2005), for example, offers a variety of strategies that teachers can adopt for enacting this right with young children:

> To achieve the right of participation requires adults to adopt a child-centred attitude, listening to young children and respecting their dignity and their individual points of view. It also requires adults to show patience and creativity by adapting their expectations to a young child's interests, levels of understanding and preferred ways of communicating. (United Nations Committee on the Rights of the Child, 2005, p. 7)

General Comment No. 12: 'The Right of the Child to be Heard' (United Nations Committee on the Rights of the Child, 2009) similarly underscores the importance of providing young children with a variety of opportunities through which to express their views through 'non-verbal forms of communication including play, body language, facial expressions, and drawing and painting, through which very young children demonstrate understanding, choices and preferences' (United Nations Committee on the Rights of the Child, 2009, p. 7). These strategies also support the emphasis contained in Article 13 that underlines the importance of children having access to relevant information to assist them to participate in different decisions and contexts:

> The child shall have the right to freedom of expression; this right shall include freedom to seek, receive and impart information and ideas of all kinds, regardless of frontiers, either orally, in writing or in print, in the form of art, or through any other media of the child's choice. (United Nations, 1989, p.4)

Research from the school sector highlights that enacting play, and the right to be heard requires teachers to reflect on what effective participation might look like in their daily educational programs so that it is not tokenistic (Horgan et al., 2015). Enacting young children's right to be heard in their learning thus requires that teachers listen to young children and engage with their perspectives and expertise (Bath, 2013). Teachers are prompted by Articles 12 and 13 to identify, promote, implement, monitor and evaluate the participation and engagement opportunities afforded to children in their daily educational programs and pedagogical practices. The 'right to be heard' relies on adults prioritising, documenting and planning how they will observe, analyse and incorporate the interests, ideas and skills of every child into aspects of their program in ways that recognise children's competence and evolving capacities to exercise their rights. Children are thus afforded opportunities to not only engage in activities, but also experience the processes by which their ideas are documented and acted upon. Building a participatory teaching and learning environment in which children play an active role, in turn, builds young children's self-esteem as learners and their social agency as they experience the ways in which their views are respected, and the influence that they can exert over their learning.

The best interests of the child

Article 3 in the UNCRC (1989) asserts that in all our interactions with young children 'the best interests of the child shall be a primary consideration' (p. 2). In this sense, the best interests of young children are to be realised through adults' interpretation and implementation of children's rights – to life and development, to be heard, to non-discrimination – and adults' ability to pay attention to young children's views when making decisions in the learning process. John Eekelaar (2015) argues that this is a complex process requiring the adult to make a distinction between decisions that indirectly and directly face the child. This, in turn, behoves adults to have regard for children's perspectives, be open to evaluating the impact of social rules and relationships on children and to consider creative solutions that will achieve the best outcomes for individual children and/or the best solution to the issues being addressed.

Tobin (2005) agrees that applying the 'best interests' principle is a negotiated process that reinforces to children the importance of capturing their lived experiences and perspectives in decision-making processes:

the act of granting children human rights confers on them the right to claim their legitimate entitlements and in doing so re-conceptualizes the power relationship between children, adults and the State. Importantly, it does not privilege children to the exclusion of all other interests within society – a child's best interests are only to be a primary and not the overriding consideration – but it does demand that they can no longer be ignored, devalued or marginalized in policy and social debates. (p. 14)

When adults apply the 'best interests' principle in their reflective practice, they gain a more nuanced understanding of the impact of decisions for individual children participating in their daily programs, and through this process, become better placed to support young children's learning outcomes.

In this section we have outlined the key principles underlying the UNCRC that position young children as holders of rights and capable participants in the learning process. We have demonstrated how these principles assist teachers to reflect on their image of young children and explore the implications that an image of 'child as human being with rights' have for our teaching values, approaches and practices.

REFLECTION POINTS

1. What is your image of the child? To what extent does your image align or conflict with the image of the child outlined in the UNCRC?
2. How familiar are you with the general principles outlined in the UNCRC? What do they mean to you and for your lived experience as a child? How do they enable you to promote young children's learning and development?
3. What do you see as your responsibilities – as teachers – towards children, as outlined in the UNCRC?
4. Have you seen examples of teachers enacting these principles into their educational programs? Describe these strategies.

RESEARCH CASE STUDY

Carol Rasborsek

AUSTRALIAN TEACHERS' UNDERSTANDINGS AND PRACTICES ON CONSULTING YOUNG CHILDREN ON QUALITY IMPROVEMENT

My research focused on teachers' understandings and practices regarding consulting young children on quality improvement. Seventeen teachers working in community-based ECEC and kindergarten centres in Victoria participated in the research. I was interested in ascertaining how teachers were responding to the expectation outlined in the NQS to consult young children when developing their Quality Improvement Plan (QIP), which details the intentions of a service regarding ongoing improvement: 'It is recommended that services adopt a collaborative approach to self-assessment and the development of their plan [QIP], involving wherever possible children, families, teachers, staff members, management and other interested parties' (ACECQA, 2011b, p. 7).

As major stakeholders, children have the right to have their perspectives included in the assessment of centre quality (United Nations, 1989). This is essential, not only to uphold children's participation rights, but also to gain a more rounded view of the quality of centres when focusing on improvement. Despite this, the majority of research on what constitutes quality in early childhood services has focused on adult perspectives, with little consideration being given to the perspectives of children. Fenech's (2011) literature review of how quality is defined and conceptualised in early childhood, for example, revealed that only 1.8 per cent of the studies reviewed included the perspectives of children. The studies that have focused on children's perspectives on quality have looked at children's likes and dislikes (Clark & Moss, 2001; Farrell, Tayler & Tennent, 2002; Harcourt & Mazzoni, 2012; Wiltz & Klein, 2001), views on decision making (Einarsdottir, 2005), perspectives on learning (Smith, Duncan & Marshall, 2005), involvement in the development of curriculum (Cremin & Slatter, 2004; Edwards, Gandini & Forman, 2011) and perspectives on teacher quality (Harcourt, 2012). Some researchers have concluded that high-quality early childhood education is directly linked to children's participation in decision making (Harcourt, 2012; Harcourt & Mazzoni, 2012; Sheridan & Pramling Samuelsson, 2001). My research provided an opportunity to ascertain teachers' perspectives on consulting young children on quality in a period of reform.

A total of 17 teachers participated. Eleven teachers believed that it is very important to include children's perspectives on quality, and more specifically, children's views on the QIP; seven stated that it was important that children are consulted on quality as they are key stakeholders of early childhood services; a further two teachers cited young children's right to be heard, adding that children offer a different perspective to adults. Another two teachers added that, while children's views were important to elicit, they would be considered alongside all stakeholders' perspectives. Three teachers reported that the process of consultation was beneficial for children. One teacher noted that she was required to consult children in the National and Victorian Learning Frameworks.

Twelve teachers noted that they mainly consulted children about activities and aspects about the educational program. They mainly spoke to children while consulting either during 'group times' or in 1:1 discussions with children. Six of these teachers consulted children on their likes and dislikes. Three teachers also noted that they consulted children about the set-up of the environment. One participant teacher, for example, said she consulted children about 'where they would like to see improvements', and another teacher noted that she asked children about 'how we can make kinder better for them'. Most teachers noted that they upheld children's suggestions for activities or change, and that this, in turn, had a positive impact on the children. To take one such example: 'The children were happy and excited that we have listened to their thoughts and ideas and we have used them throughout the day. Allows children to feel that they are active contributors and feel valued within the program'. Two teachers noted that they do not consult children; one was open to consulting children, the other less so stating that teachers 'are the ones who develop the program based on … those things we believe they need to learn at certain ages'.

The teachers in this research study noted stress and lack of time as major barriers to consulting children. Resources were mentioned, in terms of strategies and professional development. The participants were eager to consult children, but unsure of how to do so effectively. This study took place just 14 months after the introduction of the NQS and, thus, the need to write and implement a QIP within a very short space of time gave limited time to consult with children. Of interest, the main barrier expressed by participants was the perceived lack of children's understanding of quality. A few teachers did not believe that this was a barrier, but rather they would use different terminology when talking to children about quality. Participants also cited factors that supported consultation with children. These included: positive relationships, extra time and staff, resources, and fresh ideas. Children's own responses were cited as both a barrier and an enabler to consultation. Some teachers spoke about children's repetitive and 'off topic' answers while others stated that children provided fresh and different perspectives and 'really good' ideas and opinions.

This research revealed that teachers are aware of their obligations to consult young children on the QIP. While they believed that it is important to consult children regarding ECEC program quality, the degree to which children are consulted is contingent on a range of factors including time, resources and beliefs concerning children's capacities. This research highlighted that children's right to be heard in early childhood educational settings is mediated by the relationships with adults and a range of factors including the teacher's image of the child.

REFLECTION POINTS

1. How could you draw on rights-based principles to support your approaches to teaching and learning?
2. What theory and research evidence do you draw on to inform your image of the child as a competent learner?
3. Select a journal article that reports children's views. How does the report align to an image of the child as a holder of rights and a competent learner from birth with the capacities to learn in and through her relationships with others?

4. How would you describe the young child as a capable learner in your philosophy statement?

5. Have you viewed a QIP at an ECEC service? Can you establish whether children were consulted in the drafting of the QIP? Are there statements regarding the child as a competent learner? How would you describe the young child as a learner in a QIP?

6. How could you build a common language and image of the child as a competent learner in an ECEC setting?

Conclusion

In this chapter we have outlined the rights-based principles, background, policy directives and research evidence that position young children as dynamic and capable participants in the learning process. We argue that each of these bodies of knowledge contribute to understandings of ways in which teachers enact the intent of the principles underlying the UNCRC and contribute towards building respectful and participatory learning cultures with children, thereby enabling 'sustainable and empowering processes and outcomes for all children' (Tobin, 2005, p. 15).

Further reading

Ministerial Council on Education, Employment, Training and Youth Affairs (MCEETYA). (2008). *Melbourne Declaration on Education Goals for Young Australians.* Melbourne: MCEETYA.

United Nations Committee on the Rights of the Child. (2001). Article 20(1). The aims of education. General Comment No. 7, OHCHR (CRC/C/GC/1). Geneva: Office of the United Nations High Commissioner for Human Rights.

References

Archard, D. (2004). *Children, Rights and Childhood* (2nd ed.). London: Routledge.

Australian Children's Education and Care Quality Authority (ACECQA). (2011a). *Guide to the National Quality Standard.* Retrieved from http://files.acecqa. gov.au/files/National-Quality-Framework-Resources-Kit/NQF03-Guide-to-NQS-130902.pdf

Australian Children's Education and Care Quality Authority (ACECQA). (2011b). *Guide to Developing a Quality Improvement Plan.* Sydney: ACECQA.

Bath, C. (2013). Conceptualising listening to young children as an ethic of care in early childhood education and care. *Children & Society, 27,* 361–71.

Byrne, B., & Lundy, L. (2015). Reconciling children's policy and children's rights: barriers to effective government delivery. *Children & Society, 29,* 266–76.

Clark, A., & Moss, P. (2001). *Listening to Young Children: The Mosaic Approach.* London: National Children's Bureau and Joseph RowntreeFoundation.

Cloney, D., Page, J., Tayler, C., & Church, A. (2013). Assessing the quality of early childhood education and care. *Centre for Community and Child Health, Royal Children's Hospital Policy Brief, 25,* 1–4.

Coady, M. (2000). Seen and heard: children, autonomy and the U.N. Convention. *Australian Journal of Professional Applied Ethics, 2*(1), 27–40.

Commonwealth of Australia. (2009). *Investing in the Early Years – A National Early Childhood Development Strategy. An Initiative of the Council of Australian Governments.* Canberra: Commonwealth of Australia.

Cordero Arce, M. (2015). Maturing Children's Rights Theory. From children, with children, of children. *International Journal of Children's Rights, 23,* 283–331.

Cremin, H., & Slatter, B. (2004). Is it possible to access the 'voice' of pre-school children? Results of a research project in a pre-school setting. *Educational Studies, 30*(4), 457–70.

Department of Education, Employment and Workplace Relations (DEEWR). (2009), *Belonging, Being & Becoming: The Early Years Learning Framework for Australia.* Canberra: DEEWR for COAG.

Early Childhood Australia (ECA). (2016). *Code of Ethics.* Canberra: Early Childhood Australia.

Early Childhood Australia & Australian Human Rights Commission (ECA & AHRC). (2015). *Supporting Young Children's Rights. Statement of Intent (2015–2018).* Canberra: Early Childhood Australia.

Edwards, C., Gandini, L., & Forman, G. (2011). *The Hundred Languages of Children.* (3rd ed.). Santa Barbara, CA: Praego.

Eekelaar, J. (2015). The role of the best interests principle in decisions affecting children and decisions about children. *International Journal of Children's Rights, 23,* 3–26.

Einarsdottir, J. (2005). We can decide what to play! Children's perception of quality in an Icelandic preschool. *Early Education and Development. 16*(4), 469–88.

Farrell, A., Tayler, C., & Tennent, L. (2002). Early childhood services: what can children tell us? *Australian Journal of Early Childhood, 27*(3), 13–17.

Fenech, M. (2011). An analysis of the conceptualisation of 'quality' in early childhood education and care empirical research: promoting 'blind spots' as foci for future research. *Contemporary Issues in Early Childhood, 12*(2), 102–17.

Fleming, J. (2013). Young people's participation – where next? *Children & Society, 27,* 484–95.

Flottman, R., & Page, J. (2012). Getting early childhood onto the reform agenda: an Australian case study. *International Journal of Child Care and Education Policy, 6*(1), 17–33.

Freeman, M. (2000). The future of children's rights [Electronic version]. *Children & Society, 14,* 277–93.

Freeman, M. (2007). Why it remains important to take children's rights seriously. *International Journal of Children's Rights, 15,* 5–23.

Harcourt, D. (2012). Measuring teacher quality: listening to young children in Singapore. *Global Studies of Childhood, 2*(4), 260–75.

Harcourt, D., & Mazzoni, V. (2012). Standpoints on quality: listening to children in Verona, Italy. *Australasian Journal of Early Childhood, 37*(2A), 19–26.

Horgan, D., Forde, C., Parkes, A. & Martin, S. (2015). *Children and Young People's Experiences of Participation in Decision-making at Home, in Schools and in Their Communities.* Dublin: Department of Children and Youth Affairs.

James, J., & Prout, A. (Eds.). (2015). *Constructing and Reconstructing Childhood: Contemporary Issues in the Sociological Study of Childhood.* (2nd ed.). London: Falmer Press.

Joyniene, Z., & Samuelsson, P. (1999). Swedish and Lithuanian students' experience and their rights [Electronic version]. *Child and Youth Care Forum, 28*(6), 371–92.

Kaufman, N. H., & Flekkøy, M.G. (1998). Participation rights of the child: psychological and legal considerations [Electronic version]. *Children's Legal Rights Journal, 18*(1), 15–29.

Kjørholt, A. T. (2013). Childhood as social investments, rights and the valuing of education. *Childhood and Society, 27*, 245–57.

Lansdown, G. (2005). *The Evolving Capacities of the Child.* Florence: UNICEF, Innocenti Research Centre and Save the Children.

Limber, S. P., & Flekkøy, M. G. (1995). The U.N. Convention on the Rights of the Child: its relevance for social scientists. *Social Policy Report. Society for Research in Child Development, IX*(2), 1–15.

Lundy, L. (2007). 'Voice' is not enough: conceptualizing Article 12 of the United Nations Convention on the Rights of the Child. *British Educational Research Journal, 33*(6), 927–42.

Mentha, S., Church, A., & Page, J. (2015). Teachers as brokers. Perceptions of "participation" and agency in early childhood education and care. *International Journal of Children's Rights, 23*, 622–37.

Organisationfor Economic Co-operation and Development (OECD). (2001). *Starting Strong: Early Childhood Education and Care.* Paris: OECD.

Organisationfor Economic Co-operation and Development (OECD). (2006). *Starting Strong II: Early Childhood Education and Care.* Paris: OECD.

Page, J. (2007). The Convention on the Rights of the Child: creating a new global ethic for children [Electronic version]. In *The Encyclopaedia of Life Support Systems* (pp. 1–13). Oxford: UNESCO, ElossPublishers.

Schulz, M. (2015). The documentation of children's learning in early childhood education. *Children & Society, 29*, 209–18.

Sheridan, S., & Pramling Samuelsson, I. (2001). Children's conceptions of participation and influence in pre-school: a perspective on pedagogical quality. *Contemporary Issues in Early Childhood, 2*(2), 169–94.

Smith, A., Duncan, J., & Marshall, K. (2005). Children's perspectives on their learning: exploring methods. *Early Child Development and Care, 175*(6), 473–87.

Thomas, N. (2007) Towards a theory of children's participation. *International Journal of Children's Rights, 15*, 199–218.

Tobin, J. (2005). A right to be no longer dismissed or ignored: children's voices in pedagogy and policy making [Electronic version]. *International Journal of Equity and Innovation in Early Childhood, 3*(2), 4–18.

United Nations. (1989). *United Nations Convention on the Rights of the Child.* Retrieved from www2.ohchr.org/english/law/crc.htm

United Nations Committee on the Rights of the Child. (2005). '*Implementing Child Rights in Early Childhood*'. *General Comment No. 7, OHCHR (CRC/C/GC/7).* Geneva: Office of the United Nations High Commissioner for Human Rights.

United Nations Committee on the Rights of the Child. (2009). '*Implementing Child Rights in Early Childhood*'. *General Comment No. 12, OHCHR (CRC/C/GC/12).* Geneva: Office of the United Nations High Commissioner for Human Rights.

United Nations Committee on the Rights of the Child, United Nations Children's Fund & Bernard van Leer Foundation. (2006). *A Guide to General Comment 7: 'Implementing Child Rights in Early Childhood'* (pp. vii–viii). The Hague: Bernard van Leer Foundation.

Wiltz, N. W., & Klein, E. L. (2001). 'What do you do in child care?' Children's perceptions of high and low quality classrooms. *Early Childhood Research Quarterly, 16, 2,* 209–36.

Woodhead, M. (2005) Early childhood development: A question of rights. *International Journal of Early Childhood, 37*(3), 79–98.

Woodhead, M. (2006).UNESCO Education For All Global Monitoring Report 2007. Early childhood care and education. 'Changing perspectives on early childhood: theory, research and policy'. *International Journal of Equity and Innovation in Early Childhood, 4*(2), 5–48.

CHAPTER 4

Teaching for learning

Jan Deans, Jane Page and Collette Tayler

LEARNING OBJECTIVES

In this chapter you will:

1. characterise the role of the 'intentional' teacher within the Australian context, and the process of planning for learning to ensure the effectiveness of children's learning programs
2. identify evidence-based teaching strategies and interventions that are known to advance young children's learning and higher-order thinking
3. consider the balance, purpose and intent of adult-led and child-led learning in play-based educational programs.

Introduction

To make a positive difference to each child's learning and development is the core work of teachers, at once posing unique challenges and delivering great reward. Teaching children from birth to eight years of age affords real opportunity to ensure that 'none of the talents which are hidden like buried treasure in every person [are] left untapped' (International Commission on Education for the Twenty-first Century, 1996, p. 23). Delors and colleagues set four key pillars underlying education and life: 'learning to know', 'learning to do', 'learning to be' and 'learning to live together' (International Commission on Education for the Twenty-first Century), and each of these pillars affects the processes that teachers deploy to assess, plan for and promote children's learning. No matter whether teachers work with infants, toddlers, young children or children in their first years of schooling, the quality of planning to support children's learning, and the pedagogical strategies selected, will be strongly influenced by each teacher's knowledge and understandings of children and their development, interests and culture, and the learning theories and strategies available to support learning (see also Chapter 1).

In this chapter, the role of teachers in promoting children's learning and development is explored. Emphasis is placed of the role of the intentional teacher and the importance of the planning cycle, including **documentation**. Research has highlighted that what teachers know and do has the power to heighten children's motivation to learn and their love of learning, while also strengthening children's capacity to engage progressively in higher-order thinking (Hamre et al., 2013; Siraj & Asani, 2015). A core skill of teachers is to make children's learning visible to the children themselves and to others, including families who are acknowledged as the child's first teachers. Positive outcomes for children hinge on the abilities of teachers to develop curriculum and **pedagogy** that is both matched to the learner's interests and culture, and imbued with challenges that motivate the child to learn new knowledge and skills, and pose new ideas for investigation.

> **Documentation:** the process of 'observing, recording, interpreting and sharing through a variety of media; the processes and products of learning in order to deepen and extend learning' (Krechevsky et al., 2013, p. 74).

> **Pedagogy:** the teaching and learning strategies that teachers plan for and enact to advance individual children's learning and development.

The theoretical stance to teaching and learning presented in this chapter has *interactions* at the core (National Research Council, 2001; Hamre et al., 2013). Interactions among people convey meanings that link to emotion, attachment and connection to culture and language, and skills and strategies (see also Chapter 1). Interactions with others are part of life from birth and the 'engine room' of teaching and learning, having been the primary concern of numerous empirical investigations of education within early childhood and early school years settings. Notably, this stance is not intended to diminish other work that teachers do in the interests of children. Because we place everyday interactions and the salience of interactions for promoting learning at 'front-and-centre', the evidence and approaches that are profiled within this chapter are drawn from studies that have high regard for the quality of interactions in promoting children's learning.

Interactions can be observed and changed, and there are long educational and psychological traditions for conceptualising interactions in the study of teaching and learning (Wells, 1981; Good & Brophy, 2008). The nature and quality of interactions between adults and children, and among children, are fundamental to children's 'sense of comfort' within any early years setting. Daily interactions and relationships help to form children's sense of who they are, their developing thinking and who they become.

Early years teaching and learning in the Australian policy context

Australian early childhood education and care (ECEC) services policy emphasises the quality of teaching within all services for children from birth. As highlighted earlier in this text (see Chapter 2), Australia has adopted an integrated approach towards achieving this aim through the suite of legal, policy and practice-oriented frameworks that comprise the National Quality Framework for Early Childhood Education and Care. The Early Years Learning Framework (EYLF) (2009) is an important mechanism for outlining the role (and, by extension, expectations and accountabilities) of teachers in relation to raising the quality of teaching and learning support that is offered to young children. It is also a foundational document to ensure 'that children in all early childhood education and care settings experience quality teaching and learning' (DEEWR, 2009, p. 5). This assurance is provided through the expectation that teachers plan and implement rich teaching and learning opportunities. Setting clear purpose, the EYLF outlines the agreed learning and development outcomes for young children, and describes principles and practices for teaching that orient teachers in working collaboratively with families. Through the processes and practices highlighted within the EYLF, it is envisioned that teachers will actively engage children in learning, plan for learning, design an educational environment that is responsive to individual children's strengths and interests, and choose specific teaching strategies to advance learning outcomes for children.

The National Quality Standard (NQS) also provides a mechanism for considering the quality of an educational program (Quality Area 1) and the nature of relationships with children (Quality Area 5). Quality Areas 1 and 5 are core 'process' components of quality programs, and the assessment of these quality areas can help a team to reflect on the quality of the educational program and the pedagogy in their setting. As noted, the theoretical orientation of the EYLF values interactions and allows for a range of professional philosophies to guide the program.

The following case study explores a key practice embedded in the EYLF – 'intentional teaching' – and its implications for the role of the teacher within the teaching and learning process, especially when the quality of everyday interaction is at the core.

Intentional teaching: is the work of early childhood teachers who are deliberate, purposeful and thoughtful in all aspects of their interactions with children, and in their planning for learning (DEEWR, 2009, p. 15).

POLICY CASE STUDY

....

Jane Page, Collette Tayler and Sarah Young

INTENTIONAL TEACHING: FROM PLANNING THROUGH TO PRACTICE

'Intentional teaching' is subsumed within several parts of the NQS, especially National Quality Area 1, Standard 1.2.2, 'Educators respond to children's ideas and play and use intentional teaching to scaffold and extend each child's learning' (ACECQA, 2011, p. 17). The inclusion of 'intentional teaching' is a direct response to research evidence from effectiveness studies that underscore the quality, intent and content of pedagogical practices (see Chapter 1). Such practices are critical for optimal child learning and development in the early years of education (Cloney et al., 2013; Shonkoff & Phillips, 2000; Siraj-Blatchford & Manni, 2008), especially for children from disadvantaged backgrounds (Sammons et al., 2012; Tayler, Cloney & Niklas, 2015).

'Intentional teaching' is one of the eight pedagogical practices outlined in the EYLF that support teachers in advancing young children's learning, and to be 'deliberate, purposeful and thoughtful' in all aspects of their interactions with children and in their planning for learning (DEEWR, 2009, p. 15). It is enacted when teachers 'actively promote children's learning through worthwhile and challenging experiences and interactions that foster high-level thinking skills' (DEEWR, 2009, p. 15). The EYLF definition of 'intentional teaching' stems from the research literature. For example, Ann Epstein (2007) describes the 'intentional teacher' as someone who 'acts with knowledge and purpose to ensure that young children acquire the knowledge and skills (content) they need to succeed in school and in life' (p. 1). Epstein (2007) argues that in order to equip children with knowledge and skills, teachers must translate three forms of their own knowledge into the educational program and their everyday interactions:

1. knowledge of how children learn and develop
2. knowledge of academic domains – such as mathematics, science, literacy and the arts – and learning domains including cognitive, social, emotional, physical, creative and spiritual development
3. knowledge of instructional teaching strategies such as cueing and prompting, questioning, explaining, giving feedback, analysing and discussing.

These forms of knowledge are used within an ongoing planning cycle that drives pedagogical decision making.

The planning cycle illustrated within this case study (and in Figure 4.1) was adapted from the EYLF by the Victorian Curriculum and Assessment Authority (VCAA, 2013).

The first, second and third stages of planning draw upon teachers' knowledge of how children learn and develop (see also Chapter 1). Working with children from birth to age eight years, teachers gather a range of evidence of each child's learning, and draw upon theories and research understandings to interpret this evidence. The findings are used to develop learning goals for and with individual children, and their families.

Early Years Planning Cycle (EYPC): Reflection occurs at every step in the EYPC

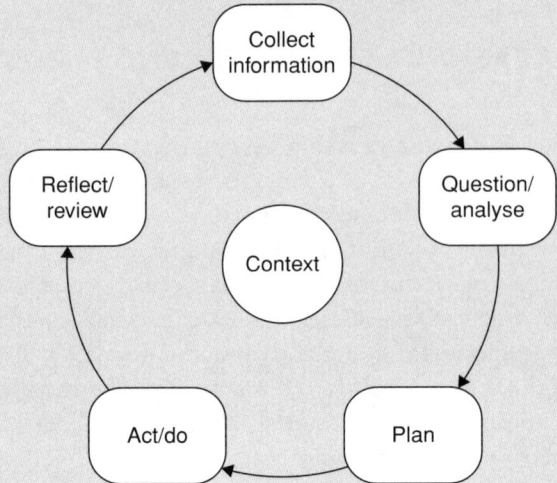

Figure 4.1: The EYPC is adapted from the *Educators' Guide to the EYLF* (2010)

Intentional teachers 'act with specific outcomes or goals in mind for children's development and learning' (Epstein, 2007, p. 1). The teachers also draw on their knowledge of academic and learning domains (VCAA, 2015), especially as children move through this age span into pre-school and school. Importantly, intentional teachers 'know when to use a given strategy to accommodate the different ways that individual children learn and the specific content they are learning' (Epstein, 2007, p. 1) as well as diverse cultures, language backgrounds and interests.

Research underpinning the policy to promote 'intentional teaching' is both widespread and compelling, and furthermore, the findings for interaction-focused teaching frameworks include results for expanding children's understanding, advancing children's higher-order thinking skills and cognition, and supporting children's participation in learning (Hamre et al., 2013; Hamre et al., 2014; Mashburn et al., 2008; Siraj & Asani, 2015; Tayler et al., 2015).

The 'act/do' and 'reflect/review' stages of a planning cycle are iterative. During these phases, 'intentional teachers' are engaging with children, documenting learning and also assessing the effect of their teaching strategies as they proceed (see also the practice case study within this chapter). Teachers progressively tailor their pedagogy and interactions in light of children's initiations and responses – responsive teaching is a mediator of child outcomes (Hamre et al., 2014). They may address children's preferred approaches and perspectives on what they have learned (DEEWR, 2009), and in so doing, teachers acknowledge children's active role in the learning process (see Chapter 3).

Hamre et al. (2012a) draw on Epstein's (2007) understanding of 'intentional teaching', identifying four elements that are fundamental to intentional teaching: 'knowing';

'seeing'; 'doing'; and 'reflecting'. 'Knowing' refers to the knowledge required to be an intentional teacher, as noted earlier. 'Seeing' refers to teachers' abilities to identify, observe and reflect on the effect of their own teaching strategies, and others' practices. 'Doing' refers to teachers' enactments of effective strategies within the moment-to-moment interactions with individuals and small groups, and the modification of these strategies in light of children's responses and learning. 'Reflecting' refers to teachers' abilities to critically consider the impact of their teaching practices on children's learning, and look for ways to improve (Hamre et al., 2012a).

Epstein (2007) and Hamre et al. (2012a) further concur that 'intentional teaching' entails creating an emotional climate that allows teachers to maximise children's engagement, the organising of experiences that extend children's learning and development, and the implementation of a range of instructional strategies to advance the learning goals set for (and agreed with) each child. (These elements of high-quality teacher–child interactions are revisited later in this chapter, when discussing effective evidence-based teaching strategies.)

Breaking down the elements of 'intentional teaching' highlights the complexity involved in advancing young children's learning and development. Children's development is dynamic, and the ways in which children take part in learning experiences are shaped by background characteristics of culture, language and child, family and community interests. All of these factors are taken into account when planning for and engaging with the very young. The use of 'reflection' supports teachers to unpack the processes, knowledge and skills that are required to advance young children's learning and development.

REFLECTION POINTS

1. Examine the ways in which 'intentional teaching' is defined. Write a list of adjectives that best describe an intentional teacher.
2. Refer to the different knowledge(s) required to be an intentional teacher. Critically reflect on yourself as an intentional teacher. Does your knowledge about children's learning and development encompass the infant, toddler, young child and child at school? If not, what sources would you need to access to build this knowledge?
3. How could you involve children to build deeper knowledge of particular concepts and ideas? How might this change as you work with children over the birth-to-age-eight lifespan?
4. Consider the four elements of intentional teaching identified by Hamre et al. (2012a) – 'knowing', 'seeing', 'doing' and 'reflecting'. Critically reflect on how you practise these different elements in your daily educational program.

5. Examine the following definitions of the instructional teaching strategies outlined in CLASS (Pianta, La Paro & Hamre, 2008). Consider how they advance young children's higher-order thinking and participation in learning. Critically reflect on your level of confidence to enact these strategies in your daily interactions with children.

- Concept development 'measures the teacher's use of instructional discussions and activities to promote students' higher-order thinking skills and cognition and the teacher's focus on understanding rather than rote instruction' (p. 62).
- Quality of feedback 'assesses the degree to which the teacher provides feedback that expands learning and understanding and encourages continued participation' (p. 69).
- Language modelling 'captures the quality and amount of the teacher's use of language-stimulation and language-facilitation techniques' (p. 75).

Pedagogy: the selection and use of evidence-based teaching strategies

In early childhood education, there is wide support for establishing a teaching and learning model that acknowledges the responsibility of teachers to work closely with children as they establish and maintain the direction of their learning. Such ideas affirm children as active co-constructors of meaning (Smith, Duncan & Marshall, 2005) and 'provide a glimpse of children's worlds as acting, doing, thinking, feeling and being through their communication and interaction with others' (Page, 2007, p. 74).

The selection and use of teaching strategies within any early years setting raises debate concerning the role of the adult and the child in the learning process, especially among teachers who align their pedagogy with socio-constructivist theory and cultural historical activity theory (Cole, 1996; Cole & Engeström, 1994; Rogoff, 2003; Vygotsky, 1978). Combined with Vygotsky's view that 'learning leads development', there is support for a teaching and learning approach that provides opportunities for young children to move beyond the known, push past prior capabilities, and achieve new understandings – with the support and collaboration of others. With these thoughts in mind, teachers can consider the relative merits of 'constructed knowledge' versus 'instructed knowledge' (Westwood, 2008). The most significant difference identified between these two approaches is that the 'constructivist' approach is understood to be child-focused and designed to encourage independent learning that brings about deeper conceptual understandings, whereas the 'instructivist' approach is recognised as being more teacher-focused and reliant on the effective provision of information and skills from the teacher to the learner (Hmelo-Silver, Duncan & Chinn, 2007; Kirschner, Sweller & Clark, 2006; Prosser & Tigwell, 2006; Rowe, 2006). Although 'constructed' and 'instructed' knowledge may appear to be in tension, current thinking notes that both sides do in fact work hand in hand to contribute to optimal learning outcomes for children.

Both human and material factors come into play as teachers make selections about optimal teaching strategies in a setting. In terms of human factors, it is acknowledged that interactions are at the core of teaching and learning, and that individual development comes about as a result of participation in joint activity with more knowledgeable others (Vygotsky, 1978; Wells & Chang-Wells, 1992) within a social and cultural context. In terms of material factors, it is recognised that mediating tools – physical, mental, material and symbolic – play an important role in supporting acting and thinking. Furthermore, curriculum content (what is to be taught and learned) across the disciplines of language and literacy, mathematics, science, the arts, physical education and information technology holds a central position for both teacher and learner.

Entering into such 'culturally valued' knowledge (Meyer & Land, 2005) takes the teacher and learner beyond the threshold of familiar space into a much riskier terrain where new knowledge awaits. The notion of scaffolding by an adult or more informed peer in this space brings into play the zone of proximal development (ZPD), a concept that has been widely embraced by educational communities to guide the practice of teaching and learning. Vygotsky (1978) defines ZPD as:

> the distance between the actual developmental level as determined by independent problem solving, and the level of potential development as determined through problem solving under adult guidance or in collaboration with more capable peers.
> (p. 86)

In addition, the idea of building curriculum from the interests of the children has long been valued in the early childhood profession. From a Vygotskian perspective, inter-subjectivity describes the contributions of all participants to the learning process and, even though contributions may not be equal, the construct implies reciprocal and responsive relationship building. Shared focus enables the co-construction of knowledge and curriculum that can expand and transform experience (Wertsch, 1985). The foundations of critical, creative thinking (Jordan, Carlile & Stack, 2008; Wright, 2010) are established through such interactions. The process offers support for sensory-rich, experiential learning that fosters choice, inquiry, shared sustained thinking, initiative, independence and self-confidence. With such a rationale in mind, teachers work together to select specific strategies, ideally from a range of strategies known for their positive effects on the learning and development of diverse young children, that will help to increase each child's skills, knowledge, understandings and attitudes towards learning.

RESEARCH CASE STUDY

Jan Deans, Jane Page and Collette Tayler

EVIDENCE-BASED TEACHING STRATEGIES FOR ADVANCING YOUNG CHILDREN'S LEARNING

Contemporary research on teaching effectiveness plays an important role in advancing knowledge of evidence-based teaching strategies that have been found to advance young children's learning and their outcomes. Numerous authors illustrate the deepening of understanding about effective teaching practices and highlight the impact of adults' interactions with children on advancing children's learning (Pianta et al., 2008; Ritchhart, Church & Morrison, 2011; Lemov, 2010; Turnbull, 2007). Three evidence-based approaches to the use of teaching strategies are presented here as case examples.

The Classroom Assessment Scoring System (CLASS)

Pianta et al. (2008) developed this empirically based and theoretically informed tool to assess the quality of interactions in any classroom. Three broad constructs – emotional support, organisational climate and instructional support – are at the core. Observers determine the presence of particular interactions and behaviours that have been found to associate positively with children's social and academic achievement.

- *Emotional support* involves:
  1. positive climate
  2. negative climate
  3. teacher sensitivity
  4. regard for the children's perspectives that are apparent.

- *Classroom organisation* involves:
  5. behaviour management
  6. productivity
  7. instructional learning formats.

- *Instructional support* involves observation of:
  8. concept development
  9. the quality of feedback
  10. language modelling
  11. the overall richness of instructional methods.

While this tool has been used to assess the quality of interactions within a class, it has also proven to be a substantiated method through which teaching quality can be significantly improved (Hamre et al., 2012b).

Project Zero

Research within this project offers insights into the processes underlying teaching and learning through an investigation of the nature of intelligence, thinking, creativity and ethics. This work is shedding light on how higher-order thinking can be enhanced across disciplines and cultures. Of particular interest is how recent research into thinking has uncovered the need for teachers to help children understand their thinking more overtly, especially in relation to identifying the different types of thinking that would be useful when children are trying to understand new concepts, ideas or events. Ritchhart et al., (2011) have identified a number of high-leverage thinking strategies that support higher-order thinking. These include:

- observing closely and describing what is observed
- developing explanations, descriptions and interpretations
- reasoning using the evidence collected
- making connections between new knowledge and previous knowledge
- considering a range of viewpoints and perspectives
- capturing the essence of the inquiry and coming up with conclusions
- wondering and asking questions
- going beyond the surface to uncover complexity.

Such strategies can help to engage children and foster the development of understandings about new concepts or ideas. There are multiple thinking routines (Ritchhart et al., 2011) that can be used to develop young children's thinking. For example, the I see, I think, I wonder (STW) routine (Ritchhart et al., 2011) supports the development of children's observation skills and then leads them into a thinking space where they are given time to think through the new information, and finally, to identify any wonderings that may have emerged through the learning process.

The Abecedarian Approach Australia (3a) project

This project generated a customised Australian version of the US Abecedarian Approach that was developed from over 40 years of research, stemming from the Abecedarian Project. The 3a Approach (see also Chapter 1) has been implemented in a diverse range of educational contexts across Australia, including playgroups in remote Indigenous communities (see Chapter 5) and in centre-based long day care services (Chapter 6). 3a is made up of four core elements, an overarching *language priority, conversational reading, LearningGames® and enriched caregiving.* These elements give priority to interactions and draw upon joint attention theory and Vygotsky's theory of social mediation. Teachers engage with each child or small group (2–3) of children in a way that is individualised, frequent and intentional. *Conversational reading* is supported through the 3S teaching technique – 'see, show, say' and *enriched caregiving* is enabled through the 3N teaching technique – 'notice, nudge, narrate'. These techniques encourage adults to engage in back-and-forth exchanges that support the teacher to assess what children hear, understand and express, and allow the teacher to expand the child's focus or frame of reference. They also help teachers offer children 'response–contingent feedback' to advance their learning.

These examples of evidence-based teaching strategies support teachers to further explore the important intersections between theory, research and practice. An important decision-making role of any teacher is to identify and implement techniques and strategies that can advance young children's learning.

REFLECTION POINTS

1. Effective teaching requires teachers to have a range of knowledge, abilities and skills, including:
   - knowledge and understanding of how children learn and how the theory–practice nexus is played out in the early years learning environment
   - the ability to focus on children's holistic learning with particular attention paid to relationship building – active engagement with learning content being taught (Hattie, 2014, p. 23), language modelling (Pianta et al., 2008) and thinking strategies (Ritchart et al., 2011)
   - the ability to plan, implement and evaluate challenging and stimulating programs that engage children in new knowledge acquisition, and big ideas and understandings (Perkins, 2014)
   - the capacity to systematically assess children's growth and development, and to provide feedback to families about developmental progress
   - the ability to create aesthetically and sensory stimulating learning environments that communicate excitement about the world (Edwards, Gandini & Forman, 1998)
   - the capacity to consider the learning and the learning environment through the eyes of the children, appreciating the many and varied learning dispositions (Carr, 2001) and learning approaches (Claxton, 1990) that exist within a group of children
   - the skills to engage using intentional, purposeful and focused teaching that supports collaborative co-construction of knowledge, and promotes shared and sustained thinking (Siraj-Blatchford 2007).

   Do you agree with these statements? Why? Why not? How would you rate your own teaching practice against these statements? What knowledge, abilities and skills do you want to further develop?

2. Critically reflect on how you access the latest research on teaching and learning. How do you communicate this knowledge to colleagues and families?

3. What teaching strategies do you use in classrooms with infants, toddlers and young children? Are there strategies you will use in light of your current reading and studies of children's learning? What are they? Why might you use these and in what setting? How do you describe and justify your selection of teaching strategies to other teachers and to families?

The balance, purpose and intent of children's learning within play-based programs

The EYLF positions the child as an active protagonist in the learning process and stresses the value in teachers providing 'a balance between child-led, child-initiated and educator-supported learning' (DEEWR, 2009, p. 15) within their educational programs. This requirement aligns with the conception of the intentional teacher as someone who is skilled at providing opportunities for individual children to pursue their own interests in learning and steps in to offer 'strategic' support when opportunities arise (Epstein, 2007), alongside planned teaching interventions that match the child's interest, further develop skills and stretch thinking. There is greater acknowledgement of the need for a more integrated approach to teaching and learning (Deans, 2014); one where child-led and teacher-led ideologies cross over to allow for effective teaching and learning to advance (DETVic, 2016) across all developmental and discipline areas.

Teachers in early years settings are required to balance the extremes of control and freedom. One end of the pendulum represents the idea of 'child-centred', 'play-based' learning as a product of experience in the world that surrounds the child (Rogoff, 1994) and the other represents 'teacher-led' instruction, or intentional purposeful teaching (DEEWR, 2009), that is deliberate and thoughtful, reflecting the Vygotskian (1978) theory that learning is a product of transmission, with learning outcomes greatly enhanced when a learner is supported by a more knowledgeable other. There has been growing interest in the impact of short, focused intentional teaching to provide 'hooks' (Lemov, 2010) that capture children's attention, and communicate what is interesting about a new idea. In the following case study, we identify some evidence-based teaching strategies that help teachers to optimise children's learning outcomes.

Children innately seek out and thrive on opportunities to push the boundaries beyond what is already known, but not so far to be beyond the individual's capacities to be able to make links with prior knowledge (Lindfors, 1999). Interest-driven teaching and learning relies on the construction of understandings from child, family or teacher-initiated content, which often leads to projects that unfold over time in unpredictable rather than predictable ways. Such an approach suggests a continuum of learning that may begin with child-initiated play-based interests, picked up by the teacher who moves the learning towards a more sophisticated inquiry about the content and, more importantly, what it means to be a learner. Moreover, Bereiter (2002) observed that young children are very often interested in topics in which they have no direct or concrete experience, such as dinosaurs, astronomy or outer space. As Bereiter (2002) claims, children are clearly interested in exploring learning content beyond their direct experience and they show interest in the conceptual challenges that are associated with learning new knowledge. The teacher's role includes balancing child-led, child-initiated and 'teacher-led' experiences in the interest of furthering a child's knowledge and skills and promoting positive attitudes to new forms of inquiry.

PRACTICE CASE STUDY

Jan Deans, Natalie Jones and Sophia Stirling

DEVELOPING BIG IDEAS AND MAKING LEARNING VISIBLE THROUGH DOCUMENTATION

Background

The following case study outlines the ways in which a group of 20 four- and five-year-old children and their teachers identified and developed a 'big idea', which emanated from a project entitled 'Toolangi Forest – Voices in the Forest'. The inquiry was initially developed in response to children learning 'in', 'about' and 'for' the environment (Palmer, 1998), with the focus quickly leading to an inquiry about the germination of the tiniest seed and its growth into the tallest mountain ash tree. As time went by, the children became knowledgeable about plant and tree growth, the value of old-growth trees, forests as habitats for wildlife, endangered species (in particular, the Leadbeater's possum), the harmful effects of logging, paper as a by-product of trees and recyclable paper.

Theory

Eisner (2002) points out that, sometimes, when teachers and children have a shared goal, surprises can occur. One of many unexpected interests that developed from the Toolangi Forest project was the idea of 'wise paper'. Consistent with the socio-constructivism and child-rights theory, the teachers employed a number of strategies, including investigating, questioning, explaining, giving feedback and acknowledging all children's contributions, to engage the children in individual, small group and large group learning. As Ritchhart et al. (2011) state: 'When there is something important and worthwhile to think about and a reason to think deeply, our students experience the kind of learning that has a lasting impact and powerful influence not only in the short term but also in the long haul. They not only learn; they learn how to learn' (p. 26).

Practice

During a group discussion about how trees, specifically old-growth mountain ash forest trees, are harvested for paper, the children and their teachers brainstormed how they could help protect the Toolangi Forest from being harvested. Several ideas were put forward by the children, including writing to the prime minister to ask him to stop harvesting in the Toolangi State Forest and using 'wise paper' in the classroom for art activities. A commitment from and by the children to 'stepping out', 'finding out' and 'speaking out' was revealed. And so began a deep inquiry that permeated all aspects of the curriculum; families were encouraged to take their children to visit Toolangi State Forest, environmental scientists were invited to speak to the children about old-growth forests, Google investigations about forest harvesting and paper making were undertaken, and drawings and letters to the prime minister were developed.

Together, the teachers and children decided that they would act to solely use recycled paper in the classroom, and they would actively support the recycling of newspapers, using the 'product' to make 'wise paper' canvases, which would provide an environmentally friendly surface for a series of mountain ash paintings. A number of influential arts teachers (Eisner, 2002; Sinclair, Jeanneret & O'Toole, 2009; Wright, 2003a, 2003b, 2010) argue for a curriculum that is rich in opportunities for children to use a range of semiotic tools for artistic creation and meaning making. In this project, the children and teachers worked together, using Celmix and PVA to laminate several sheets of newspaper before applying a wash of white paint, Celmix and PVA, to create their unique 'wise paper' canvases. The final product allowed for a transparent

newspaper print to show through, highlighting the use of recycled paper. Additionally, the layered paper created a textured surface, reflecting the natural environment
of seeds and trees in nature. This outcome connected metaphorically with the idea
of painting mountain ash trees, as the surface reflected the patterned surface of a
tree. The teachers provided the children with a sensitive colour palette consistent
with the colours of mountain ash trees as depicted in sourced photographs, which
were also provided as visual stimuli and inspiration for their paintings. The teachers
scaffolded the children, via individual and collaborative discussions, to revisit their
memories of their excursions to the Toolangi Forest. This was a strategy designed to
support meta-cognitive processes, such as recall, problem-solving and decision-making, specifically in relation to identified learning content about the shape and form of
forest trees. Over the course of the project, the inclusion of paintings on both white
recycled paper and newspaper illustrated the learning process of 'wising up' to 'wise
paper'. The documentation of 'wise paper' creation recorded both the skills children
learned and the concepts, ideas and understandings they reached.

Documentation

Many notable authors (Edwards et al., 1998; Hattie, 2012; Krechevsky et al., 2013;
Malaguzzi, 1998; Ritchhart et al., 2011; Ritchhart & Perkins, 2008; Rinaldi, 2006) write
convincingly on the significance of teachers paying close attention to the idea of
making learning, and individual learners and their thinking, visible in the educational
environment. Within early childhood, the documentation of children's learning is not
a new idea. Teachers have been using a range of approaches, such as learning stories
(Carr, 2001), to record the learning process and the outcomes. As noted by Krechevsky
et al. (2013), documentation involves 'observing, recording, interpreting and sharing
through a variety of media the processes and products of learning in order to deepen
and extend learning' (p. 74). Documentation provides a concrete way for teachers to
'capture' the interactive process of learning and communicate the depth and breadth
of the learning experience across the 'learning community' of children, families and
staff. Through observation, active listening, eliciting verbal responses, recording
reflections and recollections, and considering individual insights and feelings, the
teacher is able to build a story that has shared meaning among individuals, groups
of children, teachers and families. When teachers work to make learning and thinking visible – through the display of artworks, written records of children's voices and
photographs – they are not only honouring the voices of children but they are also
bringing the interactive learning environment to life with the collective knowledge of
what teaching and learning is being experienced. Through documentation learning
connections are established between: children and children; teachers and children;
and children, teachers and families. Also, at a time when accountability for teacher
decision making and action is expected, public documentation – that illuminates high
quality and innovative teaching and learning practice – provides a direct lens into the
practice within any early years setting. The records of any learning community, where
the rights of children to communicate their ideas and thoughts (United Nations, 1989)

are given centre stage, prove to be potent examples of the work of teachers in meeting national vision and agreed priorities for children's learning.

In this project, sequential documentation was developed by the teachers to provide evidence of the children's developing knowledge about the forest as well as the growth of their technical, linguistic and artistic skills. This evidence was used in the planning cycle, and to direct and 'nuance' teachers' decision making about balancing their role as 'supporter', 'guide' and 'leader' within a range of individual and groups experiences. The documentation was also used to highlight the voices of children as expressed through their artistic products and through their accompanying narrations. For example, individual children were able to communicate their emotional attachment to the forest.

Figure 4.2: 'Me and Adelie were looking at mountain ash trees in Toolangi. The camera was flashing; we took photos with me and Adelie next to the mountain ash. I loved Toolangi.' Clementine, five years

Figure 4.3: 'I am so happy because Toolangi is so pretty. All of the trees are so pretty … beautiful. I liked the fungi on the log; it was a nice shape – curvy.' Adelie, five years

Communications such as these draw attention to the impact of deep and wide investigations that draw children into holistic and meaningful learning. Through active participation in the inquiry, the children developed confidence to express their ideas and thoughts on a range of matters associated with the Toolangi Forest, and they also demonstrated their capacity for being active agents who were able to speak out about matters that affected them (United Nations, 1989).

Connection and community

Learning about the Toolangi State Forest, especially the 'mountain ash trees', connected the children with new knowledge about the interdependence of living things. During the learning process, the children and teachers learned that the survival of the mountain ash trees is linked to the survival of the Leadbeater's possum (now being placed on the 'critically endangered' list). They also explored how the survival of Toolangi Forest was connected to their city's water source and supply. The children's interest in this topic was shared with the families through: displays of their drawings; their writing within the educational setting; in the program book shared with families; and in the newsletter. As a result, a vibrant 'community of learners' (Rogoff, 1994) developed, with teachers, children and families co-constructing new knowledge and understandings, and together engaging in ongoing investigations. The final outcome of this project was an exhibition of paintings on wise paper that was shared with the families and the broader community.

REFLECTION POINTS

1. Review the following statements about children.
    *   Children are 'rich in potential, strong, powerful, competent and, most of all, connected to adults and other children' (Malaguzzi, 1993, p. 10).
    *   'Children are unique and have a profile of multiple intelligences for thinking and learning' (Gardner, 1985).
    *   Children learn best through playful 'self-initiated problem solving/finding and through implicitly drawn connections for self-discovered meaning-making' (St. John as cited in Connery, John-Steiner & Marjanović-Shane, 2010, p. 66).
    *   Children benefit when they master a set of mental tools (Vygotsky, 1978) or tools of the mind (Bodrova & Leong, 2007).
    *   Children actively construct knowledge, skills and attitudes by interacting with the environment and the people in it (Vygotsky, 1978; Rogoff, 1994).
    Do you agree with these statements? Why? Why not? What statements about children have you included in your philosophy statement and what is noted about children in your centre's Quality Improvement Plan? How do they align with theory or research on young children's learning and development?

2. How do you document young children's learning? How do you ensure the unique pathway of each child's learning is visible?
3. The EYLF states that 'Educators use a variety of strategies to collect, document, synthesise and interpret the information that they gather to assess children's learning' (DEEWR, 2009, p. 17). How can documentation support teachers to assess children's progression of learning over time?

In addition to understanding policy, theory and research principles regarding children's learning and also what it means to be an interventionist practitioner, teachers bring their personal values and beliefs to the educational environment. These stay at the core of the teaching and learning experience, not only reflecting the individual teacher's moral and ethical stance (Foucault, 1994), but also flowing through to professional planning and documentation, teaching strategies and the types of interactions that are enacted with children, families and colleagues. Each teacher's educational philosophy provides a solid base from which new ideas and knowledge, inconsistencies and inequities are identified, analysed, synthesised and challenged. It is understood that a range of complex ethical and politically influenced ideologies around the nature of knowledge, power, teaching and learning can stimulate teachers to question and critically reflect (Brookfield, 1995; Kolb, 1984; MacNaughton, 2000; Schön, 1987) on established foundational pedagogical truths (DEEWR, 2009; DETVic, 2016; NYAEC, 1998) that dominate early childhood literature. What is most notable in establishing a personal set of values and beliefs about teaching and learning is that these set the scene for future curriculum planning and teaching practice. They represent intrapersonal and interpersonal 'know-how of broad significance' (Perkins, 2014, p. 207) that will shape pedagogical decision making, and the collaborative learning that unfolds between the teacher and the children. Refined personal values and beliefs about teacher and learning set the scene within a teacher's classroom, and involve 'learning to know', 'learning to do', 'learning to be' and 'learning to live together'.

Conclusion

Teachers are 'among the most powerful influences in learning' (Hattie, 2012, p. 22) and as such, they are required to be passionate, energetic and accomplished when it comes to understanding the teaching and learning dyad. It is recognised that teachers are required to be skilled across three main domains:

1. by providing a learning environment that communicates a deep sense of connectedness, belonging and emotional support
2. a sense of organisation where visibility of learning is evident
3. a learning environment that allows strategically planned instructional support (Pianta et al., 2008), where teachers and children participate in, lead and co-construct new knowledge and understandings that are 'big in insight', 'big in action', 'big in ethics' and 'big in opportunity' (Perkins, 2014).

Further reading

Bruner, J. S. (1961). The act of discovery. *Harvard Educational Review,31*(1), 21–32.

Bruner, J. S. (1966). *Toward a Theory of Instruction.* Cambridge, MA: Harvard University Press.

Bruner, J. S. (1990). *Acts of Meaning.* Cambridge, MA: Harvard University Press.

Chak, A. (2007). Teachers' and parents' conceptions of children's curiosity and exploration. *International Journal of Early Years Education, 15*(2), 141–59.

Cohen, D. (1983). *Piaget: Critique and Reassessment.* London: Croom Helm.

Hattie, J.A.C, & Yates, G. (2014). *Visible Learning and the Science of How We Learn.* London: Routledge.

Ramey, C.T., Sparling, J., & Landesman, S.L. (2012). *Abecedarian: The Ideas, the Approach and the Finding.* Los Altos, CA: Sociometrics Corporation.

Trawick-Smith, J. (2012). Teacher-child play interactions to achieve learning outcomes. Risks and opportunities. In R. Pianta (Ed.). *Handbook of Early Childhood Education* (pp. 259–77). New York: The Guilford Press.

References

Australian Children's Education and Care Quality Authority (ACECQA). (2011). *Guide to the National Quality Standard.* Retrieved from http://files.acecqa. gov.au/files/National-Quality-Framework-Resources-Kit/NQF03-Guide-to-NQS-130902.pdf

Bereiter, C. (2002). *Education and Mind in the Knowledge Age.* Mahwah, NJ: Lawrence Erlbaum Associates Publishers.

Bodrova, E., & Leong, D. J. (2007). *Tools of the Mind: The Vygotskian Approach to Early Childhood Education* (2nd ed.). Columbus, OH: Merrill/Prentice Hall.

Brookfield, S.D. (1995). *Becoming a Critically Reflective Teacher.* San Francisco: Jossey-Bass.

Carr, M. (2001). *Assessment in Early Childhood Settings: Learning stories.* London: Sage Publications.

Claxton, G. (1990). *Teaching to Learn: A Direction for Education.* London: Cassell Educational.

Cloney, D., Page, J., Tayler, C., & Church, A. (2013). Assessing the quality of early childhood education and care. *Centre for Community and Child Health, Royal Children's Hospital Policy Brief, 25,* 1–4.

Cole, M. (1996). *Cultural Psychology.* Cambridge, MA: Harvard University Press.

Cole, M., & Engeström, Y. (1994). Introduction. Mind, culture and activity. *An International Journal, 1*(4), 201.

Connery, C., John-Steiner, V. P., & Marjanović -Shane, A. (2010). (Eds.). *Vygotsky and Creativity. A Cultural-Historical Approach to Play, Meaning Making, and the Arts*. New York: Peter Lang Publishing.

Deans, J. (2014). Thinking, feeling and relating: young children learning through dance. Unpublished doctoral dissertation, University of Melbourne: Victoria.

Department of Education and Training (Victoria) & Victorian Curriculum and Assessment Authority. (2016). *Victorian Early Years Learning and Development Framework*. Melbourne: Department of Education and Training (Victoria).

Department of Education, Employment and Workplace Relations (DEEWR). (2009). *Belonging, Being & Becoming. The Early Years Learning Framework for Australia*. Canberra: Commonwealth Copyright Division.

Edwards, C., Gandini, L., & Forman, G. (Eds.). (1998). *The Hundred Languages of Children: The Reggio Emilia Approach to Early Childhood Education*. Westport, CT: Ablex.

Eisner, E. (2002). *The Arts and the Creation of the Mind*. New Haven CT: Yale University Press.

Epstein, A. S. (2007). *The Intentional Teacher: Choosing the Best Strategies for Young Children's Learning*. Washington DC: National Association for the Education of Young Children.

Foucault, M. (1994). *Power*. New York: The New York Press.

Gardner, H. (1985). *The Mind's New Science*. New York: Basic Books.

Good, T. L., & Brophy, J. E. (2008). *Looking in Classrooms* (10th ed.). New York: Pearson.

Hamre, B.K., Downer, J. T., Jamil, F. M., & Pianta, R. C. (2012a). Enhancing teachers' intentional use of effective interactions with children. Designing and testing professional interventions. In R. Pianta (Ed.) *Handbook of Early Childhood Education* (pp. 507–32). New York: The Guilford Press.

Hamre, B., Pianta, R., Mashburn. A, & Downer, J. (2012b). Promoting young children's social competence through the Preschool PATHS Curriculum and MyTeachingPartner Professional Development Resources. *Early Education & Development, 23*(6), 809–32, DOI: http://doi.org/10.1080/10409289.2011.607360

Hamre, B., Pianta, R., Downer, J., DeCoster, J., Mashburn, A., Jones, S., Brown, J., Cappella, E., Atkins, M., Rivers, R., Brackett, M., & Hamagami, A. (2013). Teaching through interactions: testing a developmental framework of teacher effectiveness in over 4,000 classrooms. *The Elementary School Journal, 113*(4), 461–87.

Hamre, B., Hatfield, B., Pianta, R., & Jamil, F. (2014). Evidence for general and domain-specific elements of teacher–child interactions: associations with preschool children's development. *Child Development, 85*(3), 1257–74.

Hattie, J. (2012). *Visible Learning for Teachers. Maximizing Impact on Learning*. New York: Routledge.

Hmelo-Silver, C.E., Duncan, R. G., & Chinn, C. A. (2007). Scaffolding and achievement in problem-based and inquiry learning. *Educational Psychologist, 42*(2), 99–107.

International Commission on Education for the Twenty-first Century. (1996). *Learning: The Treasure Within. Report to UNESCO of the International Commission of Education for the Twenty-first Century.* Paris: UNESCO.

Jordan, A., Carlile, O., & Stack, A. (2008). *Approaches to Learning: A Guide for Teachers.* Maidenhead: McGraw-Hill, Open University Press.

Kirschner, P. A., Sweller, J., & Clark, R. E. (2006). Why minimal guidance during instruction does not work: an analysis of the failure of constructivist, discovery, problem based, experiential and inquiry based teaching. *Educational Psychologist, 4*(2), 75–86.

Kolb, D. A. (1984). *Experiential Learning as a Source of Learning and Development.* New Jersey: Prentice Hall.

Krechevsky, M., Mardell, B., Rivard, M., & Wilson, D. (2013). *Visible Learners. Promoting Reggio-Inspired Approaches in All Schools.* San Francisco: Jossey-Bass.

Lemov, D. (2010). *Teach Like a Champion: 49 Techniques that Put Students on the Path to College.* San Francisco: Jossey-Bass.

Lindfors, J. W. (1999). *Children's Inquiry: Using Language to Make Sense of the World.* New York: Teachers College Press.

MacNaughton, G. (2000). *Rethinking Gender in Early Childhood Education.* Sydney: Allen & Unwin.

Malaguzzi, L. (1993). For an education based on relationships. *Young Children,* November, *42*(1), 9–12.

Malaguzzi, L. (1998). History, ideas and basic philosophy: an interview with Lella Gandini by Loris Malaguzzi. In C. Edwards, L. Gandini and G. Forman (Eds.). *The Hundred Languages of Children: Advanced Reflections* (2nd Ed.) (pp. 49–98). London: Ablex Publishers.

Mashburn, A. J., Pianta, R. C., Hamre, B. K., Downer, J. T., Barbarin, O. A., Bryant, D., Burchinal, M., Early, D. M., & Howes, C. (2008). Measures of classroom quality in prekindergarten and children's development of academic, language and social skills. *Child Development, 79*(3), 732–49.

Meyer, J. H. F., & Land, R. (2005). Threshold concepts and troublesome knowledge (2): epistemological considerations and a conceptual framework for teaching and learning. *Higher Education, 49*(3), 373–88.

National Association for the Education of Young Children (NAEYC). (1998). Learning to read and write: developmentally appropriate practices for young children. *Young Children, 53*(4), 30–46.

National Research Council. (2001). *Early Childhood Development and Learning: New Knowledge for Policy.* Washington DC: National Academy Press.

Page, J. (2007). Children's discourses of emotions: rethinking citizenship. Unpublished doctoral dissertation, University of Melbourne: Victoria.

Palmer, J. A. (1998). *Environmental Education for the 21st century. Theory, Practice, Progress and Promise*. London: Routledge Falmer.

Perkins, D. (2014). *Future Wise. Educating Our Children for a Changing World*. San Francisco: Jossey-Bass.

Pianta, R. C., La Paro, K. M., & Hamre, B. K. (2008). *Classroom Assessment Scoring System [CLASS] Manual: Pre-K*. Baltimore, MD: Brookes Publishing.

Prosser, M., & Tigwell, K. (2006). Confirmatory factor analysis of the 'Approaches to teaching Inventory'. *British Journal of Educational Psychology, 76*(2), 405–19.

Rinaldi, C. (2006). *In Dialogue with Reggio Emilia: Listening, Researching, and Learning*. New York: Routledge.

Ritchhart, R., Church, M., & Morrison, K. (2011). *Making Thinking Visible. How to Promote Engagement, Understanding, and Independence for All Learners*. San Francisco: Jossey-Bass.

Ritchhart, R., & Perkins, D. (2008). Making thinking visible. *Educational Leadership, 65*(5), 57–61.

Rogoff, B. (1994). Developing understanding of the idea of communities of learners. *Mind, Culture and Activity, 1*(4), 209–29.

Rogoff, B. (2003). *The Cultural Nature of Human Development*. New York: Oxford University Press.

Rowe, K. (2006). Effective teaching practices for students with and without learning difficulties: issue and implications around key findings and recommendations from the National Inquiry into the Teaching of Literacy. *Australian Journal of Learning Disabilities, 11*(1), 99–115.

Sammons, P., Sylva, K., Melhuish, E., et al., (2012). *Influences on Students Attainment and Progress in Key Stage 3: Academic Outcomes in English, Maths and Science in Year 9*. Project Report. London: Institute of Education

Schön, D. (1987). *Educating the Reflective Practitioner*. San Francisco: Jossey-Bass.

Shonkoff, J., & Phillips, D. (2000). *From Neurons to Neighbourhoods: The Science of Early Childhood Development*. Washington DC: National Academy Press.

Sinclair, C., Jeanneret, N., & O'Toole, J. (2009). (Eds.). *Education in the Arts. Teaching and Learning in the Contemporary Curriculum*. Melbourne: Oxford University Press.

Siraj, I. & Asani, R. (2015). The role of sustained shared thinking, play and metacognition in young children's learning. In S. Robson & S. Flannery. Quinn (Eds.). *International Handbook of Young Children's Thinking and Understanding* (pp. 403–15). London: Routledge.

Siraj-Blatchford, I. (2007). Creativity, communication and collaboration: the identification of pedagogic progression in sustained shared thinking. *Asia-Pacific Journal of Research in Early Childhood Education, 1*(2), 3–23.

Siraj-Blatchford, I., & Manni, L., (2008). 'Would you like to tidy up now?' An analysis of adult questioning in the English Foundation Stage. *Early Years: An International Research Journal, 28*(1), 5–22.

Smith, A. B., Duncan, J., & Marshall, K. (2005). Children's perspectives on their learning: exploring methods [Electronic version]. *Early Child Development and Care, 175*(6), 437–87.

Tayler C., Cloney, D., & Niklas, F. (2015). A bird in the hand: understanding the trajectories of development of young children and the need for action to improve outcomes. *Australasian Journal of Early Childhood, 40* (3), 51–60.

Turnbull, J. (2007). *9 Habits of Highly Effective Teachers. A Practical Guide to Empowerment.* London: Continuum International Publishing Group.

United Nations. (1989*). United Nations Convention on the Rights of the Child.* Geneva: Office of the United Nations High Commissioner of Human Rights.

Victorian Curriculum and Assessment Authority (VCAA). (2013). *Assessment for Learning Tool. Early Years Planning Cycle.* Retrieved from: www.vcaa.vic.edu.au/Pages/earlyyears/research.aspx

Victorian Curriculum and Assessment Authority (VCAA). (2015). *The Victorian Curriculum.* Retrieved from: http://victoriancurriculum.vcaa.vic.edu.au/

Vygotsky, L. (1978). *Mind in Society. The Development of Higher Psychological Processes.* Cambridge, MA: Harvard University Press.

Wells, G. (1981). *Learning Through Interaction. The Study of Language Development,* Cambridge: Cambridge University Press.

Wells, G., & Chang-Wells, G. L. (1992). *Constructing Knowledge Together.* Portsmouth, NH: Heinemann.

Wertsch, J. V. (1985). *Vygotsky and the Social Formation of Mind.* Cambridge, MA: Harvard University Press.

Westwood, P. (2008). *What Teachers Need to Know About Teaching Methods.* Melbourne: ACER.

Wright, S. (2003a). *The Arts: Young Children and Learning.* Upper Saddle River, NJ: Pearson Education.

Wright, S. (Ed.). (2003b). *Children, Meaning-making and the Arts.* Melbourne: Prentice Hall.

Wright, S. (2010). *Understanding Creativity in Early Childhood.* London: Sage.

CHAPTER 5

Partnering with families to promote learning

Caroline Cohrssen and Frank Niklas

....

LEARNING OBJECTIVES

In this chapter you will:

1. consider research evidence that demonstrates the contribution made by the family to children's learning
2. reflect on the relationship between teachers, children and children's families in supporting children's learning
3. learn how to build strong relationships with families as a teacher.

....

Introduction

The **family** is a child's first teacher. More specifically, families are both the first *site* and the first *agents* of learning: this means that learning happens within the family setting and through interactions with family members. Children are not merely passive recipients of information (see also Chapters 1, 3 and 4). They are active participants in the process of learning and children both affect, and are affected by, the environment in which they learn. As a result of this multidirectional process, it is essential for teachers to support families in promoting children's learning and development, and working collaboratively with families is a key part of an effective teacher's practice. In the early childhood profession, this is often referred to as '**family-centred practice**'.

This chapter will address three important considerations when working with families. It sets out how the crucial role played by families in advancing young children's learning is reflected in various documents that guide early childhood practitioners. It explains what research tells us about the importance of the **home learning environment** for child development. Finally, the chapter suggests practical strategies for establishing and maintaining effective relationships and coaching family members in everyday techniques that support young children's learning.

In addition, three case studies will be presented. The first case study offers an example of a policy perspective on partnerships in learning with families. The second case study describes current research exploring the important influence of the home learning environment and how teachers can support **parents** in supporting children's learning. The third case study focuses on the Families as First Teachers (FaFT) Program, initiated in the Northern Territory, and demonstrates how families working alongside formal school settings are both supporting family interactions with schools and school personnel, and thereby enabling families and schools to collaborate in supporting individual children as they transition into school.

Family: people who have significant care responsibilities for and/or kinship relationships with the child; the child's primary caregivers.

Family-centred practice: a partnership relationship between teachers and the child's family in which family members determine what assistance they need to support the child's learning, and teachers support families to develop their own network of resources. High-quality family-centred practice takes a strengths-based and competency-based approach.

Home learning environment: all aspects of the home environment that support children's learning. These include, but are not limited to, warm, responsive engagement that supports the child's sense of well-being, as well as: reading with the child; playing learning games; telling stories; teaching sounds; letters or numbers; and visiting libraries and other places of interest in the community.

Parents: includes all adults who have a primary caregiving relationship with the child, whether biological parents or not.

The family as context of child development

The signing of the *Melbourne Declaration on Education Goals for Young Australians* (2008) reflected the growing national imperative for Australian states and territories to commit to action to ensure that all Australians become 'successful learners, confident and creative individuals, and active and informed citizens' (p. 8). Importantly, the Declaration acknowledged that achieving this goal would involve the collaboration of families, schools, other formal education institutions and institutions in the broader community.

Since 2008, the importance of the family as the child's first teacher has been systematically embedded in national guiding documents such as the *Code of Ethics* (ECA, 2016), *Belonging, Being & Becoming: The Early Years Learning Framework for Australia* (DEEWR, 2009), the *Australian Professional Standards for Teachers* (Education Services Australia, 2011), and the *Guide to the National Quality Standard* (Australian Children's Education and Care Authority, 2011). The importance of family-centred practice is similarly reflected in state-level documents, such as the *Victorian Early Years Learning and Development Framework* (VEYLDF) (Department of Education and Training (Victoria), 2016), and has filtered through to typical centre-level philosophy statements and policy documents. Families play a critical role in encouraging a love of learning both by providing opportunities for children to learn and by facilitating this learning through warm, responsive engagement with children to encourage independent problem solving and risk taking.

Family-centred practice in the guiding documents

One of the key threads that weave together the National Quality Standard (NQS) (ACECQA, 2011), the Early Years Learning Framework for Australia (EYLF) (DEEWR, 2009) and the *Code of Ethics* (ECA, 2016) is respect for the role of the family as a primary influence in children's lives. Teachers collaborate with families in order to know the child, support and extend the child's learning, and to assess the child's emerging strengths, interests and abilities. In this partnership, teachers share their perspectives of the child with the family, and parents share their special knowledge of the child with teachers. It is important to remember that families hand their children into the care of teachers and it is to be expected that parents need to feel assured that their child is receiving the best possible education and care, and that their values and beliefs are respected and upheld. The process of reconciling professional knowledge with parents' beliefs and understandings of effective education can be complex, yet it is through meaningful partnerships that children are provided with optimal opportunities for participation, engagement and learning.

The importance of educational programs and practice supporting the child's connection to community is stated in the first element of Standard 1.1 of Quality Area 1 of the NQS (ACECQA, 2011). This position is significant. By locating this priority at the forefront in the quality area that encapsulates the entire early childhood curriculum – program and practice – the child is unambiguously regarded as both an individual and a member of a community. This places an expectation on teachers to know the child and to know the child's community in order to support the child's connection to community.

Quality Area 6: 'Collaborative partnerships with families and communities', reinforces this priority. The introduction to the quality area articulates the importance of collaborative relationships for children's learning as well as the importance of 'active communication, consultation and collaboration' (p. 145) in order to achieve high-quality partnerships between teachers and families. The onus for developing and maintaining such partnerships rests with the teachers. The requirement for early childhood professionals to engage in collaborative partnerships with families is repeated in Quality Area 7: 'Leadership and service management', reinforcing the importance of involving families in making key decisions that impact on their children's learning.

Belonging, Being & Becoming: The Early Years Learning Framework for Australia (DEEWR, 2009) is also unequivocal in its expectation that teachers work in partnership with families. This is stated in the introduction to the Framework document and underpinned by the principles set out in the *United Nations Convention of the Rights of the Child* (United Nations, 1989) which states that children have the right to an education that respects their family, cultural and other identities and languages (see Chapter 3).

The vision for children's learning encapsulated in the National Framework comprises three key constructs: 'belonging', 'being' and 'becoming'. 'Belonging' is described in the Framework as 'knowing where and with whom you belong (and) is integral to human existence. Children belong first to a family, a cultural group, a neighbourhood and a wider community' (p. 7), all of which are interdependent, and all are crucial to a sense of belonging. 'Belonging', the Framework document continues, 'shapes who children are and who they can become' (p. 7). Strong partnership with families is essential for teachers to support children's sense of belonging to their families, communities and cultural groups so that children experience continuity of care across the different contexts in which they live and learn.

Early childhood professionals help children to connect concepts and activities to existing knowledge, and to children's actual lives. Partnerships with families are necessary to achieve this. Teachers strive to:

- support children's sense of identity (Learning Outcome 1)
- explore children's cultural backgrounds and traditions (Learning Outcome 2),
- promote children's sense of belonging and connectedness (Learning Outcome 3)
- build on the knowledge and language that children already possess when they attend early childhood education and care (ECEC) settings
- support children to share their knowledge, ideas and experiences that extend beyond their ECEC settings (Learning Outcome 5).

In order to achieve these goals, teachers must collaborate with families in order to access the fund of knowledge possessed by parents and other important people in children's lives.

The ECA *Code of Ethics* (ECA, 2016) places much emphasis on the importance of early childhood professionals supporting parents in the role of nurturing families and assisting them to develop a sense of belonging and inclusion. The onus for developing partnerships with families and engaging in shared decision making is described, acknowledging that families have the right to make decisions about their children. Recognition of, and respect for, the diversity of families is explicit in the document, as is the requirement to collaborate in planning, monitoring and assessing of children's learning and development, and the dissemination of information to families in ways that they understand.

POLICY CASE STUDY

Anne Kennedy

A POLICY PERSPECTIVE ON PARTNERSHIPS IN LEARNING WITH FAMILIES

In 2009, the Council of Australian Governments (COAG) established a National Quality Framework (NQF) for early childhood education and care services. The NQF is a major national policy response to the evidence of the importance of the early years for every child's learning, development and well-being for their current and future lives. Two key policy documents that flow from the NQF, the *Guide to the National Quality Standard* (ACECQA 2011) and *Belonging, Being & Becoming: The Early Years Learning Framework for Australia* (DEEWR 2009), affirm parents as 'children's first and most influential teachers' (DEEWR, 2009, p. 5) and the benefits, therefore, of enacting collaborative partnership approaches for supporting and improving outcomes for children (ACECQA, 2011, p. 147).

Informants for partnership approaches to learning

The research discussed in this chapter, along with other studies, provides policy makers with evidence that has the capacity to explain the complexity of the issues central to early learning; to envisage the outcomes that might arise from different responses to this complexity; and to provide ideas on how theorisation emanating from the research might be applied in education and care practice. Research and theorising from family-centred practice studies, for example, supports shifting policies concerned with professional partnerships with families from 'expert', 'professional-centric' models, to family-centred approaches (Espe-Sherwindt, 2008).

The Start Right Report to the UK Government (Ball, 1994) identified a 'triangle of care' framework for partnerships approaches to early learning. In the triangle of care framework, parents are at the apex of the triangle with teachers and community empowering and enabling parents as their children's most influential teachers. In this report, the *quality* of the relationship between teachers and other professionals and the family is central to ethical and effective partnerships that support children's learning and development.

The Australian Government's policy on collaborative partnerships with families, as evident in the NQS and the EYLF, extends the concept of family-centred practice and the triangle of care framework by highlighting the place or role of the child in learning partnerships. The policy documents promote an image of children as learners with rights, agency, capabilities and competence, as opposed to an image of children as passive and mere recipients of the teaching of others. The policy documents also convey an image of teachers as ethical, reflective, culturally competent, co-constructors of learning in collaboration with children, families and community, rather than an image of teachers as technicians who enact learning and teaching as a one-way process to the child.

Post-modern and post-structuralist thinking and pedagogical research also inform the images of children, families and teachers as partners in learning in the NQS and the EYLF. Ongoing research emanating from places such as Sweden and Reggio Emilia, Italy, use post-modern perspectives to inform their pedagogy:

> Is this a pedagogical space for the 'rich' child, pedagogue and parent? … The children in our project more and more start saying 'look what I can do and know' and the pedagogues are becoming more and more aware of the children's potentialities – what they actually can do and know. (Dahlberg, Moss & Pence, 2013, pp. 143–4)

The policy direction for *Australian* teachers reflects a similar approach to holding high expectations for children's learning within a partnership approach:

> Children progress well when they, their parents and teachers hold high expectations for their achievement in learning … they [teachers, families and community] continually strive to find equitable and effective ways to ensure all children have opportunities to achieve learning outcomes. (DEEWR, 2009, pp. 12–13)

Current government policy is based on the premise that teachers, families and children benefit from collaborative partnership approaches to learning because there is more likely to be:

- continuity of approaches to learning in home and ECEC settings
- a stronger sense of attachment for children
- appreciation of the strengths and diverse opportunities for meaningful learning in all settings
- shared high expectations for children's, families', communities' and teachers' competence as teachers and learners
- mutual enjoyment between families and teachers in seeing and supporting children's progress as learners
- deeper and shared understandings of each child's learning interests, strengths and abilities.

The above points are all relevant for improving learning and development outcomes for every child. When children's sense of attachment and belonging within their families, community and in an ECEC setting are strong, they feel emotionally safe and more confident to play and learn with others. As families and teachers build a deeper and shared understanding of a child's interests, strengths and abilities they are better informed when making decisions about supporting or enriching the child's learning. The Effective Pre-School, Primary and Secondary Education (EPPSE 3–16) Project research findings in the UK indicate that what families *do* is more important than who they *are*, and confirm that every family has the capacity to 'actively cultivate' their children's learning (Siraj-Blatchford et al., 2011, p. 3). The teacher's role is to support families in cultivating the rich learning opportunities in home and community-based experiences and, in turn, build on that learning in their setting.

REFLECTION POINTS

1. Why is it important that a key government policy document, such as *Belonging, Being & Becoming: The Early Years Learning Framework for Australia,* draws on multiple theoretical perspectives?
2. Reflect on the finding of the EPPSE 3–16 research showing that what parents *do* matters more than who they *are*. What does that statement mean? Why is it a positive finding for teachers?

A theoretical framework for the home learning environment

Children are members of a complex, evolving, social and cultural ecology. However, during the first few years of life, most children spend much of their time with their parents. If we position the child at the centre of his or her world, Bronfenbrenner's ecological theory (1979) (see also Introduction) demonstrates that more distal influences, such as extended family and societal institutions, impact on children's learning, but proximal factors, such as the immediate family and child care provisions, have a greater influence on children's learning. It is not surprising that the family is very influential in the development of cognitive and behavioural abilities (Wasik & van Horn, 2012). The home learning environment is thus a very important context for children's early learning.

If we apply Bronfenbrenner's ecological theory again, this time placing the family at the centre of the model, distal family characteristics, such as family **socio-economic status**, are less influential for learning than proximal features of the family context, such as the interactions between parents and children. In other words: the interactions that families have with children to support learning are far more important than family background characteristics (Niklas, 2015).

Socio-economic status: one indicator of a family's social position within broader society; associated with household income, parental education and parental occupation.

According to Vygotsky (1978), children learn through observation and interaction with knowledgeable others in social contexts. As parents interact frequently and repeatedly with their children, they are often able to identify children's current level of understanding and provide the support children need to advance their understanding. Learning can be thought of as cyclical – each time we return to a new idea, we consolidate our understanding and build on it. In the context of a child's early learning, parents play an important role by repeatedly modelling activities and supporting their children's emerging skills, providing children with multiple opportunities to rehearse new (and existing) understanding and to transfer new learning to different situations. For example, children's counting skills can be supported during routine activities from changing nappies (counting toes), to meal times (counting fruit), to open-ended play (counting teddies).

Another theoretical framework in the context of families comes from Bourdieu's social theory (1986). Bourdieu refers to social and cultural 'capital'. Here, capital does not mean money. Social capital describes the ability to 'buy into' social networks. Cultural capital comprises all cultural objects and resources a family possesses. Consequently, both access to social groups and the presence of material goods, such as books in a household, are taken into account. Further, it is the ability to make use of social and cultural capital, as well as acquired knowledge, that influences the child's learning. Closely associated with cultural capital are the cultural activities within a family. Here, cultural activities that play an important role in children's learning, such as parents' reading (modelling the value they attach to literacy) and parents reading to children, telling stories, playing dice or number games, visiting libraries or talking about books, are taken into account. Research shows that both cultural capital and cultural practice play an important role in children's learning (Niklas & Schneider, 2013, 2014).

A model of the home learning environment

Niklas (2015) provides a comprehensive model of the home learning environment and children's learning in the context of the family based on previous research (Figure 5.1).

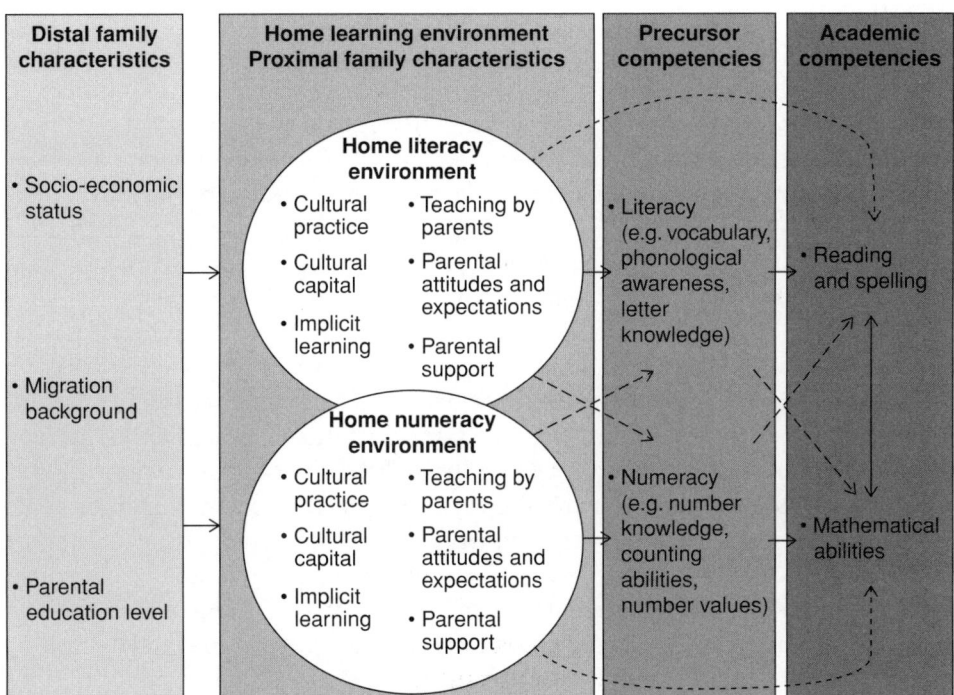

Figure 5.1: Model of the home learning environment in the context of distal family characteristics, precursor competencies and academic competencies (adapted from Niklas, 2015, p. 109)

Distal family characteristics, such as socio-economic status and parental education level or migration background, are listed on the left-hand side of Figure 5.1. In research, these characteristics are typically associated with children's cognitive abilities and their performance in academic assessment. However, research clearly indicates that the home learning environment, rather than these distal family characteristics, has a direct impact on children's early competencies. Nonetheless, both distal and proximal family characteristics are closely associated and it is often observed that parents with a higher socio-economic status, or a higher educational level, also provide higher quality home learning environments. Consequently, these parents are often the ones who, for instance, read more often to their children, interact with their children more often in a meaningful way when playing games or having conversations, or who provide more and better learning resources.

Interestingly, while the home learning environment has only small direct effects on children's academic competencies later in school (indicated by the dashed lines in the model), it is a strong predictor of competencies such as a child's vocabulary, phonological awareness, number knowledge or counting abilities in early childhood – competencies that *precede* formal literacy and mathematical skills. These specific and very important 'precursors' thus form the foundation for later learning in school and are required for academic success, demonstrating how learning is cumulative.

The home learning environment is sometimes differentiated into a home literacy and a home numeracy environment, each having a somewhat different focus. This is also evident in the model of the home learning environment presented in Figure 5.1. Elements of the home literacy environment include the number of books in a household, parental reading, and the frequency with which adults read with children and teach children letters. Elements of the home numeracy environment include the extent to which adults incorporate counting in everyday activities, dice games played with children and parental attitudes towards mathematics in general. The home literacy environment and home numeracy environment are also closely related and share characteristics. For instance, cultural capital consists of either the number of books or the number of dice/counting/calculating games at home, whereas implicit learning occurs either during reading sessions with the child or during play and everyday activities. The same applies to parental teaching of either letters or numbers, to parental attitudes towards either literacy or mathematics, and to parental support during literacy or numeracy activities at home. As the home literacy environment is a specific predictor of literacy competencies, the home numeracy environment is a specific predictor of numeracy competencies. Despite this specificity, the home literacy environment also predicts early numeracy competencies and the home numeracy environment also predicts early literacy competencies as indicated by the dashed lines in the model. In summary, Figure 5.1 clearly shows the important role that the home learning environment plays in children's early cognitive development.

The important role parents play in their children's learning is recognised in policy documents, practice and research. Consequently, every teacher must build positive relationships with children's families as well as with the children themselves. Positive partnerships are the foundations for supporting parents to create high-quality home learning environments for their children. The research case study provided below demonstrates how partnering with parents makes a significant contribution to children's learning.

RESEARCH CASE STUDY

Frank Niklas, Caroline Cohrssen and Collette Tayler

ENHANCING THE HOME LEARNING ENVIRONMENT

The research study 'Enhancing the Home Learning Environment' was conducted during 2014 in the City of Darebin, Melbourne (Niklas, Cohrssen & Tayler, 2015). One hundred and thirteen four-year-old children and their families participated in this intervention study. The study was designed to create partnerships with interested families to increase the quality of interactions between parents and children in the home learning environment. The intervention is regarded as non-intensive because the entire intervention included two brief steps: attending a group parents' evening and taking part in a follow-up 40-minute individualised session.

All families were invited to an initial parents' evening at one of four participating centres. At the parents' evenings, the 37 participating parents were equipped with general information regarding the important contribution made by the home environment to children's learning. The lead researchers suggested how children's emerging literacy and numeracy skills could be supported by families in ways that encouraged thinking and learning. Parents were also provided with a handout that offered suggestions about how to support emerging literacy and numeracy skills. These suggestions included:

- purposefully playing rhyming games during everyday conversations
- supporting children's acquisition of new words
- playing games that involved the use of dice to support counting skills
- playing memory games
- having frequent back and forth conversations with children
- visiting libraries regularly
- demonstrating that we use mathematical thinking in everyday life.

In addition, families were reminded that they are role models for their children and children are likely to mimic the literacy and numeracy behaviours that parents model, and similarly, children are likely to adopt parents' attitudes towards literacy and numeracy. To conclude the parents' evenings, families were invited to pose questions and discuss the information provided.

During the second step of the intervention, parents were introduced to the principles of counting and dialogic reading with their children during individualised play sessions that lasted approximately 40 minutes each.

Parents received coaching on supporting their child's emerging mastery of the counting principles during a dice game and were provided with a handout on the game. The dice game required each player to roll a die, identify the number rolled, and count a corresponding number of coloured counters from a pile in the centre of the table. Results were then compared between players. In response to prompts from their parents, children were required to think about concepts, such as 'more than', 'less than' and 'the same as', and to justify their answers, articulating their reasoning. Each child also received a copy of a popular children's storybook. Parents read the book with their children and were observed during this reading session. They then received feedback on their reading, along with coaching on how to enact the key aspects of dialogic reading with their child. Examples of dialogic reading strategies included: encouraging the child to complete the blank at the end of a sentence when the adult paused in a meaningful manner, asking questions about the book and encouraging the child to recall and retell the story, encouraging the child's higher order thinking by asking 'wh-questions', and linking the story with the child's real world. (Niklas, et al., 2015)

Early Childhood Education Journal, Home learning environment and concept formation: A family intervention study with kindergarten children, July 2015, pp. 1–9, Niklas, F., Cohrssen, C. & Tayler, C. (© Springer Science+Business Media New York 2015). With Permission of Springer.

It was assumed that an intervention of this nature (i.e. an intervention that supports parents' ability to provide a high-quality home learning environment) may be sufficient to increase opportunities for learning in the home environment and consequently better support children's learning than the home learning environment of families not participating in the intervention. Figure 5.2 reflects feedback on the intervention provided by parents at the end of the intervention session, indicating that only half of the parents regarded the information as new. However, all of the parents in the intervention group found it valuable and interesting, and almost 90 per cent indicated that they intended to incorporate the information in the home learning environment they provided for their children.

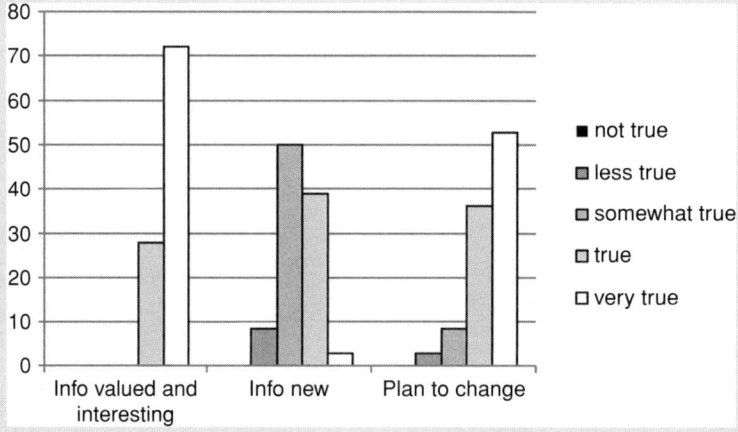

Figure 5.2: Feedback on intervention (data from Niklas, Cohrssen & Tayler, 2016)

Indeed, significantly different developments in both the home learning environment and in children's learning were found when participating families were compared with non-participating ('control') families. Participating and non-participating families did not differ significantly with regard to the initial quality of the home learning environment and their children did not differ with regard to initial cognitive abilities. However, parents in the intervention group provided higher quality home learning environments four months after the intervention and, in addition, their children showed significantly greater learning gains. These results were confirmed four months later during follow-up assessments, indicating that this non-intensive intervention had a lasting impact on families and children.

As the intervention was not intensive, the researchers believe that teachers could provide parents with information about the important impact of the home environment on children's learning, could model playful approaches to support children's mastery of the counting principles and could demonstrate the use of dialogic reading strategies.

This easy-to-apply approach does not require much in the way of concrete materials as any appropriate storybook could be used and any objects can be counted in the dice game. Consequently, a non-intensive intervention of this type could be used in different contexts and may appeal to families who, for a range of reasons, may be reluctant to participate in intensive family programs.

REFLECTION POINTS

1. When you think about families, what family structures come to mind? How might these diverse family structures impact on a child's learning and on the relationship you need to build with the family as a teacher?
2. Select the theoretical framework for the home learning environment you like best. Summarise your understanding and find other contexts in which this framework may be applied.
3. What does research tell you about the importance of the home learning environment and how you could contribute to the learning environments provided by families? Write a list of strategies you could use to support parents' efforts to develop a high-quality home learning environment.

Teachers, children and children's families

The quality of the home learning environment provided by parents for their children should not be regarded as a fixed setting but as a context that can be influenced by teachers in cooperation with parents. Successful collaboration and family-centred practice support parents in their role as children's first teachers and consequently enhances children's learning.

Collaboration and partnership

In the first few years of life, both a child's immediate family, and other people who provide care on a regular basis, have an effect on children's learning through their relationships with the child. As children grow older they are likely to interact with more people and organisations and, consequently, there are more influences on their learning: extended family, peers, neighbours, school and the community.

Young children are likely to spend most of their time in the home environment, in early childhood education settings and, later on, at school. However, in the early years, the adults who have the most influence on children's learning are their families and teachers. The more nurturing these relationships are, the more they provide a secure base to support children's learning and development. The stronger the partnerships between families and education settings, the broader the secure base will be.

Successful partnerships between teachers, primary school teachers and families are based on mutual respect, dialogue and recognition of equal status of the individuals in the partnership. This supports teachers and parents having a trusting relationship, and sharing commitment to and responsibility for children's learning (Garcia & Ríos, 2014; Waugh & Cavanagh, 2002). Parents who believe that they have the ability to support their child's learning are more likely to see involvement with the education setting as beneficial for their children. Parents need to feel positive about their parenting role and about their ability to have meaningful interactions with their child's teacher. Research shows that family practices and family involvement are far more influential on children's learning than family structure, socio-economic status, the age of the child or the size of the family – and that this applies regardless of how much formal education the parents have had, what language is spoken at home or the child's ability (Hidalgo, Epstein & Siu, 2002). All families, including families thought to be 'vulnerable' or living in disadvantaged circumstances, have the potential to draw on their strengths to support children's learning. Studies have demonstrated the benefits that community participation has for children's learning outcomes in literacy and mathematics, reducing absenteeism and improving children's behaviour at school (Diez, Gatt & Racionero, 2011).

Partnerships require commitment to participate and willingness to follow through on agreements that have been reached by teachers and families. In order for families to participate more in their children's learning they need to be involved in decision-making processes, in the evaluation of the centre or classroom program and in children's learning. Taking this approach means that the centre or school is authentically part of the community.

Australia has a multicultural society. Globalisation has led to widespread migration and, consequently, many communities are highly culturally diverse, creating challenges for children who have less access to social capital than their 'mainstream' peers. Despite this, all children have the right to an education that authentically affirms their identity and that values their cultures (Cooper & Hedges, 2014). When schools and early childhood centres have strong connections with children's families, they are more embedded in the community, teachers are more closely connected with people's lives, and children benefit from a greater sense of belonging and continuity of care. Collaborating with families may be challenging when parents and teachers have differing expectations about the nature of early childhood education and the value of the play-based approach to teaching and learning. However, by forming reciprocal relationships with families, teachers are able to draw on the expertise of children's parents in order to enact culturally responsive teaching practices. In addition, children's learning in one context is more readily transferred to other contexts, providing more opportunities for understanding to be consolidated as concepts are explored and mastered in diverse situations.

Despite the benefits for children's learning that have been demonstrated by research, other studies have found that teachers may doubt parents' involvement in schools if the parents have little formal education or belong to cultural minority groups and, at times, parents' involvement has been reduced to tokenistic roles rather than involving families in key decision making (Díez et al., 2011). A large European study was conducted from 2006 to 2011 with two of its research aims being:

1. the identification and analysis of social factors that promote integration of education systems
2. a focus on obstacles to children's educational and social inclusion.

This European Union project entitled 'Strategies for Inclusion and Social Cohesion in Europe from Education' (INCLUD-ED) was conducted in 14 countries (c.f. Diez et al., 2011; Garcia & Rios, 2014; Gatt, Ojala & Soler, 2011). Diez and colleagues (2011) highlight three noteworthy findings from this project.

1. Schools need to purposefully establish structures that make it possible for families from minority and vulnerable communities to be involved in their children's education so that children and their families are able to enact their rights to equal education.
2. More flexible and less formal opportunities for participation are needed.
3. Schools that are enacting successful partnerships with families recognise that these partnerships enable teachers to draw on funds of knowledge held by communities to which teachers who belong to mainstream cultures may not otherwise have access.

Importantly, when these strategies were enacted in schools, previously marginalised families and community members became increasingly involved in more central roles; their participation contributed to a change in their identities within the school context, and consequently, such families were likely to have a larger impact on children's learning (Diez et al., 2011).

Establishing and maintaining partnerships with families

The point at which theories and research intersect is pivotal to informing practical strategies for establishing and maintaining family-centred practice The importance of children having a strong sense of cultural and community identity is another key thread that links the NQS (ACECQA, 2011), the EYLF (DEEWR, 2009) and the *Code of Ethics* (ECA, 2016).

Establishing collaborative partnerships with families

The first step towards establishing a collaborative partnership with parents is to obtain a completed enrolment form from your service and to review the information on the form from time to time to ensure that the information remains current. If necessary, it may be appropriate to arrange for family representatives to assist with the completion of enrolment forms to ensure that families understand the questions and why they are being asked. Ensure that information about the centre or school and about the education program offered in different rooms is available to families, and made available in such a way that all families are able to understand it – this may require assistance with translation.

When children attend a new centre or start school, establish how familiar families are with early childhood education and care, and with the facilities available to them. Encourage families to spend time with the child as he or she becomes accustomed to the new environment. This transition period provides an opportunity for children, families and teachers to develop new relationships that are the foundation for future collaboration. Once the child has settled into the environment, this is the time to consolidate and strengthen the partnership with parents, building trust and mutual respect, and establishing common goals for the child's learning.

Maintaining partnerships with families

Sharing information is an important first step towards developing and maintaining relationships between families, early childhood settings and schools. It is important to recognise that families have strengths, expertise and connections to their communities that are likely to differ from your own. Finding ways to engage families in a meaningful way is important as it provides multiple learning opportunities for teachers and enables teachers not only to share their own knowledge and skills but also to learn from families who are important funds of knowledge about diverse cultures and communities. Regular opportunities to engage with families in ways that are not directly focused on learning provide informal opportunities for parents to share their opinions and ideas about their child's education.

Building enthusiasm with the children will encourage families to participate in centre and school community activities. As a starting point, teachers could consider the following practical strategies for maintaining collaborative partnerships with and between families.

- Keep channels of communication open. This will vary depending on what suits families best. The first step is to greet family members by name, showing warmth and making eye contact to show respect. Conversations at drop-off and collection times, even if brief, are a convenient opportunity to share information, and to maintain continuity of learning and smooth transitions for children from the home learning environment to the early childhood centre or school. Notebooks that remain in the child's bag for families and teachers to write in are helpful. A whiteboard near the door can be used for messages; other families may prefer text messages, emails or access to a website.

- A community noticeboard could be provided for families to share skills and resources, and to encourage community belonging that reaches beyond the early childhood setting or the school.

- A curtain ring club uses curtain rings (or a similar, inexpensive 'currency') for barter. Each member is allocated one curtain ring and uses this curtain ring to 'pay' for child-minding, assistance with odd jobs around the home or contributing other forms of assistance without needing to spend money.

- Swap groups are an opportunity for families to exchange children's clothing, toys and equipment (strollers, high chairs, scooters, books) and an informal forum for building relationships and eliciting ideas.

- A centre or school recipe book of children's favourite foods is an exciting opportunity for families to share recipes for meals that their children enjoy. This is an opportunity for families to learn about one another's food cultures while helping families to solve the 'what to eat today' dilemma.

- Working parties could be set up, enabling families to contribute their time and labour to do odd jobs around the centre or school, such as repairing equipment and furniture, painting, gardening, cleaning or collaborating on new projects. Including children in this process is an important opportunity to demonstrate teamwork, persistence and community collaboration.

- An annual 'street food' event could be held at a local park or sportsground. Inviting friends of the early childhood centre or school, such as families whose children attend (or attended) the centre or school in the past, families living in the neighbourhood and people who run local businesses, is a good opportunity to strengthen relationships within the community. Suggest that families prepare a traditional dish to share at the event.

- Hold an annual 'Storytelling Day'. Encourage families to spend the day with their children, telling (rather than reading) stories from their cultural community. They may share songs and dances.

- Regular parents' meetings that focus on 'Living with Babies', 'Living with Toddlers', 'Living with Kindies', 'Starting School' or 'Living with School Kids' are opportunities for families to share their experiences. Inviting one parent to lead the discussion at each meeting provides a chance for community members to share expertise and offer informal advice. For example, if a parent is a dentist, they could lead the conversation about dental hygiene. Depending on the skills of children's families, topics could include health, nutrition or budget management. This provides an opportunity to support children's learning by supporting community collaboration. It is also a way to address centre policies, such as exclusion or healthy eating, in a more collaborative and participative manner.

- 'What Job Do You Do?' open days are opportunities for parents to talk to children and other parents about the work they do. Careers represented could be augmented by strategically inviting additional people, such as local artists. Prioritising jobs that lend themselves to a show-and-tell approach is more appropriate with young children. These jobs could range from a carpenter bringing in wood, hammer and nails; a firefighter bringing in a hat, jacket and fire extinguishers; to an artist using local clay and ochre.

- Finally, regular family–teacher meetings are an opportunity for uninterrupted conversations about how the child is progressing and agreeing on learning goals for children. These are also opportunities to invite parents to participate in the program. Participating in the program does not necessarily mean being in the room with the children; it may mean suggesting ideas about curriculum planning or contributing resources that can be used in the program. Some parents may feel more comfortable making anonymous suggestions by writing them down and dropping them in a suggestions box.

Respecting diversity requires more than making assumptions about family skills and values based on Indigenous peoples' history, the country people come from, the languages they speak or the religions they follow. Building strong partnerships with families supports engagement with the local community and positions the centre or school as part of the community, and responsive to community developments.

Throughout, the process of establishing and maintaining family engagement and collaboration is driven by the goal of supporting children's learning; however, developing relationships with families and their communities provides rich opportunities for education professionals' learning and self-reflection. In the case study that follows, an example of best practice is provided to demonstrate how strong family-centred practice is being achieved in one particular community.

PRACTICE CASE STUDY

Louise Cooke

FAMILIES AS FIRST TEACHERS PROGRAM AS A BEST PRACTICE MODEL

The Families as First Teachers (FaFT) Program is an early learning and family support program for remote Indigenous families with children prior to school entry (0–3 years). FaFT aims to give children the best start in life through place-based programs that engage and empower families and communities. Through rigorous consultation, members of staff facilitate a program model that builds on the strengths of a community and its families. Programs are at all times respectful of cultural identity, knowledge of families and communities, and traditional child-rearing practices.

Here, we share some of the lessons that we have learnt from this exemplar program in family engagement and suggest ways in which they may be used to support other programs to ensure they are genuinely family-centred and strengths-based.

- *Respectfulness* – examining and articulating our program's core beliefs about families has helped cultivate mutual respect between families and services. The following five statements form the basis of all FaFT Program philosophies.

  1. All families want the best for their children.
  2. Families have the most significant influence on their child's development.
  3. All families have skills and knowledge.
  4. Building on family and community strengths will support sustainable outcomes.
  5. Bringing up children is everyone's business.

- *Cohesive teams* – all FaFT Programs employ a local Indigenous staff member who works closely alongside a teacher. Having local staff with deep knowledge of community, **culture** and families is essential to the success of our programs.

- *Consultation* – it is important to consider that this does not always involve simply asking direct questions such as 'what would you like to see at the service?' or 'how do you think children learn best?' There is a time and a place for such questions; however, some families respond better to more subtle ways of consulting around skills and knowledge, child-rearing practices and program development. We provide opportunities for observations and conversations through practical hands-on experiences that build relationships and a sense of trust. Running playgroups, cooking together, going on excursions or simply asking families to help prepare resources for the following day are just some examples that have led to conversations or observations helping us to better understand the skills, knowledge and aspirations of the families in our service. These experiences have also helped to build trust between families and staff, an essential component for any family-centred practice.

> **Culture:** the attitudes, customs and beliefs that generally distinguish one group of people from another. Children learn about and contribute to their culture as it is represented through language, material objects, social rituals and societal institutions, and shared from one generation to the next.

- *Reflective practice* – as FaFT employees, we consistently examine our understanding of strengths in families. We reflect on our own prejudices, values and knowledge around child development and child-rearing practices. We consider how these may differ from those of our families, where these understandings and beliefs have come from, and why we think they are important. In particular, we look at the context of these understandings and beliefs, and use such reflections to ensure programs are relevant and responsive to families.

- *Building on strengths* – we watch for strengths in all families, in particular, looking outside what our own expectations of strengths in families may be. We try to be flexible and prepared to have our own understandings and beliefs shifted to allow for a different perspective on strengths and knowledge.

- *Building capacity* – we watch carefully for opportunities to acknowledge and extend existing strengths. We always remember that we are sharing knowledge, and many families value current evidence-based practices and understandings around early learning. We try to adapt these current understandings to suit the context of our community.
- *Responsive programs* – we reflect on the practices of the EYLF, being responsive to families' needs, strengths, abilities and interests, valuing and building on these to motivate and ensure engagement in learning. Allowing for shared decision making helps to empower families and build relationships that are based on mutual respect and trust. Often this means our programs look different from what we expected as they respond to events in the community or experiences of individual families on any given day.
- *Relationships* – the importance of respectful and supportive relationships is at the heart of a successful family-centred program. Being open, honest and genuine in our desire to work with families is what drives the most successful FaFT Programs across the Northern Territory.

Implementing a truly family- and community-centred practice is no easy task. It involves being challenged on many levels, including challenging our own core beliefs about what a quality early learning service looks like. But we have learnt that if our practice is not family- and community-centred, we are not genuinely supporting families and children to grow and learn alongside us, and therefore, we are not achieving our goal of empowering families.

REFLECTION POINTS

1. Drawing on the NQS and the *Code of Ethics*, identify ways in which the FaFT Program responds to both mandated and ethical requirements to develop effective partnerships with families.
2. Reflect on new ways in which centres could encourage families to contribute to centre policies and pedagogical practice.
3. How could centres ensure that communication strategies meet the needs of all families?

Conclusion

Families play an important role in children's learning and parents are children's first teachers. It is worth noting that while teachers' primary responsibility is to provide for the education and care of children attending a program, families have many responsibilities and obligations, and consequently developing a partnership with their child's teacher may be a greater priority to a teacher than to the family. Understanding, consistency and perseverance are required as research evidence demonstrates the critical contribution made to children's learning by strong teacher–parent collaboration. In addition, this partnership approach is an explicit procedural and ethical requirement of all teachers, as they work with families to support the learning and development of the children in their care.

Further reading

Lewis, M., & Feiring, C. (Eds.). (1998). *Families, Risk, and Competence*. Mahwah, NJ: Lawrence Erlbaum.

Wasik, B. H. (Ed.). (2012). *Handbook of Family Literacy*. New York: Routledge.

References

Australian Children's Education and Care Quality Authority (ACECQA). (2011). *Guide to the National Quality Standard*. Retrieved from http://files.acecqa.gov.au/files/National-Quality-Framework-Resources-Kit/NQF03-Guide-to-NQS-130902.pdf

Ball, C. (1994). *The Importance of Early Learning*. London: Royal Society for the Encouragement of Arts, Manufactures, and Commerce.

Bourdieu, P. (1986) The forms of capital. In J. Richardson (Ed.). *Handbook of Theory and Research for the Sociology of Education* (pp. 241–58). New York: Greenwood.

Bronfenbrenner, U. (1979). *The Ecology of Human Development: Experiments by Nature and Design*. Cambridge, MA: Harvard University Press.

Cooper, M., & Hedges, H. (2014). Beyond participation: what we learned from Hunter about collaboration with Pasifika children and families. *Contemporary Issues in Early Childhood, 15*(24), 165–75.

Dahlberg, G., Moss, P., & Pence, A. (2013). *Beyond Quality in Early Childhood Education and Care: Language of Evaluation* (3rd ed.). London: Routledge.

Department of Education and Training (Victoria) & Victorian Curriculum and Assessment Authority. (2016). *Victorian Early Years Learning and Development Framework*. Melbourne: Department of Education and Training (Victoria).

Department of Education, Employment and Workplace Relations (DEEWR). (2009). *Belonging, Being & Becoming: The Early Years Learning Framework for Australia (EYLF)*. Canberra: DEEWR for COAG.

Díez J., Gatt, S., & Racionero, S. (2011). Placing immigrant and minority family and community members at the school's centre: the role of community participation. *European Journal of Education, 46*(2), 184–96.

Early Childhood Australia (ECA). *Code of Ethics* (2016). Retrieved from www.earlychildhoodaustralia.org.au/our-publications/eca-code-ethics/

Education Services Australia. (2011). *Australian Professional Standards for Teachers*. Retrieved from www.aitsl.edu.au/docs/default-source/apst-resources/australian_professional_standard_for_teachers_final.pdf

Espe-Sherwindt, M. (2008). Family-centred practice: collaboration, competency and evidence. *Support for Learning, 23*(3), 136–43.

Garcia, L. B., & Ríos, O. (2014). Participation and family education in school: successful educational actions. *Studies in the Education of Adults, 46*(2), 177–91.

Gatt, S., Ojala, M., & Soler, M. (2011). Promoting social inclusion counting with everyone: learning communities and INCLUD-ED. *International Studies in Sociology of Education, 21*(1), 33–47. DOI: http://doi.org/10.1080/09620214. 2011.543851

Hidalgo, N. M., Epstein, J. K., & Siu, S. (2002). Research on families, schools, and communities. A multicultural perspective. In J. A. Banks & C. A. Banks (Eds.). *Handbook of Research on Multicultural Education.* New York: Macmillan.

Ministerial Council on Education, Employment, Training and Youth Affairs (MCEETYA). (2008). *Melbourne Declaration on Education Goals for Young Australians.* Melbourne: MCEETYA.

Niklas, F. (2015). Die familiäre Lernumwelt und ihre Bedeutung für die kindliche Kompetenzentwicklung [The home learning environment and its significance for children's competencies development]. *Psychologie in Erziehung und Unterricht, 62*, 106–120. Retrieved from http://dx.doi.org/10.2378/peu2015.art11d

Niklas, F., Cohrssen, C., & Tayler, C. (2015). Home learning environment and concept formation: a family intervention study with kindergarten children. *Early Childhood Education Journal.* DOI: http://doi.org/10.1007/s10643-015-0726-1

Niklas, F., Cohrssen, C., & Tayler, C. (2016). Parents supporting learning: a non-intensive intervention supporting literacy and numeracy in the home learning environment, *International Journal of Early Years Education,* DOI: http://doi. org/10.1080/09669760.2016.1155147

Niklas, F., & Schneider, W. (2013). Home literacy environment and the beginning of reading and spelling. *Contemporary Educational Psychology, 38*(1), 40–50. DOI: http://dx.doi.org/10.1016/j.cedpsych.2012.10.001

Niklas, F., & Schneider, W. (2014). Casting the die before the die is cast: the importance of the home numeracy environment for preschool children. *European Journal of Psychology of Education, 29*(3), 327–45. DOI: http:// dx.doi.org/10.1007/s10212-013-0201-6

Siraj-Blatchford, I., Mayo, A., Melhuish, E., & Taggart, B. (2011). *Performing Against the Odds: Developmental Trajectories of Children in the EPPSE 3–16 Study.* Retrieved from www.gov.uk/government/uploads/system/uploads/ attachment_data/file/198924/DFE-RB128.pdf

United Nations. (1989). *United Nations Convention on the Rights of the Child.* Geneva: Office of the United Nations High Commissioner for Human Rights.

Vygotsky, L. S. (1978). *Mind in Society: The Development of Higher Psychological Processes.* Cambridge, MA: Harvard University.

Waugh, R. F., & Cavangh, R. F. (2002). Measuring parent receptivity towards the classroom environment using a Rasch measurement model. *Learning Environment Research, 5*(3), 329–52.

Wasik, B. H., & van Horn, B. (2012). The role of family literacy in society. In B. H. Wasik (Ed.). *Handbook of Family Literacy* (pp. 3–17). New York: Routledge.

CHAPTER 6

Leading for learning

Jane Page and Collette Tayler

LEARNING OBJECTIVES

In this chapter you will:

1. describe the intent underlying the role of the educational leader in the current Australian early childhood education and care policy context
2. identify key practices that enable effective educational leadership in early childhood education and care settings
3. determine the evidence needed to lead learning and track the effectiveness of the impact of educational leadership on young children's learning outcomes.

Introduction

Educational leadership is key to building high-quality early childhood education and care (ECEC) programs and driving the process of continuous improvement. Strong and effective educational leadership supports all teachers in early childhood settings to portray effective, evidence-based practices that advance children's learning. Educational leadership, however, is a complex role and requires conditions to be in place in order for it be enacted in a purposeful and systematic way. In this chapter, we will explore the role of the educational leader as outlined in national ECEC policy and international research. We outline the active ingredients that enable leading for learning.

Conceptualising educational leadership

In Australia, contemporary early years policy testifies to greater recognition of effective leadership and its impact on teachers' capacities to advance young children's learning. The importance and influence of leadership is embedded, for the first time, within the legal and policy documents that comprise the National Quality Framework for Early Childhood Education and Care (NQF). The role 'educational leader' is enshrined in national law and regulations (Parliament of Victoria, 2010; MCEECDYA, 2010) and leadership is a key aspect of Quality Area 7 of the National Quality Standard (NQS) (ACECQA, 2012). Here, the NQS confirms that effective leadership 'contributes to quality environments for children's learning and development', promotes a positive organisational culture and builds a professional learning community (ACECQA, 2011, p. 169). The NQS further outlines the knowledge, skills and characteristics required of effective leaders, noting that effective leaders have a strong understanding of their service and local context; they build a skilled team of teachers; they empower their colleagues through a continuous improvement process; and they manage change. To achieve these goals, leaders are charged to be knowledgeable across several areas, possessing in-depth knowledge of the following:

- child development (maintaining the currency of this knowledge)
- the education and care system
- the national and state ECEC policies
- effective teaching and learning processes and practices
- financial and administrative processes.

Furthermore, leaders must know how to: listen to colleagues; develop and communicate a shared vision; guide and support colleagues in a process of ongoing learning, self-reflection and continuous improvement; and build a culture of openness, trust and respect (ACEQA, 2011). Whether ECEC leaders have long or brief experience in the profession, working consistently to expand their knowledge and refine their working leadership and collaboration skills is a common goal.

By law, the *Education and Care Services National Regulations* stipulate that every centre-based long day care, family day care, outside school hours care and kindergarten service in Australia must appoint a professional as 'educational leader': 'The approved provider of an education and care service must designate, in writing, a suitably qualified and experienced educator, coordinator or other individual as **educational leader** at the service to lead the development and implementation of educational programs in the service' (MCEECDYA, 2010, Part 4.4, Division 1, 118, p. 133). ACECQA (2011) specifies further what this leading role requires of the incumbent, most notably to 'guide other teachers in their planning and reflection, and mentor colleagues in their implementation practices' (p. 85). The educational leader is defined as the professional who 'leads the development of the curriculum and ensures the establishment of clear goals and expectations for teaching and learning' (ACECQA, 2011, p. 172) and works with 'teachers to provide curriculum direction and to ensure children achieve the outcomes of the approved learning framework' (p. 178).

> **Educational leader:** a suitably qualified and experienced educator, coordinator or individual appointed as educational leader at a service to lead the development and implementation of education programs in the service (MCEECDYA, 2010).

The role of the educational leader as outlined in the national law and regulations aligns with conceptions of the pedagogical leader profiled in the research literature. Furthermore, similar educational and **pedagogical leadership** roles are found in schools (Southworth 2002). Lead teachers may take responsibility for a curriculum area, a section of the school such as Prep–Year 3, or a group of teachers working towards some priority set by the community. Pedagogical leadership, like educational leadership, has at its core 'the study of the teaching and learning process' (Coughlin & Baird, 2013, p. 1). It involves the leader:

> **Pedagogical leadership:** the process of guiding others to broader and deeper understandings of the teaching and learning process, and in particular, its impact on children's learning.

1. supporting colleagues to gain a deeper theoretical, research-based and practical understanding of learning, how children learn, and the role of the teacher, the child and the family in the learning process (Colmer, Waniganayake & Field, 2015; Coughlin & Baird, 2013; Fonsén, 2013; Waniganayake et al., 2012)
2. sharing specialist knowledge of program planning, useful teaching interventions and how they are effective for supporting child learning goals (Fonsén, 2013; Waniganayake et al., 2012)
3. fostering the growth of dispositions in staff that enhance daily practice and to build a culture that focuses on the process of learning (Coughlin & Baird, 2013; Fonsén, 2013)
4. employing strategies (coaching, mentoring, role modelling) to build the team's pedagogical knowledge and capacity (Waniganayake et al., 2012).

The attention paid to educational leadership within the NQF is based upon research highlighting the importance of educational leadership for building high-quality learning programs (Fonsén, 2013; Waniganayake, 2014) and driving the process of quality improvement (Sims et al., 2015; Gomez, Kagan & Fox, 2015). Siraj-Blatchford and Manni (2006), following their *Effective Leadership in the Early Years*

Sector Study (ELEYS) and *Researching Effective Pedagogy in the Early Years* (REPEY), identified 10 effective leadership practices for ECEC settings:

1. identifying and articulating a collective vision
2. ensuring shared understandings, meanings and goals
3. effective communication
4. encouraging reflection
5. monitoring and assessing practice
6. commitment to ongoing professional development
7. distributed leadership
8. building a learning community and team culture
9. encouraging and facilitating parent and community partnerships
10. leading and managing striking the balance.

More specifically, they examined effectiveness in relation to what practices best promoted young children's learning and development. Strong leadership was identified as core to improved outcomes for children. In the following sections, we examine these areas more deeply as we propose a model of effective leadership for learning in ECEC settings and outline the key ingredients that represent 'threshold conditions' for advancing young children's learning outcomes.

POLICY CASE STUDY

Nicole Pilsworth and Jane Page

LEADING LEARNING THROUGH COACHING

A key component of educational leadership is building staff capacity. The importance of building staff capacity is acknowledged in the NQF, most notably within Quality Area 7 of the NQS where effective leadership is illustrated as 'relationship between people', and good leaders are described as 'able to empower others' and create 'a positive organisational culture' that enables 'ongoing learning and inquiry' (ACECQA, 2011, p. 171). The educational leader is critical to providing this level of support to teachers so they can better promote young children's learning every day through their educational programs and pedagogical practices. Effective leadership produces a positive organisational culture and **professional learning** community where all teachers share experiences and expertise, and develop, in collaboration, the knowledge, skills and capacities to promote potent learning experiences for and with young children and their families. The framing of leadership in the NQS thus recognises that effective leadership is a relational process.

Professional learning: a program of activities that support early childhood teachers to reflect – individually and collectively – on the impact of their educational program and pedagogical practices on young children's learning, and to change their practices in the light of their reflection.

Coaching, in the context of educational leadership, is defined as a disciplined, structured process where two or more people form an ongoing learning relationship aimed towards the development, refinement, adaptation and improvement of educational programs and practices (Twigg et al., 2013). Coaching is a known, effective strategy to empower teachers to reflect on, modify and improve their teaching and learning practices over time. Of particular significance in the Australian 'reform' context, coaching has been proven to be effective in supporting teachers to develop and align new pedagogical practices with the expectations outlined in *Belonging, Being & Becoming: The Early Years Learning Framework for Australia* (DEEWR, 2009).

Coaches and/or educational leaders create the time, space and conditions for their colleagues to build new knowledge about teaching and learning, reflect on their current educational programs and practices, and learn new strategies to incorporate into their daily interactions with young children. Building a strong culture of learning within an ECEC setting, however, requires strategic planning that identifies how ongoing learning will benefit the organisation as a whole as well as the individuals within the organisation.

An effective learning culture helps engage colleagues in ongoing learning, and supports continuous improvement in the teaching and learning process. Schien (2010) argues that feedback and taking the time to 'reflect, analyse and assimilate the feedback' (p. 366) is at the core of effective learning cultures and communities. Feedback that is individualised, and focuses on the current knowledge, skills and capacities of teachers, supports teachers to reflect on their teaching practices and assess their effectiveness in supporting young children's learning outcomes.

In a small-scale research study in metropolitan Melbourne (see the research case study within this chapter), a professional learning program was introduced to promote the use of evidence-based teaching strategies and increase the quality of adult–child interactions. The program employed a model of coaching which focused on a collaborative, sustained engagement, both with teachers as individuals and the centre as a whole. The engagement built a shared language around teaching and learning among teachers, coach, children and families. As the program was established, clear guidelines were developed, outlining the expectations of the process as well as the responsibilities associated with each role. All parties clarified and agreed on the purpose, structure and threshold conditions that had to be evident in the environment.

An external coach was engaged to work primarily with the centre's educational leader but also with teachers in their programs. The program content goal for the coach was to support teachers to embed Abecedarian Approach Australia (3*a*) teaching strategies into their practice, through a cycle of planning, observation and reflection. During the project, the coach worked explicitly to 'role model' particular strategies, support the educational leader's 'next steps' and observe the teachers in their practice. Follow-up sessions were provided so that individual teachers could meet (either formally or informally) with the coach, to further empower them to reflect on their practice and the strategies modelled by the coach in her interactions with children during the educational program. During these sessions, the coach encouraged, stretched and supported teachers to take responsibility for their own development, set goals, integrate the teaching strategies into their educational programs, enact the strategies with individual or small groups of children, and reflect on the successes and challenges of their teaching and learning. These sessions included written but flexible plans to support both the coach and teacher to focus on specific elements of adult–child interaction. These meetings were documented to assist in ongoing reflection and learning, and to monitor progress over time.

When coaching, it is important to consider the readiness and commitment of each teacher to change. Coaching is a strategy that can utilise individual teachers' strengths as a way of reflecting on and improving practice, rather than 'fixing' people. The aim of the coaching is to build relationships based on trust rather than simply managing performance. Both formal and informal interactions within the centre can strengthen relationships within teams, and encourage a sense of ownership and responsibility for team members. Focusing on coaching as a strategy to engage teachers provides a structure to these relationships. Coaching also affords a way to monitor progress and show the impact of teacher interactions with young children. As the coaching unfolded, it became clear that some teachers needed greater support to reflect on their own practice. The coaching was further utilised to develop teachers' knowledge and understanding of reflective practice, as well as empower them to make decisions about their own practice. The staff involved had not had experience in doing this in the past.

Empowering teachers to identify their own strengths and areas for development, in turn, develops a culture of ongoing learning within a centre. This culture is at the heart of a sustainable model of continuous improvement. Leading for learning in this context is intended to involve teachers in ways that stimulate their knowledge and practice, motivation and engagement. The concept of life-long learning is an important construct to support this ongoing evolution and organisational success, and research emphasises the role of positional leaders in motivating and supporting staff in ongoing learning (Hadley, Waniganayake & Shepherd, 2015).

REFLECTION POINTS

1. How would you define an effective leader?
2. Identify someone who you think is a model leader. What skills and attributes make them a leader?
3. How would you like colleagues to describe you as a leader?
4. Why is leadership important to advancing learning outcomes for children?
5. What threshold conditions should be in place to enable effective leadership in ECEC settings?
6. What support do you need to build your leadership skills?

A model of educational leadership in ECEC settings: building the climate and commitment to advance young children's learning outcomes

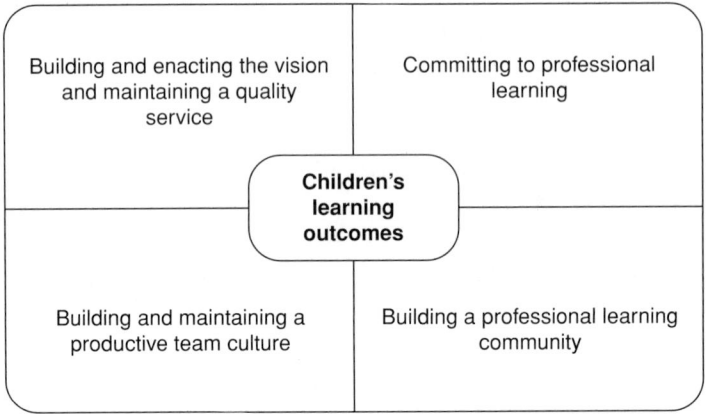

Figure 6.1: A model of educational leadership in ECEC settings

In order to promote young children's learning and improve outcomes, educational leaders need to implement a range of complementary strategies to create a workplace climate in which everyone feels they have a meaningful role to play. Constructive and purposeful relationships stem from an environment in which everyone feels safe, included, that they are treated fairly and that they share a collective purpose. These conditions form the foundations for colleagues to commit to reviewing and improving teaching practices, aligned with the expectations of Australian ECEC reform.

Building and enacting the vision and maintaining a quality service

> In the most effective settings better leadership was characterised by a clear vision, especially with regard to pedagogy and curriculum, which was shared by everyone working within the setting. (Siraj-Blatchford & Manni, 2006, p. 16)

Educational leadership involves engaging members in creating a shared vision and values, and then using these as the ongoing focus for continuous improvement (Cherrington & Thornton, 2015). In the Australian reform context, this vision centres on the image of the child as a capable learner, the role of the teacher and child in the teaching and learning process, and the importance of the adult–child interactions for supporting child outcomes. Kagan and Hallmark (2001) argue that educational leaders work with colleagues to develop the vision, inspiration, structure and direction of their broader mission – quality teaching and learning outcomes for children. Coughlin and Baird (2013) concur, and speak about the importance of educational leaders creating the systems and structures that reflect the collective vision and values. To achieve this integrated approach to quality improvement, educational leaders need to work with management (owners or licensees of services, and/or agencies that auspice the services) to explore how time, money and resources can be best employed to support the vision (Coughlin & Baird, 2013). This requires a form of administrative leadership where the educational leader understands that creating quality outcomes for children rests in part on having quality ECEC systems, organisational cultures and threshold conditions in place. These conditions, in turn, enable educational leaders and teachers to have the time and space to build and enact their vision (Cherrington & Thornton, 2015; Twigg et al., 2013). Ensuring that the vision flows into all the documents related to children's learning, such as the quality improvement plan and educational programs, will further assist in monitoring how the vision is enacted within the setting over time.

Building and maintaining a productive team culture

'Distributed', 'participative', 'facilitative' or 'collaborative' models of leadership call for a shift away from the traditional vision of leader as one key individual towards a more collective vision, one where the responsibility for leadership rests within various formal and informal leaders. (Siraj-Blatchford & Manni, 2006, p. 20)

While educational leaders work to ensure adherence by all to the collective vision and values, it is also vital that they draw on individuals' strengths and expertise, and provide opportunities for team members to deploy their strengths, and accordingly lead different aspects of pedagogy and the program plan (Cherrington & Thornton, 2015). Research demonstrates that distributed leadership positively affects each teacher's level of commitment, shared decision making and professional identity – distributed leadership is capacity building and empowering (Cherrington & Thornton, 2015; Siraj-Blatchford & Manni, 2006; Torrance, 2013; Waniganayake, 2014). However, although distributed leadership elicits many positive outcomes, it requires time, considered planning and attention to being purposeful and fair. Distributed leadership itself requires monitoring (Torrance, 2013; Waniganayake, 2014), and is dependent on the commitment, dedication and effort of individual teachers (Siraj-Blatchford & Manni, 2006).

Educational leaders can also explore possibilities for their own and colleagues' leadership development through connecting with the wider community. Shonkoff (2014) notes that a long-term strategic approach is necessary if the early childhood sector is to raise child outcomes: this involves the whole community. He argues that enacting the aspirations embedded in policy into daily programs and practices is contingent on building alliances at a macro level, and includes specialists and stakeholders within the local community, as well as policy makers, researchers and investors. This approach can enable educational leaders to formulate and enact goals that are specific to their local learning community. Waniganayake (2014) concurs and proposes a model of distributive leadership that recognises 'both the micro perspective located within an early childhood centre, and the macro perspective of the environment beyond the centre' (p. 74). This model of distributive leadership requires a form of advocacy leadership on the part of the educational leader where a connectedness to and engagement with the broader community can bring lasting change (Kagan & Hallmark, 2001).

Building a professional learning community

> Learning communities are made up of people who share a common purpose. They collaborate to draw on individual strengths, respect a variety of perspectives and actively promote learning opportunities. The outcomes are the creation of a vibrant, synergistic environment, enhanced potential for all members and the possibility of new knowledge. (Whitehead, Boschee, & Decker, 2013, p. 243)

Relationships within early childhood education and care communities are key to driving the creation of new knowledge about young children's learning. Marsick and Watkins (1999) argue that building new understandings is enhanced when there is a professional learning culture that promotes trust, the sharing of knowledge, dialogue, inquiry and risk taking, and gives constructive feedback to people at all levels. Stoll (2011) agrees and adds that sharing a learning focus within a community hinges, in part, on leaders':

- cultivating involvement and shared leadership
- nurturing trust and collaboration
- promoting collaborative inquiry that leads to deep learning within the community of learners.

Coming together, in the cause of a common vision, typically involves change for some or all members. Considering change theory, and models of change, can assist a team to account for different feelings and changing priorities, including the 'letting-go' of some ideas or practices and the 'bringing-in' of others. According to Bridges (2004), change is a process that involves endings, transitions and beginnings. During a change process all are in the position – either voluntarily or involuntarily – of having to end an attachment to doing things one way and begin another way. Although realising that change is inevitable in any professional context, especially in light of new knowledge or reform stemming from changes in policy direction, any member may struggle to 'let go', or may end up carrying some 'emotional baggage'. By recognising this, and within a trusting environment, the group can work through the processes of change and transition. Transitions to new approaches or practices involve having the direction and goals clarified, even if these are sketchy at first. Eventually, as the direction and goals are clarified and become more concrete, all members of the learning community are able to comfortably 'end the old' and 'begin the new'– to align towards a common purpose. When this occurs individual members of the learning community can begin to work together collaboratively to create new knowledge and deeper levels of understanding of young children's learning.

Committing to professional learning

The NQF places expectations on teachers to develop new theoretical, research-based and practical knowledge of learning, how children learn, and the role of 'teacher', 'child' and 'family' in the learning process (Coughlin & Baird, 2013; Fonsén, 2013; Waniganayake et al., 2012). Professional learning is an important vehicle through which educational leaders and teachers can build new knowledge.

Research confirms that professional learning can positively impact on teacher confidence, professional growth and improved practice if it:

1. is aligned with standards for practice and organisational goals, and has explicit objectives (US Department of Education, 2010)
2. is continuous (Hadley et al., 2015; Nolan, Morrissey & Dumenden, 2013)
3. is delivered by academics, mentors or coaches (Degotardi, Semann & Shepherd, 2012; Hahs-Vaughn & Yanowitz, 2009)
4. is supported by the management/leadership team (Walter & Briggs, 2012)
5. is designed to align teaching strategies to teachers' qualifications and experience in the sector, and their knowledge (Hadley et al., 2015)
6. enables the collective participation of all teachers in the educational setting (US Department of Education, 2010)
7. supports teachers to reflect on how to teach children and the impact of their practices (Colmer et al., 2015; Opfer & Pedder, 2011),
8. combines theory, research and practice to promote deeper contextualised knowledge (Colmer et al., 2015).

The following case study showcases the impact that a targeted professional learning program, incorporating these features into its design and implementation, has on the quality of the teacher–child interactions across a centre.

RESEARCH CASE STUDY

Jane Page and Collette Tayler

THE VICTORIAN ADVANCING EARLY LEARNING STUDY: PROFESSIONAL LEARNING TO ADVANCE TEACHING EFFECTIVENESS

Researching the impact of evidence-based strategies on the quality of programs within Australian early childhood settings is important. As outlined in Chapters 1 and 4, the intent, frequency and content of teachers' interactions with young children is core to advancing their learning and development. Yet, Australian research evidence from the E4Kids study (outlined in Chapter 1) indicates that there is a low presence of instructional support offered to young children in ECEC programs. The following case study describes the effects of a professional learning intervention aimed at raising the quality of learning support offered to young children, and highlights the value of generating evidence that tracks the effectiveness of professional learning on the program. The study adopted a collaborative model that privileged the integration of new (not used in the settings) evidence-based teaching strategies within daily pedagogical practices. Teachers were supported in critically reflecting on the impact of their teaching on children's learning, and adjusting their pedagogical approaches over a sustained period of time.

The Victorian Advancing Early Learning (VAEL) Study (2014–17), funded by the Victorian Department of Education and Training (DET), is conducted by researchers at the University of Melbourne in partnership with managers, educational leaders and teachers from the Moonee Valley and Hume City Councils, Gowrie Victoria and the Broadmeadows Valley Primary School. The study addresses three questions.

1. How does the quality of teacher–child interaction change in settings where teachers are coached in the use of one-to-one teaching techniques?
2. What strategies do educational leaders apply to improve the quality of pedagogy within their centre?
3. What is the impact of consistent implementation of teaching techniques on children's learning?

In this case study we focus on question one – the change in educator–child interactions over time.

The study design involved two key elements:

1. a *treatment year* – involving educational leaders and teachers in a program of professional learning, and fortnightly on-site interactive coaching sessions to support implementation of the teaching strategies (for more detail see the practice case study later in this chapter)
2. a *maintenance year* – involving the educational leader supporting teachers in continuing to implement the teaching strategies into their programs and daily practices. This project tested the effect of this professional learning model on the quality of teachers' interactions with young children and their ability to sustain improved practice over time.

Data collected includes time sample evidence (to capture how teachers were spending their time in classrooms and the type of talk they used during interactions) and 'room-level' evidence of the quality of interactions, collected using CLASS (Pianta, LaParo & Hamre, 2008). This data was captured four times a year across all rooms of the services. The findings below represent changes that occurred across the treatment year and the first half of the maintenance year, at a centre-level, in one of the sites (18 months in total).

The professional learning goal was to shift the focus of program and daily interactions in the setting towards enhanced support for children's learning. Analysis of the time sample reveals that the teachers increased the amount of time they spent with children, including interacting with one child, two to three children (small group) and four or more children (large group), from 34 per cent at the outset to 81 per cent 18 months later. Furthermore, the teachers reduced the time they spent in activities that took them away from children, such as cleaning or organising, managing routines, supervising passively, or working with another teacher, from 42 per cent at the outset to 7 per cent 18 months later.

The content of adult interactions additionally impacts on children's learning. In the second year of the study, an additional set of time–sample data was collected on the type of talk individual teachers modelled in their interactions with the children. We focused on 'supervisory talk', 'educational talk' and 'responsive talk'. 'Educational' talk was defined as 'back-and-forth exchanges between child and teacher where the teacher discusses concepts with the children'. The data highlighted that the level of educational talk that occurred between teachers and children increased from 26 per cent at the outset to 41 per cent 18 months later. These sets of time–sample data highlight the merit of collecting evidence of practice alongside a professional learning and coaching program. The program had an impact, changing the amount of time teachers spent with children, and the intent and content of their interactions.

These data were complemented by room-level evidence of the interactions, collected using the toddler and 'Pre-K' *CLASS* tools noted in Chapters 1 and 4. For example, the toddler-room data rendered evidence regarding the level of emotional and behavioural support, and engaged support for learning. Across 18 months, emotional and behaviour support increased by close to two points on a seven-point scale and engaged support for learning increased by two and a half points.

These preliminary findings highlight the impact that deliberate and focused professional learning, and coaching, that is focused on supporting the ongoing implementation of evidence-based strategies, have in educational programs and practices. Setting and agreeing on goals to adjust pedagogy in a preferred direction chosen by the group, and tracking progress towards the goals, is a potent way to raise the quality of ECEC programs and, by extension, to increase children's learning outcomes. The study-in-progress is tracking child learning outcomes, with the data being used to further enlist teachers' pedagogies over time as children progress into school.

REFLECTION POINTS

1. What is your vision for curriculum and pedagogy? How does it contribute to quality outcomes for young children? How are the teacher and the child positioned in this vision?
2. What impact does the organisational climate have on teacher confidence, professional growth and improved practice?
3. Consider the notions of shared vision, productive team culture, professional learning and professional learning communities outlined in this chapter. What contribution do they make to advancing young children's learning? What challenges may arise as you engage with these notions?

4. 'Research on educational leadership has rarely included the voice of the learners in the settings … it would be interesting to ask children about what they have learnt about leadership from the adults in their lives – both within their family contexts as well as from staff at the early childhood centres' (Waniganayake, 2014, p. 73). How could educational leaders and teachers incorporate children's perspectives on leadership into their approach to building a learning community whose goal is to advance children's learning outcomes?

A model of educational leadership: tracking the effectiveness of educational leadership on young children's learning outcomes

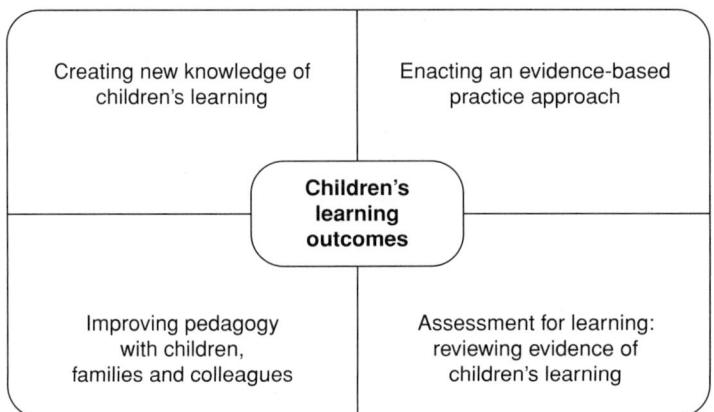

Figure 6.2: A model of educational leadership: tracking the effectiveness of educational leadership on young children's learning outcomes

Creating new knowledge of children's learning

As highlighted in Chapter 2, the policies and frameworks that make up the NQF draw on contemporary theory and research related to learning, development and teaching effectiveness, and, as such, present new challenges for teachers charged with enacting this Australian 'vision' for early childhood education and care programs. One of the key roles of the educational leader is to expose colleagues to new theoretical, research-based and practical knowledge, and to create the conditions that enable teachers to explore how theory and practice are interlinked (Coughlin & Baird, 2013). The EYLF (DEEWR, 2009) names a range of theories – developmental theories, socio-cultural theories, socio-behaviourist theories, critical theories and post-structuralist theories – that teachers can draw on in their daily practice and outlines several benefits to teaching and learning:

Drawing on a range of perspectives and theories can challenge traditional ways of seeing children, teaching and learning, and encourage teachers, as individuals and with colleagues, to:

- investigate why they act in the ways that they do
- discuss and debate theories to identify strengths and limitations
- recognise how the theories and beliefs that they use to make sense of their work enable but also limit their actions and thoughts
- consider the consequences of their actions for children's experiences
- find new ways of working fairly and justly (DEEWR, 2009, p. 11).

In addition, educational leaders can support teachers to deepen their understanding of teaching and learning by creating a culture of reflective practice. McLeod (2015) outlines nine steps of reflection to support teachers as they develop a sustained focus and approach to reflection on the educational challenges they face in daily practice.

1. **Readiness** to be open, develop self-awareness and consciousness of one's practice
2. **Recalling** a situation accurately as part of own practice
3. **Recognising** personal influences, views, biases
4. **Reflecting** (on, in) the child's experiences from their own perspective. What are their feelings? How do you know?
5. **Reviewing** together by sharing and comparing own understandings and thoughts
6. **Relating** to relevant reading and research
7. **Re-appraising** relevance. Evaluating what this shows and means personally, looking at the implications for own practice
8. **Responding** by making appropriate changes (letting go and letting come) and
9. **Remembering** the benefits of new learning (for you and the children) so reflection is sustainable.

Reflecting on reflection: improving teachers' readiness to facilitate participatory learning with young children, N. McLeod, *Professional Development in Education*, copyright © International Professional Development Association (IPDA), reprinted by permission of Taylor & Francis Ltd, www.tandfonline.com on behalf of International Professional Development Association (IPDA).

When teachers are supported to reflect on their daily practice, they develop a deeper and more nuanced understanding of their impact on children's learning and development.

Enacting an evidence-based practice approach

Research on teaching effectiveness has further raised an awareness of the importance of teachers' interactions with young children and the specific impact that teaching strategies have on children's learning outcomes in the early years (Cloney et al., 2013). Educational leaders need to build knowledge of research, and of evidence-based teaching and learning strategies that have been proven to make a difference to children's learning outcomes, and to trial and implement such strategies in daily practice alongside their colleagues. Kagan and Hallmark (2001) underscore the importance of pedagogical leaders applying their knowledge and skills to the local realities of a setting. 'A pedagogical leader functions as a bridge between research and practice. With knowledge and information provided by researchers and academicians, and armed with first hand experiences, pedagogical leaders serve as interpreters of research and theory' (p. 9). Through systematic review of evidence, educational leaders can build new meaning into their daily practice, and assess and monitor the impact that selected strategies have for individual children. The final case study in this chapter offers an educational leader's perspective on her involvement in research where she supported colleagues to implement evidence-based strategies into their daily practices, and the impact this had on the quality of interactions and the amount of time they spent with individual and small groups of children.

Assessment for learning: reviewing evidence of children's learning

Reviewing evidence is central to identifying areas for improvement in teaching and learning practices in early years settings. Assessment for learning is a practice principle outlined in the EYLF for Australia (DEEWR, 2009) and is defined as the process of gathering and analysing information about what children know, can do and understand (p. 17).

Supporting assessment for learning practices is core to the role of the educational leader as it offers a systemic approach to collecting evidence of children's learning, analysing children's learning, tailoring teaching interventions to promote learning and assessing the impact of interventions on children's learning. Building this systematic approach with colleagues, throughout the planning cycle, offers a robust way to document and assess the diverse ways in which children express their learning, and to draw on research and theory to assess the impact, intent and content of teachers' educational programs and interactions.

Improving pedagogy with children, families and colleagues

> Assessment, when undertaken in collaboration with families, can assist families to support children's learning and empower them to act on behalf of their children beyond the early childhood setting. When children are included in the assessment process they can develop an understanding of themselves as learners and an understanding of how they learn best. (DEEWR, 2009, p. 17)

Developing respectful and collaborative relationships with families, children and other professionals supporting learning, health and well-being, enables educational leaders and teachers to build deeper understandings of children. They can tailor educational programs in a more responsive and meaningful way to suit children's capacities and interests. This knowledge can be integrated at all stages of the planning cycle – collecting evidence of young children's learning, analysing young children's learning, tailoring teaching interventions to promote young children's learning and assessing the impact of these interventions on young children's learning – and assists teachers to check the relevance of their assessments against the perspectives of the learner and other key players in the process. Educational leaders play a key role in supporting all those engaged with the child.

While this chapter has highlighted the central role of the educational leader in building high-quality programs and driving the process of continuous improvement, it should be noted that the successful enactment of educational leadership is dependent on a range of factors including the person (e.g. the educational leader), the position (the authority and autonomy the educational leader is given to enact the role) and the place (the ECEC setting) (Waniganayake et al., 2012). Fonsén (2013) further argues that there are four key dimensions that impact on the successful enactment of pedagogical leadership:

1. the context
2. the organisational culture
3. the professionalism of directors
4. management of substance.

Educational leaders should be mindful of these factors and work with management (or service owners) to ensure that they have the appropriate support and resources.

REFLECTION POINTS

1. Kagan and Hallmark (2001) advocate for a 'systems approach' to leadership in the early childhood education and care sector that incorporates five forms of leadership: community; pedagogical; administrative; advocacy; and conceptual. These forms of leadership are interconnected and contribute to the effectiveness of the whole approach.
   - Community leadership – links vision, programs and practices to needs of the local community. Creates links with members of the local community and builds awareness within the community of the value of education, health and well-being of children.
   - Pedagogical leadership – serves to make connections between research, theory and practice. Targets gaps in knowledge and provides new information, shaping agendas in relation to the realities of ECEC practices.
   - Administrative leadership – provides the 'vision, inspiration, structure, and direction' (p. 9) required to create a quality ECEC system.
   - Advocacy leadership – requires knowledge of policy, legislation and current priorities for ECEC, and links to vision, exploring how to bring positive and lasting change through policy and legislation.

- Conceptual leadership – builds a vision for ECEC that transcends a local organisation, understanding reform in the context of social movements, fields and change.

  What forms of leadership are you familiar with? What new knowledge and skills would you need to develop to enact these styles of leadership? How do these forms of leadership support educational leaders to guide and support their colleagues in their planning, reflection and implementation practices?

2. Discuss the perspectives on: creating new knowledge of children's learning; leading colleagues to implement evidence-based practice approaches; reviewing evidence of children's learning; and improving pedagogy with children, families and colleagues that are outlined in this chapter. What contribution do they make to advancing young children's learning? How might you benefit from being engaged in the learning approaches?

PRACTICE CASE STUDY

Gracie Pupillo

EDUCATIONAL LEADERSHIP: SUPPORTING COLLEAGUES TO IMPLEMENT EVIDENCE-BASED STRATEGIES IN DAILY EDUCATIONAL PROGRAMS

I am an educational leader working in an inner west region in Melbourne in a centre-based long day care setting catering for 100 children from six months to four years of age, and 85 families. In 2014 and 2015, my educational leader role was shaped by the participation of all professionals at our centre in the VAEL Study. I have been working in conjunction with a coach to support my colleagues to implement strategies from the 3a. I have worked to build competence and confidence in implementing 3a in daily interactions with individual or small groups of children (2–3).

I attended the professional learning sessions that were held with all the teachers at three-monthly intervals throughout the year. These sessions focused on one particular strategy each time, and the theory and research underlying the practices. Each following day we began implementing the strategies. This professional learning was vital in supporting me as an educational leader to build the required knowledge and skills to implement the strategies into our daily programs. It helped me to realise that, as an educational leader, it was valuable to build specific knowledge of teaching and learning strategies alongside colleagues. This shared learning helped us to discuss how 3a teaching techniques supported individual children's learning, how they aligned with our goals for individual children, and how they could be introduced and implemented into our educational programs over time in a systematic way.

The main focus of my role was to support teachers in the implementation of teaching techniques. A highly experienced mentor/coach from the project worked with and supported me in my role. This was critical in assisting me to gain more knowledge, skills and confidence to support my colleagues' implementation work. At the start of the study, my mentor visited me fortnightly for 'educational leader' sessions. Each session would begin with a check-in to understand how things were going at the centre then we would review a particular strategy that we were implementing. For example, I would give examples of how I implemented the enriched caregiving strategy in the kindergarten room, and my successes and challenges. We would then practise and role play the strategy. Depending on how the centre was coping, my mentor would provide me with further information. For example, when I felt my colleagues and I were struggling with the implementation of certain strategies and the change to our practice, she gave me a reading about change and the stages that professionals can experience and progress through during change – denial, commitment, resistance and exploration. This helped me to understand and identify where I and my colleagues sat in terms of these stages. With this new understanding, I approached discussions with colleagues differently – I was more open to and considerate of their individual needs – and this was helpful for building a respectful and supportive community of practice. The final part of the visit was most beneficial as my mentor and I would go into each teacher's room and observe interactions and engagement. I found this extremely valuable, as I was also able to learn from her modelling about how to approach teachers, give constructive feedback and observe the implementing of strategies with the children – such as modelling one-on-one interactions with children during mealtimes, demonstrating rich language exchanges, and the positioning of the adult to see what children were looking at and interested in – in order to begin an exchange. The sessions with my mentor/coach were pivotal to my professional development in the area of coaching and **mentoring**. I particularly found the hands-on role modelling and instantaneous feedback the most valuable in supporting my role as educational leader.

Mentoring: a component of professional learning (see definition earlier) in which an educational leader, or another knowledgeable and experienced professional colleague, works alongside individual teachers to develop their capacity to advance young children's learning.

The study required each colleague to choose one or two focus children who were 'vulnerable' or known to be living in disadvantaged circumstances. Each week, they had to plan for these children using 3a techniques. In addition to aligning techniques with individual children's learning goals, at the end of the week each teacher would record the daily strategies they implemented. At the beginning, I did not have a focus child or children myself, but then it was suggested that I choose two children who I believed needed additional support, and I therefore completed these processes alongside my colleagues. This was very beneficial as I experienced the same struggles and challenges as the teachers, and I was able to understand their frustrations as I was experiencing similar things. This helped us to support each other and continue our work.

As my colleagues and I began learning more about 3a, we felt progressively more confident in sharing the details of what we were doing with families. After having discussions with families about our new teaching approaches, we found that they started to share with us the differences that they noticed in their children's learning. The teachers then began showing families the specific strategies so that they could implement them at home with their children. With this growing confidence, the teachers started creating displays to make the learning visible at the service, and together we organised a very successful evening event for families. The families' feedback was that they found the videos presented of teachers implementing the strategies with their children very useful, since they were able to see techniques in action, and realise how teachers engaged and interacted with their children to extend their learning. Receiving positive feedback from families was a turning point for us, as we saw the impact that our new approaches had on building collaborative approaches to extend children's learning.

Support from management (in this case, the local government) is vital for any program to be sustained throughout the service. It is of utmost importance that management understands and recognises the purpose and value of teachers' chosen practices to children's learning, and the time and support required to enact new techniques and practices. The centre coordinator attended our 3a training and as a result, understood the outcomes and benefits of the program. This supported me in my role as educational leader as she supported this work in many ways. She added 3a to the monthly meeting agenda, and supported teachers to develop skills and set goals in relation to 3a. Coordinators of services and assistant coordinators are vital to the success of this work as they can also offer support to the educational leader and teachers with any issues they may face. When inducting new families into the service, the study is explained, and information is given about 3a teaching techniques and their benefits to children and families.

I believe that, through this experience, the teachers and I have transformed our practice. We have become increasingly self-aware when interacting with children during routine times, reading one-on-one with children and when implementing LearningGames®. Our relationships with children and families have strengthened because we know and understand them at a deeper level, and we are focused on children's learning. This new knowledge gained and strategies learnt have impacted on our practices and enabled more intentional teaching in our daily interactions with children. As an educational leader, I feel that this process has enabled me to support every colleague to attain better outcomes for children.

Conclusion

The role of the educational leader is complex and multifaceted. As educational leaders acquire and practise new knowledge and skills, and develop a strategic approach to guiding and supporting their colleagues in their planning, reflection and implementation practices, professional work becomes more refined. Purposeful leadership has the power to transform organisational cultures, empower colleagues to feel part of a collective teaching and learning endeavour, and raise the quality of support offered to young children and their families.

References

Australian Children's Education and Care Quality Authority (ACECQA). (2011). *Guide to the National Quality Standard.* Retrieved from http://files.acecqa.gov.au/files/National-Quality-Framework-Resources-Kit/NQF03-Guide-to-NQS 130902.pdf

Australian Children's Education and Care Quality Authority (ACECQA). (2012). *National Quality Standard Assessment and Rating Instrument.* Retrieved from http://files.acecqa.gov.au/files/Assessment%20and%20Rating/1-NQS_Assessment%20and%20Rating%20Instrument_120522_%20FINAL-1.pdf

Bridges, W. (2004). *Transitions, Making Sense of Life's Changes* (2nd ed.). Cambridge: Da Capo Press.

Cherrington, S., & Thornton, K. (2015). The nature of professional learning communities in New Zealand early childhood education: an exploratory study. *Professional Development in Education, 41*(2), 310–28.

Cloney, D., Page, J., Tayler, C., & Church, A. (2013). Assessing the quality of early childhood education and care. Centre for Community Child Health Policy Brief, *25.* Retrieved from www.rch.org.au/uploadedFiles/Main/Content/ccch/Policy_Brief_25_Quality.pdf

Colmer, K., Waniganayake, M., & Field, L. (2015). Implementing curriculum reform: insights into how Australian early childhood directors view professional development and learning. *Professional Development in Education, 41*(2), 203–21.

Coughlin, A. M., & Baird, L. (2013). Pedagogical leadership. Paper. Ontario Ministry of Education. Kingston, ON: Queens Press.

Degotardi, S., Semann, A., & Shepherd, W. (2012). Using practitioner inquiry to promote reflexivity and change in infant-toddler early childhood programs. In P. Whiteman & K. De Gioia (Eds.). *Children and Childhoods 1: Perspectives, Places and Practices* (pp. 36–57). Newcastle-upon-Tyne: Cambridge Scholars.

Department of Education, Employment and Workplace Relations (DEEWR). (2009). *Belonging, Being & Becoming: The Early Years Learning Framework for Australia.* Canberra: DEEWR for COAG.

Fonsén, E. (2013). Dimensions of pedagogical leadership in early childhood education and care. In Hujala, E., Waniganayake, M. & Rodd, J. (Eds.). *Researching Leadership in Early Childhood Education* (pp. 181–92). Tampere: Tampere University Press.

Gomez, R. E., Kagan, S. L., &. Fox, E. A. (2015). Professional development of the early childhood education teaching workforce in the United States: an overview. *Professional Development in Education, 41*(2), 169–86. DOI: http://dx.doi.org/10.1080/19415257.2014.986820

Hadley, F., Waniganayake, M., & Shepherd, W. (2015). Contemporary practice in professional learning and development of early childhood teachers in Australia: reflections on what works and why. *Professional Development in Education, 41*(2), 187–202.

Hahs-Vaughn, D., & Yanowitz, K. (2009). Who is conducting teacher research? *Journal of Educational Research, 102*(6), 415–26.

Kagan, S. L., & Hallmark, L. G. (2001). Cultivating leadership in early care and education. *Child Care Information Exchange, 7*(1), 7–11.

Nolan, A., Morrissey, A., & Dumenden, I. (2013). Expectations of mentoring in a time of change: views of new and professionally isolated early childhood teachers in Victoria, Australia. *Early Years, 33*(2), 161–71.

Marsick, V. J., & Watkins, K. (1999). Envisioning new organisations for learning. In D. Boud. & J. Garrick (Eds.). *Understanding Learning at Work* (pp. 199–216). London: Routledge.

McLeod, N. (2015). Reflecting on reflection: improving teachers' readiness to facilitate participatory learning with young children. *Professional Development in Education, 41*(2), 254–72.

Ministerial Council for Education, Early Childhood Development and Youth Affairs (MCEECDYA). (2010). *Education and Care Services National Regulations under the Education and Care Services National Law.* Melbourne: MCEECDYA. Retrieved from www.education.nt.gov.au/__data/assets/pdf_file/0019/24085/EducationCareServicesNationalRegulations.pdf

Opfer, V. D., & Pedder, D. (2011). Conceptualizing teacher professional learning, *Review of Educational Research, 81*(3), 376–407. DOI: http://doi.org/10.3102/0034654311413609

Parliament of Victoria. (2010*). Education and Care Services National Law Act, No. 69 of 2010.* Retrieved from www.legislation.vic.gov.au/

Pianta, R. C., LaParo, K. M., & Hamre, B. K. (2008). *Classroom Assessment Scoring System [CLASS] Manual: Pre-K.* Baltimore, MD: Brookes Publishing

Schien, E. H. (2010). *Organizational Culture and Leadership,* (4th ed.). San Francisco: Jossey-Bass.

Shonkoff, J. (2014). The need for strategy: translating inspiration into concrete goals and plans we develop together. Keynote presentation at *The IDEA Conference.* The LEGO Foundation. 8–10 April, Billund, Denmark. Retrieved from www.theideaconference.com/

Sims, M., Forrest, R., Semann, A., & Slattery, C. (2015). Conceptions of early childhood leadership: driving new professionalism? *International Journal of Leadership in Education: Theory and Practice, 18*(2), 149–66.

Siraj-Blatchford, I., & Manni, L. (2006). *Effective Leadership in Early Years Sector Study (ELEYS) Study.* London: Institute of Education, University of London.

Southworth, G. (2002). Instructional leadership in schools: reflections and empirical evidence. *School Leadership & Management, 22*(1), 73–91. DOI: http://doi.org/10.1080/13632430220143042

Stoll, L. (2011). Leading professional learning communities. In J. Robertson & H. Timperley (Eds.). *Leadership and Learning* (pp.103–17). London: Sage Publications.

Torrance, D. (2013). Distributed leadership: challenging five generally held assumptions. *School Leadership & Management 33*(4), 354–72.

Twigg, D., Pendergast, D., Fluckiger, B., et al. (2013). Coaching for early childhood teachers: an insight into the effectiveness of an initiative. *International Research in Early Childhood Education*, 4(1), 73–90.

US Department of Education. (2010). *Toward the Identification of Features of Effective Professional Development for Early Childhood Educators*. Washington DC: US Department of Education. Retrieved from www2.ed.gov/rschstat/eval/professional-development/literature-review.pdf

Walter, C, & Briggs, J. (2012). *What Professional Development Makes the Most Difference to Teachers?* Oxford: University of Oxford Department of Education.

Waniganayake, M. (2014). Being and becoming early childhood leaders. Reflections on leadership studies in early childhood education and the future leadership research agenda. *Journal of Early Childhood Education Research*, 3(1), 65–81.

Waniganayake, M., Cheeseman, S., Fenech, M., Hadley, F., & Shepherd, W. (2012). *Leadership: Contexts and Complexities in Early Childhood Education*. Melbourne: Oxford University Press.

Whitehead, B M., Boschee, F., & Decker, R. H. (2013). *The Principal: Leadership for a Global Society*. Thousand Oaks, CA: Sage.

CHAPTER 7

Advocating for learning

Collette Tayler, Tim Gilley and Jane Page

LEARNING OBJECTIVES

In this chapter you will:

1. explore the nature of advocacy and how it can be applied to advance children's learning and development outcomes
2. consider how research has informed advocacy efforts in the Australian context and influenced policy change
3. recognise how advocacy can be applied to support high-quality practice in early childhood education care programs.

Introduction

> To be an advocate and to engage in advocacy is to adopt a stance, advance a cause, and attempt to produce a result on behalf of an interest of a person, group or cause. (Cohen, 2004, p. 9)

Teachers need to be powerful advocates for the children in their programs. **Advocacy** is an important dimension of the professional role of the teacher as it can produce significant positive effects on children's learning and development. Advocacy can also be complex work – it may involve not only children but also children's families, teacher colleagues, other professionals and potentially other organisations, such as agencies concerned with health and well-being issues, governments and unions. This chapter considers the nature of advocacy, and the way collective action can be a helpful tool for improving the lives of young children and their families, especially in settings where behaviour reflecting racism, intolerance, gender bias and other forms of discrimination results in the marginalisation of some. The material invites you to consider the context of advocacy work in early childhood settings, and the skills and strategies of working as an advocate for the purpose of enhancing children's outcomes.

Advocacy: speaking, listening, writing and acting in the interests or on behalf of an individual or group who may be disadvantaged by conditions present in a system, an institution or environment, with intent to influence decision making, and achieve change and improvement for those who may not be powerful enough to represent their own interests effectively. Advocacy may be conducted in partnership with others.

Nature of advocacy

The power of education to transform lives is the reason behind centuries of effort making access to basic education universal, and the initiatives enabling young children access to high-quality early education and care. A strong start to life-long learning is thought to ensure overall well-being. Helen May, a highly esteemed advocate for the quality of life experience of the very young in New Zealand, notes:

> Since the nineteenth century, early childhood advocates have sought to persuade society in general and politicians in particular as to the benefits of early childhood care and education for children prior to school entry, which in New Zealand is at age five years. Dreams of social and political change have fuelled the beginning of many early childhood institutions. In contrast, rationales of social and political order have underpinned the gaze of political patronage and government interest. The contradiction between the dream and the political reality has been mediated as early childhood services have sought to negotiate a sustainable future. (May, 2006, pp. 245–6)

This commentary is a sharp reminder that advocacy work in regard to early childhood is situated within the history of a country and its political order, and the reformers' dreams of social and political change for alternative (better) institutions for children. In brief, the *nature* of advocacy is political and advocacy work depends upon the level of 'community will' to change the status quo. To this end, every individual has a part to play and can make a difference.

All people are shaped and affected by the environment of their community and advocacy activity is often driven by particular issues within the lived experience of individuals. Some light on the nature of advocacy in a democracy is shed by Salt-marsh (1996) who records John Dewey's contribution to pedagogy that links community involvement with intellectual and moral development. He deploys Dewey's big ideas regarding 'democratic community', 'social service', 'reflective inquiry', 'education for social transformation' and 'linking education to experience' to highlight the challenge of work involving social reconstruction. Democratic values and citizenship are developed through processes that afford members the opportunity to thrive, and that carefully address the individual and collective human rights of all.

A vision of high-quality care and education for the very young provokes action that will help ensure each child is able to realise her or his full potential. To this end, the ecological framework conceived by Bronfenbrenner (1979) (see Introduction) is a helpful conceptual device to consider the context of the child and what specific action may be necessary to afford the child optimal conditions for learning and development. A teacher who observes a 'present social order' as marginalising some children and families, for example, may be provoked to build a campaign that reaches out and welcomes them, and ensures that the centre or school community adjusts any behaviour that marginalises. Ensuring that children are surrounded by warm kinship, community networks, and cultural environments that welcome and encourage curiosity, inquiry and strong dispositions towards learning is the nature of advocacy within the early childhood profession. Moreover, the principles underlying the *United Nations Convention on the Rights of the Child* (UNCRC) (1989) and the concept of children as rights holders is foundational in guiding the nature of advocacy in early childhood education care (ECEC) settings (see Chapter 3).

Agencies: organisations that directly provide a service or are responsible for particular areas or activities related to service provision. In the ECEC context, there are a range of different agencies including private businesses, non-government, not-for-profit organisations and government institutes and authorities.

Sometimes, advocacy will be personal and 'low-key' in the way it is done, and at other times advocacy may involve engaging with a wide range of actors across a wide range of **agencies** and professions that are linked to ECEC settings and schools. As Cohen notes, advocates may also come from a range of different interests and backgrounds:

> Advocates may be friends or family members of the beneficiary [or beneficiaries], attorneys for the individual, public interest lawyers, government attorneys, representatives of organised groups, for-profit and not-for-profit organisations, labour unions, social workers in public and non-public agencies, legislators at all levels of government, other public employees, as well as journalists and teachers. (2004, pp. 9–10)

In this way, advocacy can be seen to have a broad scope across most elements of human society. Advocacy occurs when people work alone or join together to promote the universal aspirations encapsulated within United Nations declarations and conventions (Petrasek, 2014). It may involve support for an individual or for a small or large group. Advocacy occurs when the resolution of issues that affect or marginalise some are being addressed. An advocate works to support those who may lack the power to assert their own rights or argue the case for change (e.g. for greater equity). The target audience for an advocate is any person or group who is impeding the opportunities or rights of those without power to change their situation. Because teachers work with very young (non-voting) members of the community, they have special responsibility to consider children's interests in any setting where children are found.

A policy stance on advocacy and change

In Australia, contemporary early years policy papers and documents note the importance and value of advocacy in early years settings. The National Early Childhood Development Strategy, for example, positions advocacy as part of a three-pronged approach to creating the optimal conditions for enhancing young children's learning and development:

> Government, non-government providers and private providers have an important service delivery, community development and advocacy role. This includes providing quality, accessible and affordable services which have a central focus on supporting positive development of children as well as supporting the participation of parents in community life. Providers also have a responsibility to offer good conditions and professional development for the early childhood and family support workforce. (COAG, 2009, p. 7)

Furthermore, National Quality Standard (NQS), Element 6.3.4 notes advocacy as an important vehicle that supports services to build relationships with children and families and engage with their local community. It notes that assessors can discuss with services how they 'promote child-friendly communities and advocates for universal access to a range of high-quality early childhood and school age care programs for all children' (ACECQA, 2011, p. 161). In this way, the advocacy work of teachers is embedded within the Australian ECEC policy system (see also Chapter 2).

Early Childhood Australia (ECA) and the Australian Human Rights Commission (AHRC) collaborated to address ways in which teachers can support young children's rights, agreeing on a statement and key areas for action that 'assists ECA and its members to be clear and credible advocates in campaigning for the rights and wellbeing of young children' (ECA & AHRC, 2015, p. 1). The agencies worked collaboratively to identify key areas for action to advocate for young children's rights in Australia. In addition, the *Code of Ethics* (ECA, 2016) also underscores the multifaceted nature of advocacy in early years services. In the preamble, the Code aligns advocacy with ethical responsibility and speaks to the importance of teachers taking action 'in the presence of unethical practice' (p. 1). The Code's preamble states that it has been informed by the key 'principles in the United Nations Convention of the Rights of the Child (1991) and the Declaration on the Rights of Indigenous Peoples (2007)' and in its core principles section aligns action and ethics with children's rights, stating that teachers should 'respect and maintain the rights and dignity of children, families, colleagues and communites' (p. 2). The Code promotes the importance of just legal and policy frameworks for children and families, and states that teachers should 'advocate for the development and implementation of laws and policies that promote the rights and best interests of childern and families'. Advocacy activity related to enabling the best conditions for professions to be the most effective is also addressed. In embracing the Code, teachers may 'advocate for my profession and the provision of quality education and care' (p. 4), and further, the value of professional knowledge and research knowledge is noted to support the optimal outcomes for children. The Code states that ECEC teachers 'use research and practice-based evidence to advocate for a society where all childern have access to quality education and care' (p. 3).

REFLECTION POINTS

1. In your role as a teacher, reflect on the nature of advocacy and discuss how advocacy touches the work that you do.
2. What implications does advocacy hold for the child and the broader range of actors in the child's life: their family, the communities in which their family participates, and the broader society and its institutions?
3. What new insight does 'advocacy' provoke when you consider the role of 'teacher'? How should advocacy help shape your understanding of your role as a teacher in designing a curriculum to advance young children's learning and development?
4. How can the 54 articles in the UNCRC be used to help shape advocacy efforts?

Levels of ECEC policy advocacy and change

ECEC policies can be viewed on a continuum operating from the level of day-to-day practice to major policies adopted by governments and pertaining to social well-being, education, health, housing, transport and employment. A number of examples at different levels are identified below.

*   At room level within an ECEC centre: are children treated as active agents of their own learning; are meals at a time when teachers intentionally promote conversation and learning in relation to the eating of food; how is the management and clearing up of lunch items used to expand children's sense of community?
*   At a centre level: how many children can be enrolled; how are the rooms and the outdoor spaces organised; what is the philosophy of teaching; what fee levels are set; how are government health and safety regulations implemented; how is child protection assured?
*   At a local government level: how is ECEC policy and provision promoted in the community; what operations policies are in place for the administration and management of ECEC services? At this level, provision of professional

development, maintenance of buildings and equipment, and support to the networks of early childhood providers and professionals can be part of a holistic focus on supporting children's development.

- At state or regional levels: what funding is provided and what are the purposes and intentions of this funding; how is the regulation of services promoted; what procedures are in place to assess the level of service improvement; what processes exist for maintaining the currency of legislation and how is inter-government cooperation achieved?
- At national levels: what funding is provided and what are the purposes and intentions of this funding; what legislation is in place and what departments or institutions are set up to manage this; how are the policy efforts aligned across jurisdictions, agencies and program areas related to children's education, health and well-being, security and safety?

In Australia, the establishment of a National Quality Framework (NQF) to drive improvements in ECEC quality is an example of advocates using evidence of the importance of early learning and development to bring about change, and working concurrently across local, state, regional and national levels (refer to Chapters 1 and 2). However, the evidence base for policy may be limited or conflicting, and policy change also happens contrary to evidence because it can be driven by popular emotion raised after sudden events in the community. Policy change may also be expedient for political or instrumental reasons, such as cutting spending on economic grounds, with the achievement of one goal (e.g. reduction of expenditure) at the cost of another (e.g. quality ECEC provision). Here are some examples.

- In the late 1980s, Victoria introduced legislation to require mandatory reporting of child abuse by a range of professionals. An advocacy organisation produced a report which argued against this legislation on the basis of evidence that there were better ways to spend scarce resources on this important and complex social problem (Carter, 1988).
- The Australian Government policy of keeping children of asylum seeker families in immigration detention centres is in place despite evidence from reputable professionals that the practice is highly damaging to their health and well-being (Penovic & Sifris, 2005; Newman, Dudley & Steel, 2008).
- ECEC is also a contested national policy area because of historical roots of separate 'childcare' and 'early childhood education' agendas: policy related to delivering affordable 'childcare' to allow the workforce participation of families continues to be in tension with policy focused on the provision of high-quality early learning in the years before school (Productivity Commission, 2014).

In advocating for change, it is important to understand the levels of government engaged in policy work in order to locate where the decisions are made and to identify key decision makers.

POLICY CASE STUDY

Rachel Flottman

IMPLEMENTING A NEW POLICY: THE SPACE BETWEEN TEXT AND ACHIEVEMENT OF THE INTENDED OUTCOMES

'Advocacy within the early childhood sector needs to consider strategies for working with governments both to protect early childhood pedagogy and provision as well as to influence and change government policy and practice' (May, 2006, p. 262). The Australian early childhood advocacy sector is characterised by multiple, vocal groups that are geared towards generating stronger outcomes for all children. In Australia, this group constitutes broad stakeholder groups, such as ECA, as well as smaller groups that represent particular issues such as Early Learning Association Australia and Early Childhood Intervention Australia (just to name a few). These groups work together, with teachers and also independently, to influence government's early childhood service provision for all children generally, for their particular interests specifically, as well as for quality pedagogy. Over recent years, these advocating bodies have been particularly challenged as the early childhood sector has been through transformational change in Australia (Flottman & Page, 2012).

In 2007, the then newly elected Australian Government announced a broad range of reforms aimed to improve the quality of the early childhood system. These reforms included the introduction of a new NQS, a National Early Years Learning Framework (EYLF) and a quality and rating system to provide information on the performance of early childhood education and care provision against each of the NQS. While government developed the reforms, the broader early childhood sector played a large and significant role in both influencing the government's human capital reform agenda to include early childhood education and care in the way that it did, and then in shaping it once the reform momentum was set in place.

The advocacy sector was vital in advocating for regulatory and pedagogical changes in Australia. Advocates argued for the inclusion of particular elements of early childhood quality, ones that treasuries might look past, but early childhood specialists know cannot be overlooked, such as the inclusion of better staff:child ratios for children under three years to support quality adult–child interactions (1:4 in Australia).

Advocates argued strongly for the inclusion of high-quality and excellent ratings in the assessment and rating system, which go beyond assessing and reporting on a minimum standard. Negotiating the importance of standards higher than a minimum with governments can be difficult, but this was a negotiation worth having, and Australia now has a comprehensive world-leading system of early childhood quality assessment and rating that integrates regulatory compliance and quality improvement. Further, it provides information to families and governments about the quality of children's early education and care, and the transparency of ratings provokes services to continue to drive-up the quality provision.

Beyond advocating on regulatory matters, pedagogical advocacy is also important as it is the teacher's pedagogy – what they do day-to-day, moment-to-moment with children – that significantly affects the children's learning and development experiences within settings, centres and schools. Unfortunately, however, translating policy into practice, in particular policy that requires pedagogical change, remains one of the biggest challenges in any reform process (Coburn, 2005). Research suggests that the process of turning policy into practice is most effective when practitioners can be supported to understand how they can accommodate the new changes into their own teaching practices at the classroom level (Spillane, Reiser & Reimer, 2002; Coburn, 2005). This is a process of knowledge translation and accommodation whereby teachers make sense of the policy through their existing set of beliefs, values and experiences in order to change and influence their practice in the future.

Throughout the current reform process, early childhood advocacy groups have worked together, and with teachers, to use their collective influence on government to design, develop and deliver professional learning opportunities in ways that can be accessible to the professionals working every day with infants, toddlers and young children. For example, ECA has material about the varying ways in which the EYLF can be put into practice on many of its web-based platforms; it publishes a monthly journal and magazine, as well as hosting blogs and convening a biannual conference. Gowrie Victoria and other professional support groups have provided professional learning and consultancy support across the ECEC sector. These strategies are important means by which advocates take the policy that governments have agreed to and support the ECEC sector to translate this into practice. In doing so, the advocacy sector has been able to work with teachers to interpret the reforms for themselves and support the knowledge translation process, as Spillane, Reiser and Reimer (2002) and Coburn (2005) suggest above.

Taking this approach is empowering for the early childhood profession, whose members actively engage with policy initiatives that come from government, and the implementation processes, rather than simply accepting and implementing reforms without critical reflection and local customisation, or ignoring them. Early childhood advocates and teachers have a mechanism through advocacy to provide input to reform ideas, feedback on reforms and to interpret these so that they can be understood locally and applied in their own particular and most appropriate way.

The place of research in advocating for children and their learning rights

Using well-chosen and designed research as an advocacy tool can help to make the case for change, assist in the planning of change and record the effect of the advocacy effort. For the advocacy work of teachers to be effective, consideration needs to be given to: the preferred outcomes; the evidence available to help advocate for change in direction, policy or practice; the time that it may take to see a change; and who may hold the keys to successful change that reflects success. Research evidence may be used in a range of advocacy contexts, for example:

- justifying the need for a program or support, for example, through child observations: what is the extent of the problem or issue that needs a remedy?
- establishing the likelihood of advocacy efforts having some level of success: what does research on similar advocacy efforts reveal?
- identifying the decision makers who will need to be influenced: who are the potential allies and how to elicit their support; who is likely to block any change?
- assessing the effectiveness of the program or intervention: what methods can be used?
- communicating the results of the advocacy: who needs to know?

The potential of research to support advocacy is conditioned upon the quality of the research available and its relevance to the issue being addressed. Robust evidence can be helpful in persuading key players to change direction, or move attention and resources towards a specific group needing support, or a problem needing to be resolved. Research moves beyond a simple collection of opinion and/or anecdote to the provision of evidence that can be used to demonstrate the status of a situation nationally, regionally or in a local community. Research can be used to support or refute a position or stance on a particular issue and to help persuade those who have the power to make change at the system, service, constituent group or local level. An analysis of international research literature related to advocacy suggests that the work of teachers is influenced by three domains, each supplying a rich array of policy, research and practice evidence, and direction:

- studies related specifically to ECEC provision, including the quality of programs (Ang, 2014; Gromada & Greenspan 1974; Tayler et al., 2013); approaches to multiculturalism (Han & Thomas, 2010); inclusion of children with disabilities (Hutchinson et al., 2014); supporting refugee children (Newman, 2005); and the need to develop a public narrative about the importance of ECEC (Oberklaid, 2014)
- studies related to broader well-being and development issues faced by young children and their families, including the need to advocate for children (McDonald, 1995; Pithouse & Crowley, 2007); domestic violence (Thiara & Humphreys, 2015; Humphreys & Absler, 2011); child sexual abuse (Jackson, 2004); child maltreatment and the need for child protection (Briggs, 1991; Cummins, Scott & Scales, 2012); separated parents (Bond, 1998; Parkinson, 2013); and children in detention centres (Penovic & Sifris, 2005)
- studies related to broader social issues and debates, including gender policy making (Rolandsen Agustin, 2008); children in out-of-home care (Kiraly & Humphreys, 2015; Delfabbro, Barber & Cooper, 2002; Tarren-Sweeney & Hazell, 2006); human rights (Petrasek, 2014); poverty and class (Bullock & Lott, 2001); minorities (Bowes & Sim, 2006); and underprivileged groups as actors on their own behalf (Cashmore, 2002; Ross, 1977).

It is important to distinguish the use of major research study evidence and small-scale research undertaken locally. Both are important tools for advocacy, and both need to demonstrate the use of rigorous methods. Longitudinal studies that identify, for example, poorer outcomes for children growing up in low-income families can be used to advocate for earlier and more effective intervention. In another example, a small-scale longitudinal study conducted by the Brotherhood of St Laurence (Gilley & Taylor, 1995; Taylor & Nelms, 2008) found that low income, in comparison to living in a family on a higher income, substantially reduced the life chances of children, particularly in relation to success in education. While all children in the study had opportunities for successful lives, the findings also suggested that children from more advantaged backgrounds were likely to have multiple opportunities for success, while those from disadvantaged backgrounds were more likely to have one major chance – publicly funded education. These findings have been used in advocacy efforts targeted at State and Commonwealth Governments for additional public assistance for low-income families in order to improve child outcomes; for example, advocating for the reinstatement of funds that had been cut for kindergarten programs, which had led to higher fees and a subsequent drop in the attendance rates of children from low-income families.

Furthermore, in a classroom context, sustained observation of an individual child's progress can provide vital evidence to support a teacher's advocacy effort on behalf of a child. Teachers who have strong capacity both to assess published research for its relevance, validity and reliability, and to design their own research, have a powerful set of skills for use in any advocacy effort. Research can help inform all stages involved in advocacy. The discipline of clarity on how information is collected, manipulated and applied, how results can be repeated and how to draw conclusions that do not go beyond the extent and quality of the data, are foundational skills to develop (see Chapter 8). Teachers must be research literate and research-design capable.

Finally, Laney (2003) identified four reasons why it may not be easy to clearly or quickly see the result of advocacy effort.

1. Outcomes may emerge over lengthy periods of time, beyond the scope of many research efforts to track change. For this reason, longitudinal studies of any planned interventions can be valuable because they can track change over time, and the sustainability of the change.

2. It can be difficult to attribute change to a particular action or intervention. There are so many influences on children's social and cognitive abilities, and their academic success, that it is difficult to disentangle the effects of a particular action or intervention by the teacher from other factors. Research using randomised controlled trial methods (for controlling these other influences) to test the efficacy of certain actions, approaches or practices can be invaluable. However, as with longitudinal research more generally, these studies can be highly resource intensive.

3. There may be other planned interventions with similar goals operating at the same time, making it difficult to disentangle their respective influences.

4. There are complexities in clearly defining the outcomes that constitute success, given that preferred outcomes are rarely fully articulated and operationalised.

REFLECTION POINTS

1. How can you best use research in advocacy for improving children's learning and development outcomes?
2. What resources would you require to access existing research, and plan and carry out your own research?
3. How could you and your colleagues in a centre or school use research to advocate for children and their families?
4. What are ways of using theories, research studies and policy documents to advocate for children in your program, in your local community or with government?

RESEARCH CASE STUDY

Jeff Borland, Tamera Clancy, Nichola Coombs, Kate Cotter, Alice Hill, Brigid Jordan, Anne Kennedy and Yi-Ping Tseng

CHANGING THE TRAJECTORY OF CHILDREN'S LIVES: RESEARCH AND ADVOCACY

The Early Years Education Program (EYEP) is an innovative program designed to protect and enhance the development and learning of young children in and on the edge of the child protection system, to ensure that they arrive at primary school developmentally and educationally equal to their peers. The Early Years Education Research Program (EYERP) is a randomised controlled trial to test the effectiveness of the EYEP.

There is strong scientific evidence that early intervention for highly vulnerable children provides the most favourable outcomes and costs less than later remediation (National Scientific Council on the Developing Child, 2007). According to data from the states and territories, there are 36 000 pre-school children in the child protection system in Australia (AIHW, 2015). It is highly likely that all these children would benefit from access to high-quality ECEC services. However, because of a lack of funding, few of these children have consistent access to ECEC. Furthermore, many ECEC services do not have the capacity to address the complex needs of highly vulnerable children and their families.

EYERP is intended to assist with advocacy for improved access to ECEC for vulnerable children. The findings from the trial will provide a major increase in knowledge about 'what works' in the design of programs for these children in an urban environment in Australia. There is also the potential for establishing a stronger case for funding through the overall benefit–cost analysis of EYEP that is being done.

About the Early Years Education Program

The EYEP is offered by the Children's Protection Society (CPS), an independent not-for-profit child welfare organisation based in the north east of Melbourne. The CPS designed EYEP to target the particular needs of children in their early years who have been or are at risk of being abused or neglected.

There is substantial evidence that exposure to physical, emotional and/or sexual abuse and traumatic experiences early in life may have profound adverse effects on children's brain development (Perry, 2002; Shonkoff, 2012). Disruption to brain development affects the ability to learn, with recent studies, for example, showing that self-regulation is linked to the development of literacy and numeracy skills (Raver et al., 2011). Deficiencies in cognitive and social skills that develop before the age of five are likely to become the basis of problems such as low education attainment, unemployment, teenage pregnancy, and involvement in crime (Heckman, 2008).

EYEP has a dual focus: addressing the consequences of abuse and neglect on children's brain development, and redressing their learning difficulties. Key features of EYEP are: high staff:child ratios (1:3 for children under three years and 1:6 for children over three years), qualified staff, a rigorously developed curriculum, and the use of relationship-based pedagogy. An innovative feature of the program is an inter-disciplinary model, which includes an education leader who has graduate qualifications in early childhood curriculum (supported by a part-time early childhood curriculum consultant), an in-house infant mental health consultant, and family support consultant.

The objective of care in EYEP is to foster significant attachments for children who are likely to be experiencing disrupted and compromised attachment relationships in their home environments. The education model in EYEP is a pedagogically driven reflective teaching model that is child-focused and built on the EYLF (DEEWR, 2009). The EYEP model actively engages with parents to encourage ongoing participation in the program, as well as enhance their usage of all available health, educational and social services available, in order to improve outcomes for children.

The Early Years Education Research Program

The objective of the randomised controlled trial of EYEP is to determine whether the program can improve the school readiness of participants. Specific hypotheses to be tested are whether participation in EYEP causes: improved child outcomes such as better health and development outcomes; a higher level of academic ability and achievement; improved emotional and behavioural regulation; and reduced incidence of poor parenting practices and increased engagement by parents with neighbourhood and community services.

To be eligible for participation in EYEP, children must be aged from 0–3 years, assessed as having two or more risk factors as defined in the Best Interest Case Practice Model (a list of criteria specified by the-then Victorian Department of Human

Services, 2012), be currently engaged with family services or child protection services, and have early education as part of their care plan. Referrals of potential participants in the EYERP are made by case workers from child welfare services funded by the Victorian Department of Health and Human Services. Families who consent to participate in EYERP are randomly assigned into either the EYEP participation group or the control group. The participation group remain in EYEP for three years (or until school entry). The control group receives 'usual care' – a mix of parental and guardian care, as well as education and care provided by other local childcare centres or kindergartens. The usual care is determined by the child's parent(s) without any direction from EYERP or EYEP staff.

Data are being collected on an extensive set of outcome measures for participants in EYEP and the control group at baseline, at yearly intervals for three years, and six months after commencing the first year of school. The research will evaluate the impact of EYEP by comparing changes in outcome measures (at time of data collection minus at baseline) for children participating in EYEP with children in the control group. Estimates of the net impacts of EYEP will be translated into estimated monetary values, and these benefits aggregated to compare against the program costs, to provide a benefit–cost evaluation.

Advocacy at the practice level

Teachers who use advocacy as a strategy for advancing young children's learning and development have greater opportunity to make a difference to the quality and effectiveness of children's experiences. Influences on children's learning and development that are subject to advocacy effort are twofold in nature:

1. factors that *mediate* the child's sense of well-being, and his or her social and academic achievement outcomes. These exist within the child's ECEC or school setting and include: the nature of teacher–child and child–child interactions; the emotional, organisational and instructional support; the chosen curriculum and the activities available to engage the child and promote learning; the opportunities afforded to children to shape and influence the education program; the qualifications of staff; the staff:child ratio and size of the class group; and the materials and equipment available. In most cases, each of these factors is open to adjustment by teachers and leaders within the setting, and can be altered in the interest of better supporting children's learning and development
2. factors that *moderate* the child's outcomes. These may be found by reviewing the ecological systems surrounding the child (Bronfenbrenner, 1979) (see Introduction). They include:

   - material living conditions – such as the level of poverty in a household and the level of education of the child's primary caregivers
   - unemployment and government income support

- the cost and availability of housing
- the availability, quality and cost of health care
- the existence of discrimination or prejudice against groups – such as refugees (Newman, 2005; Penovic & Sifris, 2005), Indigenous peoples (Lampert et al., 2014), same-sex couples raising children (Rosato, 2006) and children with disabilities (Parish & Cloud, 2006; Hutchinson et al., 2014)
- relationship issues related to separation and custody arrangements (Parkinson, 2013)
- the availability and effectiveness of child advocacy and complaints mechanisms (Pithouse & Crowley, 2007).

Teachers who are committed to the best interests of children pay attention to issues for critical reflection, research evidence and risk minimisation. The importance of wider family and societal influences on the life chances of children, beyond what is in the direct control of teachers in their daily practice, is clearly acknowledged, yet some effort made to collaborate with other agencies towards the improvement of conditions surrounding the child and family can have a positive effect. In addition, building strong collaborative relationships and partnerships with families, community members and other early years professionals supports continuity of learning for children across the contexts in which they learn and grow. Sharing information enables teachers to create stronger links between the centre or school program and children's learning at home and in their communities. Parents can also discuss and implement learning activities at home with their children to consolidate and enhance the children's learning. Teachers can build on these partnerships to ensure that children and families are provided with the appropriate guidance to support the transitions across services and settings. These activities collectively build the conditions required to best support children's learning and development in the early years.

REFLECTION POINTS

1. Plan your advocacy response to the following two scenarios, by addressing the following questions:
   - How is change in the best interests of children?
   - Who are the decision makers? What advocacy has already been done in this area and what can you learn from it? Who might resist a change in decision and why?
   - How can the teacher document this effort and communicate it to others?

Scenario 1

A recent teacher graduate is one of three ECEC staff employed in a centre and working with 12 children aged 0–24 months. Over her first few weeks in the position she carefully observes the children and informally assesses their capabilities, having regard to all aspects of infant and toddler development.

She also studies the specific policies for practice in the room and takes notes about the practice. The teacher concludes that the children have good relationships with the other teachers, are emotionally well supported and have a range of interesting activities in which they engage; however, the quality of learning support for children is low. She feels confident in this judgement as she received training in how to assess the quality of learning support in ECEC rooms. She feels she needs to be an advocate for improving the learning support to children in the room in which she teaches.

Scenario 2

A teacher works in an area where the local council announces the cancellation of their professional development program. For the past 10 years staff received four training days per year and the teacher valued the content of this program and the opportunity to network with other teachers in her area. The teacher believes that the training has been important in improving the quality of local ECEC programs but has not collected any evidence to verify this. She also believes that the council decision will lead to poorer quality programs over time.

2. How will you remain alert to the possibilities to advocate for changes to practice in your setting?

PRACTICE CASE STUDY

Isabel Brookes

IMPLEMENTATION OF A COLLECTIVE VISION FOR SOCIAL EQUITY IN EDUCATION, HEALTH AND DEVELOPMENT

This case study represents a high-stakes response to redress widespread inadequacy within an existing early childhood education program at a site catering to children and families facing extensive disadvantage. The service is attended by some of the most vulnerable children within the community, and complex trauma from early experiences accounts for a high prevalence of clinical, behavioural and emotional disorders. The response is to develop and implement an improvement strategy focused on ensuring that children access a high-quality learning program that integrates health and development support.

Background

Children identified as experiencing high levels of disadvantage, neglect and trauma have a markedly increased risk of poor outcomes. National data indicates that

Aboriginal children are especially vulnerable to these factors, illustrated through low levels of engagement with education and high levels of chronic health problems within Aboriginal cohorts (Wise, 2013; Silburn et al., 2009; Urbis Australia, 2014). In acknowledgement of these data, the executive responsible for a remote multifunctional Aboriginal children's service are taking action to improve the service provision and management of children's learning and development in the birth-to-five-years age span.

Response plan

The team arranged internal and external assessment of the centre practices, consulted within all levels of the organisation and with external parties, and produced an improvement plan focused on:

1. achieving positive learning and development outcomes
2. aligning daily operations with the NQF
3. transitioning to an 'approved service' enabling 'childcare benefit' revenue to sustain improvements beyond the initial investment.

To meet these outcomes, effort was concentrated on three areas: the educational program, the workforce and inter-professional collaboration.

The educational program

A plethora of evidence was available about early learning experiences and conditions that ameliorate disadvantage, and the components of high-quality programs, especially for vulnerable children. Young children who are vulnerable, because of familial and community characteristics, are demonstrated to be at persistent risk of doing poorly over time, with intervention by pre-school age ineffective at improving poor developmental trajectories (Tayler, Cloney & Niklas, 2015). There was a strong need to act to ensure the children currently accessing the centre received high-quality early learning experiences.

Drawing on the research literature, and existing programs targeted at changing the trajectories of children experiencing adverse life courses (Jordan et al., 2014), the structural components of the educational program were adapted to meet children's requirements for education and care. An educational leader was appointed with greater non-contact than teaching time to provide staff support, adult:child ratios were improved (1:3 for 0–35 months, 1:6 for 36–60 months) to enhance 1:1 interactions; each child was assigned a primary caregiver for consistency of care; and a trauma-informed, evidence-based children's learning program was put into place.

The workforce

Deficiencies in the program stemmed in part from negative workplace culture that was present, manifest through persistent staff absenteeism, poor service management and toxic staff relationships. Over time, this resulted in an inability to meet the basic requirements of service provision. To change this culture and build staff capacity: training was provided; position descriptions were revised; casual contracts were changed to fixed-term appointments; and expectations of staff to deliver against the outcomes of the improvement plan were incorporated into performance appraisals. The leadership team and teachers together engaged in professional learning to build knowledge about child trauma, effective interactions, and conditions in the environment to support children's sense of security and connectedness.

Inter-professional collaboration

Despite the centre being co-located with child and allied health service programs, prior to the development of the response there was little interaction between the education and health services. This disconnect had a dual impact: children at the centre were not receiving the additional support they required to participate in the learning program, and staff were unable to develop and deliver an appropriate program due to high incidences of disruptive behaviour. A strong enabler of this collaboration was the unswaying agreement among all involved that change *must* occur, and that improving children's educational and health outcomes was a common endeavour. New referral pathways are developed for the children at the centre, and individual learning and development plans are created. To maintain focus on the intended outcomes, and build relationships between the education, health, development and family support programs, the staff are engaged in shared professional learning experiences.

Governance

A steering committee was established to oversee the development and implementation of the improvement strategy, with membership including internal representatives from across the education, health and family support service teams and external representatives, including child protection agents and researchers working with the organisation in child learning and development research. It was clear that a number of 'threshold conditions' needed to be in place to achieve the massive change necessary to implement the improvement plan. These conditions included significant investment in human and material resources, cohesion across the early years division, and stipulations about engagement from all levels of leadership. Each condition was mapped to the NQF and, when collectively addressed, allowed for a strong foundation for improvement. An improvement strategy leadership was defined within the organisation responsible for leading and monitoring the implementation of the response.

Many challenges still exist, including navigating the integration of existing services and building the coordinated approach to service provision across education, health and family support activities. However, the demands of pursuing this approach are not to impact negatively on the ability of programs to deliver their services to existing clients, and the integration must be meaningful. Furthermore, the engagement of families and carers is complex since children living with child protection orders have diverse care arrangements ranging from foster care, to family day care operators and group care. Buy-in across these carer categories is mixed and children often move between each type of care with little warning. Developing a response that provides appropriate pathways for engagement for each of these care types is an ongoing priority. Early efforts have included regular communication about the implementation of improvement strategy, and increasing the number of family and carer events at the centre. Brokering and navigating a collective of people, and mobilising a community to make a coordinated effort to make a difference to children's learning and development, demands effective leadership and the commitment of all involved.

Conclusion

The case has been made in this chapter for advocacy to be considered as an important part of the teacher's role in improving children's learning and development outcomes. Using research evidence helps frame advocacy efforts within a strong professional and ethical position. This is essential. The level of any policy change sought has implications for what alliances may be necessary in attempting to bring about change. Being a strong advocate for children can lead to significant improvements in children's learning and development and, after all, that is the main purpose of the profession.

Further reading

Australian Human Rights Commission. (AHRC). (2015). *Immigration detention statistics*. Retrieved from www.humanrights.gov.au/immigration-detention-statistics

Cloney, D., Cleveland, G., Hattie, J., & Tayler, C. (2015). Variations in the availability and quality of early childhood education and care by socioeconomic status of neighbourhoods. *Early Education and Development*. Advance online publication. DOI: http://doi.org/10.1080/10409289.2015.1076674

Cohen, K. R., Lee, C. M., & McIlwraith, R. (2012). The psychology of advocacy and the advocacy of psychology. *Canadian Psychology*, *53*(3), 151–8. DOI: http://doi.org/10.1037/a0027823

Council of Australian Governments (COAG). (2015). 'Closing the Gap in Indigenous Disadvantage'. Retrieved from www.coag.gov.au/closing_the_gap_in_indigenous_disadvantage

Gilley, T., Tayler, C., Niklas, F., & Cloney, D. S. (2015). Too late and not enough for some children: Early childhood education and care (ECEC) program usage patterns in the years before school in Australia. *International Journal of Child Care and Education Policy*, *9*(1). DOI: http://doi.org/10.1186/s40723-015-0012-0

Victorian Department of Education and Training (2015). 'About VCAMS'. Retrieved from www.education.vic.gov.au/about/research/Pages/infosystem.aspx

References

Ang, L. (2014). Vital voices for vital years in Singapore: one country's advocacy for change in the early years sector. *International Journal of Early Years Education*, *22*(3), 329–41. DOI: http://doi.org/10.1080/09669760.2014.911695

Australian Children's Education and Care Quality Authority (ACECQA). (2011). *Guide to the National Quality Standard*. Retrieved from http://files.acecqa.gov.au/files/National-Quality-Framework-Resources-Kit/NQF03-Guide-to-NQS-130902.pdf

Australian Institute of Health and Welfare. (AIHW) (2015). *Child Protection Australia 2013–14*. Child Welfare Series No. 61. Canberra: Australian Institute of Health and Wellbeing.

Bond, M. (1998). Advocating for children of separating parents. *Children & Society*, *12*(1), 12–24. DOI: http://doi.org/10.1111/j.1099-0860.1998.tb00041.x

Bowes, A., & Sim, D. (2006). Advocacy for black and minority ethnic communities: understandings and expectations. *The British Journal of Social Work*, *36*(7), 1209–25. DOI: http://doi.org/10.1093/bjsw/bch383

Briggs, F. (1991). Child Protection Programs: can they protect young children. *Early Childhood Development and Care*, *67*, 61–72.

Bronfenbrenner, U. (1979). *The Ecology of Human Development*. Cambridge, MA: Harvard University Press.

Bullock, H. E., & Lott, B. (2001). Building a research and advocacy agenda on issues of economic justice. *Analyses of Social Issues and Public Policy*, *1*(1), 147–62.

Carter, J. (1988). *Mandatory Reporting and Child Abuse. Policy in Practice Series (2)*. Melbourne: Brotherhood of St Laurence.

Cashmore, J. (2002). Promoting the participation of children and young people in care. *Child Abuse and Neglect, 26*(8), 837–47.

Coburn, C. (2005) The role of non-system actors in the relationship between policy and practice: the case of reading instruction in California. *Educational Evaluation and Policy Analysis, 27*(1), 23–52.

Cohen, E. S. (2004). Advocacy and advocates: definitions and ethical dimensions. *Generations, 28*(1), 9–16. DOI: https://search.ebscohost.com/login. aspx?direct = true&db = sih&AN = 13579484&site = ehost-live

Council of Australian Governments (COAG). (2009). *Investing in the Early Years – A National Early Childhood Development Strategy*. An initiative of the Council of Australian Governments. Canberra: Commonwealth of Australia.

Cummins, P., Scott, D., & Scales, B. (2012). *Report of the Protecting Victoria's Vulnerable Children Inquiry Volume 1*. Melbourne: Department of Premier and Cabinet.

Delfabbro, P., Barber, J., & Cooper, L. (2002). Children in out-of-home care in South Australia: baseline analysis from a three-year longitudinal study. *Children & Youth Services Review, 24*(12), 917–32.

Department of Education, Employment and Workplace Relations (DEEWR). (2009). *Belonging, Being & Becoming: An Early Years Learning Framework for Australia*. Canberra: DEEWR.

Early Childhood Australia (ECA). (2016). *Code of Ethics*. Canberra: Early Childhood Australia.

Early Childhood Australia & Australian Human Rights Commission (ECA & AHRC). (2015). *Supporting Young Children's Rights. Statement of Intent (2015–2018)*. Canberra: Early Childhood Australia.

Flottman, R., & Page, J. (2012). Getting early childhood onto the Reform Agenda: an Australian case study. *International Journal of Child Care and Education Policy. 6*(1), 17–33.

Gilley, T., & Taylor, J. (1995). *Unequal Lives? Low Income and the Life Chances of Three Year Olds*. Melbourne: The Brotherhood of St Laurence.

Gromada, H., & Greenspan, E. (1974). Working together for children: a child advocacy system. *Child Welfare, 53*(6), 380–5. DOI: https://search.ebscohost.com/login. aspx?direct = true&db = sih&AN = 24411724&site = ehost-live

Han, H. S., & Thomas, S. (2010). No child misunderstood: enhancing early childhood teachers' multicultural responsiveness to the social competence of diverse children. *Early Childhood Education Journal, 37*(6) 469–76.

Heckman, J. (2008). Schools, skills and synapses. *Economic Inquiry, 46*(3), 289–324.

Humphreys, C., & Absler, D. (2011). History repeating: child protection responses to domestic violence.*Child & Family Social Work, 16*(4) 464–73.

Hutchinson, N. L., Pyle, A., Villeneuve, M., Dods, J., Dalton, C. J., & Minnes, P. (2014). Understanding parent advocacy during the transition to school of children with developmental disabilities: three Canadian cases. *Early Years: Journal of International Research & Development, 34*(4), 348–63. DOI: http://doi.org/10.1080/09575146.2014.967662

Jackson, S. L. (2004). A USA national survey of program services provided by child advocacy centers. *Child Abuse and Neglect, 28*(4), 411–21. DOI: http://doi.org/10.1016/j.chiabu.2003.09.020

Jordan, B., Tseng, Y., Coombs N., Kennedy A., & Borland, J. (2014). Improving lifetime trajectories for vulnerable young children and families living with significant stress and social disadvantage. *BMC Public Health, 14,* 965. Retrieved from www.biomedcentral.com/1471-2458/14/965

Kiraly, M., & Humphreys, C. (2015). A tangled web: parental contact for children in kinship care. *Child & Family Social Work, 20*(1), 106–15.

Lampert, J., Burnett, B., Martin, R., & McCrea, L. (2014). Lessons from a face-to-face meeting on embedding Aboriginal and Torres Strait Islander perspectives: 'A contract of intimacy'. *Australasian Journal of Early Childhood, 39*(1), 82–8. DOI: http://search.informit.com.au/documentSummary;dn = 192656106444395;res = IELHSS

Laney, L. (2003). *Advocacy Assessment Guidelines.* Wallingford, UK: CIMRC.

May, H. (2006). 'Being Froebelian': an Antipodean analysis of the history of advocacy and early childhood. *History of Education: Journal of the History of Education Society, 35*(2), 245–62. DOI: http://doi.org/10.1080/00467600500528586

McDonald, M. J. (1995). The citizens' committee for children of New York and the evolution of child advocacy (1945–1972). *Child Welfare, 74*(1), 283–304. DOI: https://search.ebscohost.com/login.aspx?direct = true&db = sih&AN = 24227235&site = ehost-live

National Scientific Council on the Developing Child. (2007). The science of early childhood development: closing the gap between what we know and what we do. Working Paper. Retrieved from www.developingchild.net

Newman, B. (2005). From classrooms to the streets and back again: real rights for refugee children. *International Journal of Equity and Innovation in Early Childhood, 3*(2), 90–3.

Newman, L. K., Dudley, M., & Steel, Z. (2008). Asylum, detention, and mental health in Australia. *Refugee Survey Quarterly, 27*(3), 110–27. DOI: http://doi.org/10.1093/rsq/hdn034

Oberklaid, F. (2014). Advocacy for early childhood framing the message. *Every Child, 20*(4), 3. DOI: http://search.informit.com.au/documentSummary;dn = 734763771764805;res = IELHSS

Parish, S., & Cloud, J. (2006). Financial wellbeing of young children with disabilities and their families. *Social Work, 51*(3), 223–32.

Parkinson, P. (2013). Violence, abuse and the limits of shared parental responsibility. *Family Matters, 92*(1), 7–17. DOI: http://search.informit.com.au/documentSummary;dn = 439256220455683;res = IELFSC

Penovic, T., & Sifris, A. (2005). Like a bird in a cage: children's voices and challenges in Australia's immigration detention scheme. *International Journal of Equity and Innovation in Early Childhood, 3*(2), 32–44.

Perry, B. (2002). Childhood experience and the expression of genetic potential: what childhood neglect tells us about nature and nurture. *Brain and Mind, 3,* 79–100.

Petrasek, D. (2014). Global trends and the future of human rights advocacy. *Sur: International Journal on Human Rights, 11*(20), 44–55.

Pithouse, A., & Crowley, A. (2007). Adults rule? Children, advocacy and complaints to social services. *Children & Society, 21*(3), 201–13. DOI: http://dx.doi.org.ezp.lib.unimelb.edu.au/10.1111/j.1099-0860.2006.00051.x

Productivity Commission (2014). *Child Care and Early Childhood Learning Draft Report.* Canberra: Commonwealth of Australia.

Raver, C. C., Jones, S. M., Li-Grining, C., Zhai, F., Bub K., & Pressler, E. (2011). CSRP's impact on low-income pre-schoolers pre academic skills: self-regulation as a mediating mechanism. *Child Development, 82,* 362–78.

Rolandsen Agustin, L. (2008). Civil society participation in EU gender policy-making: framing strategies and institutional constraints. *Parliamentary Affairs, 61*(3), 505–17.

Rosato, J. (2006). Children of same-sex parents deserve the security blanket of the parentage assumption. *Family Court Review, 44*(1), 74–86. DOI: http://doi.org/10.1111/j.1744-1617.2006.00068.x

Ross, R. J. S. (1977). Problems of advocacy. *Journal of Sociology and Social Welfare, 4*(8), 1246–59.

Saltmarsh, J. (1996). Education for critical citizenship: John Dewey's contribution to the pedagogy of community service learning. *Michigan Journal of Community Service Learning, 3*(1), 13–21.

Shonkoff, J. P. (2012). Leveraging the biology of adversity to address the roots of disparities in health and development. *Proceedings of the National Academy of Sciences, 109*(Supplement 2), 17302–7.

Silburn, S., Brinkman, S., Ferguson-Hill, S., Styles, I., Walker, R., & Shepherd, C. (2009). *The Australian Early Development Index (AEDI) Indigenous Adaptation Study.* Perth: Curtin University of Technology and Telethon Institute for Child Health Research.

Spillane, J., Reiser, B., & Reimer, T. (2002). Policy implementation and cognition: reframing and refocusing implementation research. *Review of Educational Research, 72*(3), 387–431.

Tarren-Sweeney, M., & Hazell, P. (2006). Mental health of children in foster and kinship care in New South Wales, Australia. *Journal of Paediatrics and Child Health*, *42*(3), 89–97.

Tayler C., Cloney, D., & Niklas, F. (2015). A bird in the hand: understanding the trajectories of development of young children and the need for action to improve outcomes. *Australasian Journal of Early Childhood*, *40*(3), 51–60.

Tayler, C., Ishimine, K., Cloney, D., Cleveland, G., & Thorpe, K. (2013). The quality of early childhood education and care services in Australia. *Australasian Journal of Early Childhood*, *38*(2), 13–21.

Taylor, J., & Nelms, L. (2008). *School Engagement and Life Chances at 15 and 16*. Melbourne: Brotherhood of St Laurence.

Thiara, R. K., & Humphreys C., (2015). Absent presence: the ongoing impact of men's violence on the mother–child relationship. *Child & Family Social Work*. Published online 5 January. DOI: http://doi.org/10.1111/cfs.12210

United Nations. (1989). *United Nations Convention on the Rights of the Child*. Geneva: Office of the United Nations High Commissioner for Human Rights.

Urbis Australia. (2014). *Evaluation of the National Partnership Agreement on Indigenous Early Childhood Development. Final Report*. Canberra: Australian Government. Retrieved from www.coag.gov.au

Victorian Government Department of Human Services. (2012). *Best Interests Case Study Practice Guide*. Melbourne: Victorian Government Department of Human Services.

Wise, S. (2013). Improving the early life outcomes of Indigenous children: implementing early childhood development at the local level. Issues Paper No. 6 for Closing the Gap Clearing House Canberra: Australian Government, Australian Institute of Health and Welfare, Australian Institute of Family Studies.

CHAPTER 8

Research for learning and teaching

Amelia Church, Jane Page, Susan Wright and Collette Tayler

LEARNING OBJECTIVES

In this chapter you will:

1. consider the role of research in building understanding of how children learn and how teaching can affect positive outcomes for children
2. learn about methodologies commonly used in research in early childhood education and care programs, and how teachers and young children can be active researchers
3. discover how research methods inform a systematic and intentional approach in supporting learning and teaching
4. consider the ethical issues particular to research with young children in early childhood programs.

Introduction

Research in early childhood education and care (ECEC) programs is increasingly focused on the practices or process of high-quality teaching in early learning settings

Research: systematic, transparent and replicable inquiry.

and the primacy of learning with families in the home environment. Furthermore, research in ECEC is drawing policy attention to the importance of very early learning in the period from birth to the age of three, as evidence from neuroscience underscores the significance of early experiences for a child's brain development

Methodologies: approaches to research, informed by the paradigmatic (worldview) and philosophical stance of the researcher.

and functioning (see also Chapter 1 and Chapter 2). Research in ECEC necessarily acknowledges children's rights (see also Chapter 3) as a core consideration of research design. Over the past four decades, a great deal of work has been done in adapting or

Methods: the strategies, tools or techniques researchers use to gather evidence.

establishing **methodologies** and **methods** that enable children's voices to be heard. This chapter is informed by these two key influences – how evidence contributes to our understanding of

learning and teaching in the early years, and how research ethics is a central platform of ECEC research – and focuses on approaches to research. Each case study in this chapter is drawn from contemporary research projects in early childhood and they each illustrate methods that are productive in eliciting children's experiences and knowledge. These three research case studies in turn highlight the role research plays in shaping practice and policy in early learning and teaching.

The role research plays in shaping practice and policy in early learning and teaching

Research plays an important role in the lives of teachers. Throughout this text we highlight the ways in which research:

- provides evidence of what constitutes effective high-quality teaching, and learning practices and processes
- influences the policies that frame the roles of teachers
- provides insights into the complexities and nuances of advancing young children's learning across diverse social and cultural contexts
- supports families with distinct and differing learning interests and priorities.

As teachers, it is important that we have an understanding of research, how it has influenced policy, how it impacts on our roles, how we can interpret it to build improved learning outcomes for children, and how we can build contemporary knowledge of evidence-based teaching and learning practices, and policies for interpretation and integration, into our educational programs.

In the past decade in Australia, we have seen a strong emphasis on the development of research-informed policy. The National Early Childhood Development Strategy (NECDS), for example, outlined neuroscience and economics research findings to argue a case for investing in early childhood education (Commonwealth of Australia, 2009, p. 9). The policy also drew on Australian data to establish the inequities that exist for Australian children to further establish priorities for how that investment could be directed. For example, the NECDS used research data which established that Australian children, especially Indigenous children, have lower health and well-being outcomes compared with those from other OECD countries (Commonwealth of Australia, 2009, p. 10). At the same time, the NECDS outlined international research that established the impact early learning relationships have on young children's future learning and health, identified the multiple risk factors impacting on young children's learning and development, and named the teaching and learning interventions that are known to positively impact on young children's learning outcomes and development (Commonwealth of Australia, 2009, pp. 4, 8, 33). In this way, research was key to providing the evidence required to justify investment in early childhood education, and shaping the strategic directions and priorities required for building stronger educational futures for young children.

Importantly, the NECDS was an across-governments (Federal, State and territory) initiative that identified research as a major means through which government could monitor and evaluate its priorities and, in turn, inform future policy and strategy (Commonwealth of Australia, 2009, p. 25). The NECDS outlined several key ways in which research would be used for this purpose including:

> consistent unit record information and a comprehensive national minimum data set to support the early childhood development strategy; improving the dissemination of the evidence about early childhood development; improving reporting (building on existing data development and reporting initiatives); implementing a national research agenda; building the evidence base around innovative and integrated service delivery. (2009, p. 30)

At the same time, the NECDS supported governments in being transparent about the impact and outcomes of their policies and strategies, and how they informed future policy directions so to 'ensure effective policy responses for Australian children and their families' (Commonwealth of Australia, 2009, p. 7). This, in turn, has led to a commitment at national, State and local levels of government to develop the capacity to produce evidence of the impact of their policy initiatives. The Commonwealth Government has invested in the following significant new national data collections to evaluate and monitor Australia's early childhood policy objectives in recent years.

- *The Australian Early Development Census* (AEDC, 2015) monitors children's development every three years for children in their first year of primary school.
- Children's access and participation in pre-school programs and child care are reported annually (ABS, 2015).
- *The National Early Childhood Education and Care Workforce Census* has been conducted in 2010 and 2013 (Social Research Centre, 2014).

The following case study highlights the ways in which the Victorian Curriculum and Assessment Authority (VCAA), along with the Victorian Department of Education and Training (then known as DEECD), actively engaged in research with researchers and practitioners to build evidence of teachers' experiences in implementing new assessment practices outlined in their then-new *Victorian Early Years Learning and Development Framework* (VEYLDF), and the impact this had on providing further support for teachers in the context of reform.

POLICY CASE STUDY

Carmel Phillips and Jane Page

BUILDING EVIDENCE OF TEACHERS' IMPLEMENTATION OF ASSESSMENT FOR LEARNING PRACTICES IN A PERIOD OF RAPID REFORM AND CHANGE

As an independent statutory body responsible to the Victorian Minister for Education, the mission of the VCAA is to provide high-quality curriculum, assessment and reporting that promotes individual life-long learning. The key role of the VCAA Early Years Unit is to support implementation of the VEYLDF (DEECD, 2009). This implementation support is enacted within a collaborative partnership with the Department of Education and Training (DET), formerly the Department of Education and Early Childhood Development (DEECD).

The VEYLDF was released in November 2009 for implementation from 2010. It adopted the five learning outcomes from the National Early Years Learning Framework (EYLF) (2009) (whose scope is children from birth to age five years) and developed eight practice principles to support young children's learning and development from birth to eight years. The Victorian early childhood system is envisioned as an integrated system, including maternal and child health services and schools. The introduction of the VEYLDF created new challenges for teachers in relation to advancing positive outcomes for children. Ongoing implementation of the VEYLDF requires, and has produced, significant change in practice for many teachers. The new challenge and opportunity for the VCAA was to develop collaborative research partnerships with researchers, policy makers and a broad range of multidisciplinary practitioners to strengthen the confidence, knowledge and skills of teachers implementing the VEYLDF.

It is understood that effective implementation of a new learning framework, in a period of national reform, will occur when teachers have the opportunity to build their knowledge base and skills, and build confidence in new practices (VCAA, 2012). This is particularly important in relation to assessment practices. In 2009, an independent trial and validation of the draft VEYLDF identified a staged implementation with progressive feedback on successes and challenges as a useful communication mechanism supporting teachers' knowledge engagement and application of the VEYLDF. In 2010, a project charter was developed to support the successful implementation of the VEYLDF. This charter was formulated around six key intentions that included:

1. improving outcomes for all Victorian children from birth to eight years of age
2. improving collaborative, effective and reflective practices of all early childhood professionals
3. strengthening family and community awareness of the importance of the early childhood period for learning and development
4. improving integration of practice across services within the early childhood system to advance children's learning and development
5. supporting families to support young children's learning and development in the home and community
6. building strong and equal partnerships between all early childhood professionals (VCAA, 2012).

The VCAA designed and delivered a series of professional learning programs with researchers and professionals to advance teachers' effective implementation of the VEYLDF: the Outcomes Project 2010–11 (VCAA, 2012), the Assessment for Learning and Development Project 2012 (VCAA, 2013) and the Inquiry to Implementation Project 2013 (IIP) (Monash University, 2014). From the outset of this process, the VCAA identified a collaborative research model as a key platform on which the intent and content of this suite of professional learning programs would be built and evaluated. The content of these programs was developed in collaboration with key researchers, policy makers and teachers, and informed by research on the most effective way for teachers to work together with children and families to support a continuum of learning and development. The programs positioned teachers as researchers building assessment evidence and high-quality practices with children, their families and other across-disciplines early childhood professionals.

The programs adopted a professional inquiry/action research approach to learning where participants focused on an issue relevant to their context, and observed, documented and analysed evidence of children's learning. This occurred within an action research cycle of problem formulation, planning action, taking action, data collection, critical evaluation of the data and reporting outcomes for further planning (VCAA, 2012). Throughout these projects, data and evidence were collected from participants. The VCAA used the data to monitor and measure the usefulness of each professional learning program in supporting teachers' implementation of the VEYLDF. Practice changes from the learning programs were documented to support engagement with the VEYLDF. The data, in turn, informed the development of future professional learning programs with a strengthened focus on assessment practice. This approach ensured that the VCAA was responsive to the experiences of teachers working across a diverse range of early years settings in Victoria. This included maternal and child health, family day care, supported playgroups, early childhood intervention services, long day care, kindergarten, outside school hours care and the early years of school.

In addition, two external and independent evaluations, commissioned by VCAA, provided additional information about the next steps. The first was a state-wide process evaluation of the implementation of VEYLDF from 2010–11. This research provided important additional data on the reach, engagement and impact of the implementation of the VEYLDF activities and resources, and identified the barriers, enablers and inhibitors experienced by early childhood professionals (Griffith University, 2012). The second was a review and evaluation of the IIP (Monash University, 2014). It provided independent feedback on the impact of the IIP and explored the implications for up-scaling this work across professional learning networks in the future.

These collaborative research partnerships continue to play an important role in VCAA directions to build evidence of the daily experiences of teachers critically reflecting on practice in a period of reform. This evidence is vital in informing VCAA and DET directions to design a range of learning opportunities and resources that continue to challenge, influence and advance assessment practices across the early years. Systematic evidence-based research, within a period of rapid reform and change, is the key to disrupting long-held beliefs and practices in relation to assessment practices. The opportunity to be part of this sustained engagement and focus has strengthened attention, knowledge, regard and respect between teachers, early childhood professionals and researchers. The documented transformation in collaborative practices through targeted professional learning programs continues to improve the everyday learning experiences of young children, and informed the project to update the VEYLDF and produce a second edition in 2016.

REFLECTION POINTS

1. How familiar are you with the international and Australian research that has informed polices at national, State and local levels of government? What research has been most influential in shaping the recent National Reform Agenda?
2. Select a policy and note the ways in which it has been informed by research. How does this research frame contemporary teaching and learning in the early years? What questions or issues does this research raise for you? How might this research impact on your thinking and actions regarding what constitutes high-quality learning support to young children and families?
3. How will you access research as a practising teacher to keep informed of contemporary research findings and design your own local research studies? What journals, websites and organisations can support you to keep abreast of research?

Types of research in the early years

Understanding how research has informed and influenced major ECEC systems-reform priorities supports teachers to see the praxis between research, policy and practice, and the ways in which research has actively shaped contemporary understandings of teachers' and children's roles in the teaching and learning processes. This knowledge is further supported by an exploration of what research involves, the challenges of doing research, and the common approaches and methods that can be used to generate new knowledge about teaching and learning in the early years.

There are number of approaches that can be used when researching in the early childhood profession. Some common approaches that are used include surveys, ethnography, case studies and action research (Mukherji & Albon, 2015). Studies can range from large-scale, longitudinal research (e.g. Effective Pre-School and Primary Education Project (EPPE), Effective Early Educational Experiences (E4Kids)) to closely honed, detailed analyses (e.g. 20–60 minute interactions between an adult and child, e.g. Wright, 2010; Church, 2010). Decisions about what approach to use in ECEC research are strongly aligned with the purpose of the research. For instance, large-scale longitudinal research aims to study trends across a period of time, and across the population, and requires a big enough sample to be able to run sophisticated statistics to describe such trends. By comparison, closely honed case studies aim to understand and illustrate the particular rather than the general, such as the *how* of teaching and learning, through detailed analyses of child–teacher interactions, often involving a small number of participants. Furthermore, contemporary research into ECEC may combine large-scale study that seeks to generalise findings to populations or systems with small-scale, probing studies that are nested within the large-scale design. This approach can produce specific, fine-grained details of processes or experiences and outcomes related to certain subject matters or for particular constituent groups. For example, the findings about shared sustained thinking were generated from case studies that were conducted within a large-scale EPPE research project (Sylva et al., 2004; Siraj & Asani, 2015). In brief, contemporary study designs, that are set to investigate problems related to ECEC and children's learning, development and well-being, may draw from both quantitative and qualitative methodologies and investigate both at scale and locally – 'in situ' – in order to learn about the impact of different practices on the experience and outcomes of children (Cresswell, 2013). Both large-scale and small, closely honed studies generate new knowledge about teaching and learning in the early years, and provide valuable insights that can be applied across systems and services depending on the scope and approach of the research.

Decisions about what 'drives' the research, what is considered to be most important for the particular study, are linked to the researchers' epistemology – their fundamental beliefs about what constitutes knowledge. What is knowledge and how is it acquired? And what knowledge is pertinent to the field of ECEC, or to the processes of learning, or to the development of 'child agency', or to cognitive and embodied meaning making through the arts, and so on. In addition, research is influenced by the theoretical orientations that the researcher employs to frame the research. The theoretical lens employed in the research will, in turn, influence the design of the research, including its rationale, aims, methods and analysis of the data. New understandings of teaching and learning in the early years has been generated through many theoretical perspectives including, for example, developmental, socio-cultural, economic, post-structural, post-modern, critical, post-colonial and ethics of care. Researching through different theoretical lenses assists us to rethink teaching and learning from multiple perspectives and to address the diverse range of factors that shape teaching and learning processes in the early years. Understanding the theoretical orientation of research can support us to recognise the beliefs that drive the research and to situate it in the broader research literature.

Decisions about how data are to be interpreted and reported are closely linked to the research project's rationale, aims, specific questions or hunches, and the level and type of detail that are required to present defensible 'claims' about what the research tells us. To illustrate, one means of interpretation, which is particularly relevant to the projects reported within this chapter, is *hermeneutics*. Hermeneutics covers the 'theory of understanding and interpretation of linguistic and non-linguistic expressions' (Ramberg & Gjesdal, 2005). In other words, expression covers a broad range of symbolic means of communication – visual, physical, spatial – such as graphic communication, gestural communication or human relational communication within space (e.g. proximity versus far apart).

Research that focuses on 'human life and existence' (the fundamental concern of hermeneutics) sits well with contemporary ECEC praxis. This is because 'social constructivism', a common theoretical lens used to understand 'knowledge' and how knowledge is acquired, is often used in fields involving young children (e.g. Reggio Emilia, Vygotskian principles of zone of proximal development (ZPD), learner-centeredness, social and cultural emphasis on knowledge acquisition). For instance, the Reggio Emilia metaphor of the '100 languages' of childhood is to see all symbolic communication – language, dance, drawing, music, play – as important in the early years. Indeed, as Vygotsky emphasised, the arts are a 'first' language or literacy of the young child (McArdle & Wright, 2014).

In terms of the link between ECEC and artists' 'languages', one particular social-constructivist orientation that is helpful for understanding 'quality' learning and teaching, which is particularly pertinent to this chapter, is 'qualities of quality' (Seidel et al., 2009, pp. 29–45). A fundamental tenet of 'qualities of quality' is that the most important indication of excellence in arts education is the quality of students' learning experiences, rather than the quality of the artworks they produce. For example, emphasis is given to adults engaging with students in explicit conversations about the artistic decisions they are making and these artworks, in turn, are regarded as evidence of learning. Such evidence is gathered over time through the use of portfolios, reflections, photographs, videos and audio recordings. The role of the documentation of learning in action is a valued component of this process, as it provides a record of what actually happens during artistic experiences

(Chemi, 2014), and becomes a catalyst for discussing the learning taking place in these experiences in reflective, analytic ways (Rinaldi, 2006) (see Chapter 4). An important component of this work is that teachers must view the artworks of their students as more than aesthetic objects, viewing them instead as sites of learning and evidence of understanding (Leavy, 2009).

Evidence of understanding is a common goal for researchers interested in young children's learning but what constitutes this evidence depends on the theoretical orientation, main research question(s) and methodology of the research project. For example, what counts as evidence in rights-based research with young children would include communication strategies that harness and build on children's capabilities and talents to express their views, and will assist young children to participate more directly and effectively in research (O'Kane, 2000). This could include activities and materials such as drawing, mapping, flow diagrams, diaries, photography, dolls, puppets, play dough, drama stories and songs, narratives, videos and social interactions. Rights-based research would also acknowledge the range of languages that are possible to engage young children meaningfully, and individual children's preferred modes of communication, including gaze, facial expression and body movement (Flewitt, 2005; Samuelsson, 2004), sign language, expressive body language or sounds (Alderson, 2001).

Communicating research

Researchers have a responsibility to communicate the findings of their research not only to participants but to the broader community. Findings may be communicated through action, including change to practices and provision, and research practitioners may seek to share the findings of their research with their own professional network, as the issues instigating the research are likely to be of interest to the immediate local settings. Typically, research dissemination would take the form of presenting papers at academic and professional conferences, and peer-reviewed articles in journals concerned with learning and teaching in the early years. Yet researchers should also seek to share the 'so what' of the project outcomes, making details accessible to practitioners through websites, reports, briefings, professional newsletters, and professional development where appropriate and possible.

Importantly, the reader is not a passive recipient of published research; instead ECEC teachers review research for the relevance of their own professional contexts and the learning needs of the children in their care. Developing the capacity to be a critical reader of research is a graduate skill required of all practitioners in the field, so that they can draw on available and useful research to inform practice and reflections on practice. As professional learning is an ongoing process, so is the progress of research in ECEC that seeks to contribute to knowledge, and acknowledge the work of others with an awareness that each small piece adds to our greater understanding of children's abilities. The following case studies provide examples of small, recently published studies that add to our understanding of the *process* of learning and teaching in the early years.

RESEARCH-PRACTICE CASE STUDY

Wan Yi Lee

ADULT–CHILD INTERACTIONS: PROMOTING CREATIVITY IN CHILDREN'S DRAWING

This study investigated children's creativity in their drawing processes, focusing on creative thinking and creative processes in relation to modes of meaning making, as well as how adult–child interactions promote creativity while the child is drawing. The goal of the study was to increase the appreciation of children's creativity in their graphic, narrative-embodied play and to advocate the part played by adults in supporting children in their play.

Within an interpretivist paradigm, this was a small-scale practitioner-based case study undertaken in a kindergarten located in an inner-west suburb of Melbourne. A total of 10 children's drawing experiences, with adult–child interactions, were video recorded in a kindergarten room setting. Video observation allowed the researcher to revisit data that contained aesthetic, emotional and intellectual responses, such as in the graphic, narrative and embodied modes in children's drawing processes, as well as the verbal and non-verbal interactions between participants. The transcriptions of video were read, coded and analysed for creative thinking and creative processes, using the frameworks for children's creativity in relation to modes of meaning making (see Wright, 2010; Robson, 2014).

The EYLF states that 'Developing dispositions such as curiosity, persistence and creativity enables children to participate in and gain from learning' (DEEWR, 2009, p. 33). This educational focus on creativity is based on the belief that creativity is foundational for success in all learning areas and that promoting creativity enables children to understand and appreciate the genuine meaning of becoming literate and numerate (Robinson, 1999).

Despite the uniqueness of each child, there seems to be a number of similar themes and conditions between children's drawings that the adult can be aware of to better understand and support the child in his/her drawing experience. Firstly, the drawings in this study suggest some common themes that children at kindergarten age are interested in exploring. These themes may include spatial relationship, elements in the sky, weather, buildings, people and colours. In Figure 8.1, for example, the child is using verbal and embodied expressions to explain how a drawn thunderstorm unfolds – saying 'thunder, thunder, thunder' while shaking the drawing paper in the air to make thundery noise. The adult asks the child earlier if she heard the thunderstorm the other night, linking the child's drawing to real experience. Making this link supports the child's meaning making and creativity. Yet these themes should not be considered as things to look for in children's drawings; rather the teacher tries to understand the intentions and meanings behind drawings to support the child's creativity. Furthermore, intertextuality was evident in the children's drawings, highlighting the prevalence of popular media in children's meaning-making process. Knowing the child's favourite stories, films, toys and TV programs is helpful in understanding the child's drawing and narratives.

Figure 8.1: How a thunderstorm unfolds

Encouraging spontaneous drawing is fundamental in supporting the child's agency and ZPD: 'As children develop skills and abilities related to psychological needs for self-expression and competence, they will claim areas of autonomy related to the exercise of these abilities, in accordance with the possibilities afforded by different cultural environments' (Helwig, 2006, p. 459). From the experience of interacting with the children during their drawing, it was evident that the children were self-motivated and knew what they wanted to draw as they sat down with drawing materials. Last, and by no means least, adult–child interaction is not a rigid or 'one-size-fits-all' strategy. Instead, interaction is sensitively attuned to each child's learning interest, learning modalities and learning needs. It also requires the adult to improvise, imagine and co-create with the child in a happy and relaxed environment.

Practice-based research is particularly common in educational research, where practitioners research their own practice in the hope of exploring and identifying better teaching solutions (O'Toole & Beckett, 2010). Combining this case study with practice-based research provided a powerful, context-specific and highly practical approach to examining the research questions of this study. I would recommend practitioner-based research to teachers who are interested in improving their own teaching practice and children's learning as this research methodology can provide holistic, practical and context-specific findings.

REFLECTION POINTS

1. How do the methods of this study respond to the aim of studying the role of the teacher in promoting creativity?
2. How is 'knowledge' positioned in this type of research?
3. As a teacher, how can you facilitate children's creative thinking and creative processes through play and intentional teaching?

Research participation in the early years: teacher and children as co-researchers in learning

Research in the sociology of childhood has informed a shift over the past few decades from research on children to research with children as active contributors to the design (what matters to children?) and procedure (how do children express views about issues that matter to them?) of research studies. Indeed, there has been a growing recognition that teaching and learning, as an ongoing participatory process in which adults and children co-construct, assess and document their new knowledge and understandings of their worlds, is in itself a form of research. As Alison Clark (2005) states 'the distinctions between research and teaching can blur' (p. 29). Rinaldi (2006) argues the need for greater recognition of the teacher as researcher: 'we want our research, as teachers, to be recognised. And to recognise research as a way of thinking, of approaching life, of negotiating, of documenting' (p. 192). Within this frame, the teacher and the child are viewed as key protagonists in the teaching and learning process. Clark (2005) proposes several key elements that enable a multi-method (mosaic) approach to researching with children:

- multi-method: recognises the different 'voices' or languages of children
- participatory: treats children as experts and agents in their own lives
- reflexive: includes children, practitioners and parents in reflecting on meanings, and addresses the question of interpretation
- adaptable: can be applied in a variety of early childhood institutions
- focused on children's lived experiences: can be used for a variety of purposes including looking at lives lived rather than knowledge gained or care received
- embedded into practice: a framework for listening that has the potential to be both used as an evaluative tool and to become embedded into early years practice. (pp. 30–1)

These approaches highlight the multidimensional nature of the teaching and learning process, and the detailed planning required to ensure that children are active participants in the teaching and learning process.

RESEARCH-PRACTICE CASE STUDY

Rachel Pollitt

ASSESSMENT OF NUMBER IN A PLAY-BASED PROGRAM

This study explored the effectiveness of using children's representations of number symbols and quantity as a formative assessment strategy. The aim of this study was to better understand the various ways in which young children communicated existing mathematics knowledge within the context of a play-based curriculum, and to consider the implications this may have for assessment, planning and teaching practices. This research focused on the gap between formative assessment strategies in the early childhood setting and teaching practice, aiming to explore the effectiveness of using representations of quantity and numerals as a formative assessment strategy within a play-based curriculum.

The study adopted a narrative inquiry approach, aligned with its focus on the narration of the experience as it unfolded, and the final product – in this case, the child's drawing. This study explored the diverse ways in which 47 four-year-old children at three different early learning centres in metropolitan Melbourne demonstrated their number knowledge while they traced around wooden numerals, drawing and discussing values of quantity (see Figure 8.2). By analysing the product and the narrative together, each artefact provided evidence of what children know and understand, based on 'what they make, write, draw, say and do' (DETVic, 2016, p. 15). This approach provided opportunities for verbal and non-verbal modes of communication that were integral to the meaning-making processes and allowed for the experiences of an individual to emerge. Essentially, children's mark making, and accompanying narratives, provided an insight into their mathematical reasoning, facilitating authentic assessment. The method is child-centred, as it is the child who actively decides how and what to represent, what to say and what the relationships between numerals and quantity mean to them. In summary, drawing and talking included three important approaches: 1. the guided questions that were used like a script and modified for each assessment situation; 2. quality interactions for supporting the child's increased engagement with the activity; and 3. sustained shared thinking (Siraj & Asani, 2015) to develop and extend the narrative.

The following prompts were used to sustain conversations with children about their representations of 'how many' the numerals meant to them.

- Is there anything you would like to show/tell me about the number you have chosen?
- Would you like to draw me a picture of how many the number (5) is?
- How do we know it is (5)?
- Would you like to show/tell me about the number (5)?
- Would you like to tell me about your drawing?
- I wonder … what do you think would happen if …?

Children took 7 to 12 minutes to complete the activity once. On completion, a photograph was taken of each child's work for inclusion in the data set. Later, the handwritten observations were paired with corresponding photographs then analysed for evidence of accuracy of representation of the selected numeral, numerical understanding, using the developmental progression points of the Learning Trajectories Approach (Clements & Sarama, 2009), and mastery of the counting principles (Gelman & Gallistel, 1978). By analysing the product and the narrative together, each artefact provided evidence of 'what children know and understand, based on what they make, write, draw, say and do' (DEECD, 2009, p. 13). The following (see Pollitt et al., 2015) provides an example of one activity.

Figure 8.2: Children chose wooden numerals to trace around

Tom incorporated a combination of numbers, people, Star Wars figures, a car stuck in traffic, a rocket launch, letters and a self-portrait to represent his understandings of numerals and quantity (see Figure 8.3). Throughout his narration of his work, Tom used mathematical language to describe the elements of his work using comparative terms such as 'larger than', 'shorter', 'faster', 'heaviest', 'the oldest' and finally 'running late' (Clements & Sarama, 2012; Klibanoff et al, 2006; van Oers, 2010).

Figure 8.3: Tom's work (4.9 years)

As he was working, the tail of a creature he drew reminded Tom of the number '8', prompting him to write '8' beside it. He tapped eight figures in his work and counted to eight using one-to-one correspondence. Tom practised writing the numeral 5 three times before shouting out 'I can do it!' When asked 'how many' the numeral

5 represented, Tom replied that he is 'that many' and drew a self-portrait. As the conversation continued, Tom said that, now that he could 'make a 5', he wanted to make a card for his father's 50th birthday. It is through Tom's detailed explanations and drawing that his recognition of the number symbols of '5', '8' and '50' could be identified and built upon.

The aim of this assessment approach was to determine the extent to which children recognised the relationship between numerals and quantity, as counting and cardinality are one of the first and most fundamental developmental progressions of mathematical learning (Clements & Sarama, 2009). It should, however, be emphasised that the success of the strategy relied on several key elements: firstly, the purposeful use of guided questions to engage children's thinking, sustain their attention, and elicit evidence of their mathematical understandings; secondly, the provisions of wooden numerals provided an unequivocal focus on number; and thirdly, the open-ended nature of the activity enabled children to articulate their individual understandings of quantity rather than requiring them to provide the 'right' answer.

Analysis of this type of activity with these children revealed the following key findings.

- Children's mathematical reasoning is creative and inventive. Informal, formative assessment is critical if teachers are to provide contingent learning experiences that both consolidate children's current understanding and keep pace with children's evolving understanding.
- Providing children with a range of resources with which to explore mathematical concepts supports their learning and encourages the transfer of knowledge from one context to another.
- Children's understandings of numerals and quantity are grounded in real, everyday experiences. Teachers can encourage mathematical thinking and language in real, everyday experiences across all aspects of their programs. Formative assessment that takes place during the typical play-based program provides a familiar setting for children to engage with materials used for assessment. The assessment strategy is developmentally appropriate and enables children to document and communicate their individual mathematical understandings.
- Children's understandings of number and quantity are interrelated, complex and unique. In order to assess children's understanding of mathematical concepts, teachers need to ask open-ended questions and engage in sustained conversations that provide opportunities for children to take the lead. Collaborating with children during mathematical assessment helps teachers to identify teachable moments as they emerge. This further informs intentional teaching strategies and supports ideas for planning effective learning experiences to meet the child's unique needs, while also building strong foundations for future mathematical learning.
- Small group activities provide opportunities for children to share their knowledge with their peers. Using this assessment strategy with small groups of

children facilitates peer learning and the sharing of perspectives, providing insights into the ways in which children co-constructed mathematical learning. This assessment strategy promotes discussion about mathematical concepts and demonstrates that mathematics can be a social and engaging experience for children and teachers, with positive assessment and learning outcomes.

- Children's representations of numerals alone do not always reflect their depth of mathematical knowledge. Evidence provided by children's narrative, in conjunction with their drawings, provides greater insights into their existing and emerging mathematical knowledge.

Assessment that is play-based supports the many ways in which children's thinking spontaneously flows through their ideas as they emerge, evolve and unfold. This form of assessment is well-suited to a play-based curriculum and to the site of child–teacher interactions in early learning environments. In the same way that teachers strive to provide authentic learning experiences, so too can assessment tools be constructed from the child's existing and emergent mathematical knowledge.

Research-practice case study content and images used with permission from Pollitt, R., Cohrssen, C., Church, A., & Wright, S. (2015). 'Thirty-one is a lot!' Assessing four-year-old children's number knowledge during an open-ended activity. *Australasian Journal of Early Childhood, 40*(1), 13–22.

REFLECTION POINTS

1. What can teachers learn from the principles of good research design?
2. How does data collection in research compare with collecting information about children's learning in ECEC settings?
3. What principles of play-based assessment in this case study could you apply to your own practice?

Research ethics in the early years

Ethical principles

Although the process for monitoring the ethical conduct of research varies from country to country and across different disciplines, the principles that inform the conduct of research are universal. The *National Statement on Ethical Conduct in Human Research* (NHMRC, 2015) guides the conduct of research in Australia, identifying four key values and principles of ethical conduct (merit and integrity, justice, beneficence and respect) and two key themes (risk and benefit, and informed consent). These values, principles and themes guide research with all participants, but children and young people are identified as a group with specific issues, namely maturity to consent to their own participation in research. We provide some overview of the issues in the sections that follow, with particular emphasis on consent and respect.

Researchers in early childhood education and care have a responsibility to demonstrate that the design of their study will lead to valid results, and that the question they pose can be answered within the proposed scope of the research. Assessing research merit and integrity ensures that the aims of a study are feasible and that the study seeks to contribute to our understanding of an important issue, practice, policy or provision in ECEC. The burden to participants is to be limited where possible and, as such, sharing their time and experiences should be valued in productive methodologies and reliable methods, resulting in outcomes which contribute to our understanding of young children's lives. The integrity of the research is demonstrated not only in the robust design and conduct but also in how researchers manage the process – with skill, design and implementation fidelity, honesty and a commitment to contributing to public knowledge.

Beneficence underscores the importance of minimising possible risk – primarily for children, parents or teachers who may participate in the research but also for practitioners or academics involved in the study. All research in ECEC must demonstrate that the benefit of any study outweighs the possible risk to those involved. The consideration is one of relativity; for example, recent research at the Murdoch Children's Research Institute into peanut allergy poses considerable risk of severe physical reaction, and children's participation takes place in the hospital with clinical supervision and access to immediate treatment. The possible benefit of the research, however, is to find a viable form of immunotherapy to prevent possibly fatal reaction to the ingestion of peanuts. Ethics committees at universities review applications for research with human participants to consider the foreseeable risks in relation to proposed benefits of a study. Yet, as children and their parents are informed about the aims, possible consequences and requirements before agreeing to take part, essentially the participants decide the beneficence of any given project. Importantly, the values and principles of ethical research are interdependent and evident in the process of informed and *voluntary* consent.

The principle of justice asks us to consider the fairness of research with children, their families, teachers and professionals working in the field. Is the process of recruitment fair? Will the participant group have access to the benefits of the research findings? There is a concern of the burden of research in over-sampling particular communities; although this may be addressed if the research directly benefits those communities involved. The outcomes of research – at the very least a summary of key findings – should be accessible to participants. Not only must the aims of a study be clearly explained but a principle of fairness for participation in the *benefits* should govern our research with children, families and professionals engaged in learning and teaching.

Informed consent

Ethical research in learning and teaching recognises that the needs of the participants are always more important than the aims of a research project. Research with very young children demands that the researcher or research practitioner gives due consideration to informed consent. Parents are asked to provide consent for any child who does not have the demonstrable maturity to agree to both the requirements and repercussions of their involvement in a research study. In Australia, the *National Statement on Ethical Conduct in Human Research* (NHMRC, 2015) – unlike guidelines in the UK and the US – does not actually make provision for children's *assent* to research but, in practice, children themselves should have the opportunity to agree to their participation in any data collection. The challenge for the researcher lies in providing opportunities for children to express their willingness to be part of observations, testing, interviews or ethnographic enquiry that provides evidence for the study in the research process.

Research in the sociology of childhood is particularly concerned with opportunities for children to participate as researchers, recognising that children are experts in relation to their own lives and have the right to contribute to decisions that immediately affect their lives (e.g. Mayall, 2000; see Groundwater-Smith, Dockett & Bottrell, 2015, for a summary and Chapter 3 in this book for a more detailed discussion of children's rights). In seeking to invite young children to be involved in a study, the researcher is reminded to consider children's competencies, which are 'important not only for judging when children or young people are able to give their consent for research; even young children with very limited cognitive capacity should be engaged at their level in discussion about the research and its likely outcomes' (NHMRC, 2015, p. 50).

Respect for participants

All researchers must demonstrate respect for the people, practices, cultures and communities they seek to involve in the research process. Inevitably, this requires expertise or experience in working with, or knowledge of, the communities invited to participate, and may involve the researcher undertaking specific cultural competence courses as part of initial, establishment work for a study. For example, if we respect children's rights to assent to participate in research, relative to their ability to recognise what is being asked of them, any researcher or research assistant working with infants should be able to respond to and recognise demonstrable resistance during data collection. Respectful practice necessitates minimisation of discomfort – for example, acknowledging that questions around pedagogy or beliefs may be disconcerting for teachers – and the anticipation of participants' needs (see Harcourt, Perry & Waller, 2011, for further examples of respect in the ethical design, conduct and communication of research).

Scholars who work in ECEC should be mindful of issues of power, even where the research seeks to involve children, professionals or parents as co-researchers. Ethical symmetry (see Groundwater-Smith, Dockett & Bottrell, 2015, for a review) recognises the institutional, situational and individual positioning of power relationships, and seeks to address how adequately the procedures and conduct of research enables people to share their existing knowledge and experiences of the world. These considerations are necessary in all social research but also provide a framework for ECEC professionals to reflect on their own practice.

All research with human participants requires ethical approval to ensure that the needs of participants are considered above the requirements of the study. Most importantly, ethical considerations guide the practice of research through every stage of a project. The needs of participants – be they babies, toddlers, pre-school-aged or school-aged children, parents, teachers, healthcare professionals or policy leaders – are considered in the design of the study while collecting data, and in thinking about the fidelity of the data; that is, how well the data captures the contribution of the participants to the research. Ethical conduct should also be paramount in communicating the results of the research; ensuring confidentiality and respectful practice when sharing information that participants have been generous enough to share, to improve our understanding of learning and teaching in the early years.

Conclusion

This chapter provided an overview of the practice of research in Australian ECEC, briefly identifying prominent research issues and focusing on research-in-action that informs teachers' understandings of children's learning. Although there is significant research on children's learning conducted as part of large-scale studies, evidence of and about children's day-to-day learning experiences provides teachers with critical information that can inform teaching and pedagogical decisions. The case studies illustrated a research-in-action approach which responded directly to teachers' responsibilities to children's learning outcomes as set out in the EYLF (DEEWR, 2009). This chapter provided an introduction to the approaches and methods that teachers can use to collect evidence of children's learning, evidence to inform teaching and to engage others (including families) in children's learning.

Further reading

Australian Bureau of Statistics (ABS). (2014) *National Early Childhood Education and Care Collection: Concepts, Sources and Methods 2013*. Retrieved from www. abs.gov.au/ausstats

MacNaughton, G., Rolfe, S. A., & Siraj-Blatchford, I. (2010). *Doing Early Childhood Research: International Perspectives on Theory and Practice*. Sydney: Allen & Unwin.

References

Alderson, P. (2001). Research by children. *International Journal of Social Research Methodology [Electronic version]*, 4(2), 139–53.

Australian Bureau of Statistics (ABS). (2015). *Preschool Education, Australia, 2014*. Retrieved from www.abs.gov.au/ausstats

Australian Early Development Census (AECD). (2015). *The Australian Early Development Census*. Melbourne: The Social Research Centre. Retrieved from www.aedc.gov.au/early-childhood

Chemi, T. (2014). The artful teacher: a conceptual model for arts integration in schools. *Studies in Art Education*, 56(1), 370–83.

Church, A. (2010). Opportunities for learning during storybook reading at preschool. *Applied Linguistics Review*, 1(1), 225–51.

Clark, A. (2005). Ways of seeing: using the mosaic approach to listen to young children's persepctives. In A. Clark, A. Kjørholt & P. Moss (Eds.). *Beyond Listening: Children's Perspectives on Early Childhood Services* (pp. 29–50). Bristol: Policy Press.

Clements, D., & Sarama, J. (2009). *Early Childhood Mathematics Education Research: Learning Trajectories for Young Children*. Florence, KY: Routledge.

Clements, D., & Sarama, J. (2012). Mathematics learning, assessment and curriculum. In R. Pianta (Ed.), *Handbook of Early Childhood Education* (pp. 217–39). New York: The Guildford Press.

Commonwealth of Australia. (2009). *Investing in the Early Years – A National Early Childhood Development Strategy. An Initiative of the Council of Australian Governments*. Canberra: Commonwealth of Australia.

Cresswell, J. W. (2013). *Research Design. Qualitative, Quantitative and Mixed Methods Approaches* (4th ed.). Thousand Oaks, CA: Sage.

Department of Education and Training (Victoria) & Victorian Curriculum and Assessment Authority. (2016). *Victorian Early Years Learning and Development Framework*. Melbourne: Department of Education and Training (Victoria).

Department of Education, Employment and Workplace Relations (DEEWR). (2009), *Belonging, Being, & Becoming: The Early Years Learning Framework for Australia*. Canberra: DEEWR for COAG.

Flewitt, R. (2005). Conducting research with young children: some ethical considerations [Electronic version]. *Early Child Development and Care, 175*(6), 553–65.

Gelman, R., & Gallistel, C. (1978). *The Child's Understanding of Number.* Cambridge, MA: Harvard University Press.

Griffith University. (2012). *Evaluation of the Implementation of the Victorian Early Years Learning and Development Framework: For All Children from Birth to Eight Years. Early Childhood Professionals' Perceptions of Implementation Activities and Resources 2010–2011. Final Report. May 2012.* Melbourne: Victorian Curriculum and Assessment Authority.

Groundwater-Smith, S., Dockett, S., & Bottrell, D. (2015) *Participatory Research with Children and Young People.* London: Sage.

Harcourt, D., Perry, B., & Waller, T. (2011). *Researching Young Children's Perspectives: Debating the Ethics and Dilemmas of Educational Research with Children.* Abingdon: Routledge.

Helwig, C. C. (2006). The development of personal autonomy through cultures. *Cognitive Development, 21,* 458–73.

Klibanoff, R., Levine, S., Huttenlocher, J., Vasilyeva, M., & Hedges, L. (2006). Preschool children's mathematical knowledge: the effect of teacher 'math talk'. *Developmental Psychology, 42*(1), 59–69.

Leavy, P. (2009). *Method Meets Art: Arts-based Research Practice.* New York: Phaidon.

Mayall, B. (2000). The sociology of childhood in relation to children's rights. *The International Journal of Children's Rights, 8*(1), 243–59.

McArdle, F., & Wright, S. (2014). First literacies: art, creativity, play, constructive meaning-making. In G. Barton (Ed.). *Literacy in the Arts: Retheorising Learning and Teaching* (pp. 21–37). London: Springer.

Monash University. (2014). *Review and Evaluation of the Inquiry to Implementation Project.* Melbourne: Victorian Curriculum and Assessment Authority.

Mukherji, P., & Albon, D. (2015). *Research Methods in Early Childhood: An Introductory Guide.* London: Sage.

National Health and Medical Research Council (NHMRC). (2015). *National Statement on Ethical Conduct in Human Research 2007 (Updated May 2015).* Retrieved from www.nhmrc.gov.au/book/national-statement-ethical-conduct-human-research

O'Kane, C. (2000). The development of participatory techniques. Facilitating children's views about decisions which affect them. In P. Christensen & A. James (Eds.). *Research with Children. Perspectives and Practices* (pp. 136–59). London: Falmer Press.

O'Toole, J., & Beckett, D. (2010). *Educational Research: Creative Thinking and Doing.* Melbourne: Oxford University Press.

Pollitt, R., Cohrssen, C., Church, A., & Wright, S. (2015). 'Thirty-one is a lot!': Assessing four-year-old children's number knowledge during an open-ended activity. *Australasian Journal of Early Childhood, 40*(1), 13–22.

Ramberg, B., & Gjesdal, K. (2005). *Stanford Encyclopedia of Philosophy*. Retrieved from http://plato.stanford.edu/entries/hermeneutics

Rinaldi, C. (2006). *In dialogue with Reggio Emilia. Listening, Researching and Learning*. London: Routledge Taylor and Francis Group.

Robinson, K. (1999). *All Our Futures: Creativity, Culture and Education. Report to the National Advisory Committee on Creative and Cultural Education*. London: National Advisory Committee on Creative and Cultural Education.

Robson, S. (2014). The Analysing Children's Creative Thinking Framework: development of an observation-led approach to identifying and analyzing young children's creative thinking. *British Educational Research Journal, 40*(1), 121–34.

Samuelsson, I. (2004). How do children tell us about their childhoods? [Electronic version]. *Early Childhood Research and Practice, 6*(1), 1–12.

Seidel, S., Tishman, S., Winner, E., Hetland, L. & Palmer, P. (2009). *The Qualities of Quality: Understanding Excellence in Arts Education*. Cambridge, MS: Project Zero, Harvard Graduate School of Education.

Siraj, I., & Asani, R. (2015). The role of sustained shared thinking, play and metacognition in young children's learning. In S. Robson & S. Quyinn (Eds.). *The Routledge International Handbook of Young Children's Thinking and Understanding* (pp. 403–15). London: Routledge.

Social Research Centre. (2014). 2013 *National Early Childhood Education and Care Workforce Census*. Retrieved from www.srcentre.com.au/

Sylva, K., Melhuish, E., Sammons, P., Siraj-Blatchford, I., & Taggart, B. (2004). *The Effective Provision of Pre-school Education [EPPE] Project. Final Report*. Nottingham: DfES Publications.

van Oers, B. (2010). Emergent mathematical thinking in the context of play. *Educational Studies in Mathematics, 74*(1), 23–37. DOI: http://doi.org/10.1007/s10649-009-9225-x

Victorian Curriculum and Assessment Authority (VCAA). (2012). *Report on the Outcomes Project 2010–2011 Shining a Light on Children's Learning*. Melbourne: VCAA.

Victorian Curriculum and Assessment Authority (VCAA). (2013). *Report on the Assessment for Learning and Development Project 2012.Transforming Practice in the Early Years*. Melbourne: VCAA.

Wright. S. (2010). *Understanding Creativity in Early Childhood*. London: Sage.

Index